# DEADLY DOUG

# DEADLY DOUG

## BEHIND THE SCENES AT ASTON VILLA FC

## DOUG ELLIS

JOHN BLAKE

Published by John Blake Publishing Ltd,
3, Bramber Court, 2 Bramber Road,
London W14 9PB, England

www.blake.co.uk

First published in hardback in 2005

ISBN 1 84454 162 2

British Library Cataloguing-in-Publication Data:

A catalogue record for this book is available from the British Library.

Design by www.envydesign.co.uk

Printed in Great Britain by Creative Print and Design Group.

1 3 5 7 9 10 8 6 4 2

Papers used by John Blake Publishing are natural, recyclable products made
from wood grown in sustainable forests. The manufacturing processes conform to
the environmental regulations of the country of origin.

Every attempt has been made to contact the relevant copyright-holders,
but some were unobtainable. We would be grateful if the appropriate people
could contact us.

# PREFACE

I was three years old when my father died, leaving my mother as a young widow in the aftermath of the First World War, and with very sparse means of support. Like other ladies of that era, when a generation of husbands and sons had been decimated by war, my mum simply had to cope, without the help of the welfare state as it exists today.

As a widow with two young children to support, she had to find ways of earning a living. She took in a lodger to bring in a few shillings a week. She also took in washing and I have hazy memories of helping her by turning the handle on the old-fashioned mangle.

I was heartbroken when she died and will always regret realising too late that all she really wanted in return for the start she gave me in life, against all the odds of those difficult days, was more of my time.

The story of my life is dedicated to her memory.

# FOREWORD BY ANDY GRAY

Deadly Doug has been much maligned over the years, but ever since I met him and came to understand him, I have never doubted either his passion for football or his passion for Aston Villa. Anyone who questions that doesn't know Doug Ellis at all – and has probably never even met him.

Don't get me wrong, Deadly is the sort of character who can rub people up the wrong way. He has a huge ego and he has his critics, so I am not trying to paint him as the game's Mr Perfect. However, the guy *is* Aston Villa-mad, he's daft about football and his heart is in the right place – particularly now that he's had a triple bypass!

In fact, most people who really have got to know him over the years have a Doug Ellis story to tell – I have plenty – but there is one in particular that always makes me chuckle.

I came into Villa Park one day with a new girlfriend and introduced her to the chairman. Now Doug has always been a bit of a ladies' man – and the fact that he married such a pretty woman bears testimony to that fact – so he was extremely welcoming.

'Hello, young lady, where are you from?' he inquired.

'I'm from Malvern,' she told him.

'Yeah,' said Deadly, quick as a brick. 'I know Malvern – it's £200,000 an acre!'

Now that's Doug for you. He knows the value of most things, and although he has been attacked for being a miser, the facts don't bear that out. There has been something of an ugly witch hunt against him – a witch hunt from a group of people who have wanted him out for the best part of the thirty years that I have known him. They have been trying, unsuccessfully, to remove him as chairman, and it's been a personal crusade for them.

But it's never going to happen, because Deadly is made of sterner stuff; he is a tough character and has worked hard for the benefit of Villa. I like him and I respect what he has done – and is still doing – for Aston Villa FC. I can see beyond all the hysteria. Of course, he has a seemingly harsh exterior that tends to put people off, but I can assure you that there are few people who have given more for Villa.

His greatest achievement has been to keep the club solvent. His critics may call him a miser, but he has spent £100 million over a ten-year period: a figure that makes Villa about the fifth or sixth biggest spenders in the top flight. We've seen the spend-or-bust policy of Leeds United and that should make every club realise the folly of over-stretching themselves. For that reason, because of the way that Doug has kept Villa safe, he is the Top Man as far as I am concerned.

# CONTENTS

# CHAPTER ONE

# U-TURN FROM DISASTER

Villa Park, the home of Aston Villa plc. My second home... Despite the almost-daily experience of arriving there, the sensation is always the same. Villa Park is not merely a place of work, in 1997 a £126 million public company or an office block with a football pitch. Yes, it is all those things, but it is also a uniquely special place to me.

Lifetime supporters know what I mean. They share a similar emotion when the stadium comes into view before a match. There is always a sense that something special could be about to happen.

This is especially the case for night games in the winter: when you arrive at Villa Park, the floodlights provide a halo effect and give the impression of a giant, outdoor theatre.

We've seen many a drama played out there over the years, that's for sure. In the last forty years, countless millions have been spent on transporting the stadium, and the entire football club, from Victoriana to the demands of the new century.

The simple act of arriving at the ground for a normal day's work never fails to provide me with what politicians would call 'the feelgood factor'. Everything is smart and ship-shape. No effort or expense has been spared as the season-by-season improvements have been completed.

There always seems to be a buzz of activity in the air, particularly when preparations for a match are underway. Maintenance staff are going about their business. Members of the public are calling in at the main office, the ticket office, or the Villa Village on the far side of the car park. The souvenir shop exudes the ambience of a top city-centre store.

A succession of fans of all ages emerges from it, many of them often clad in club replica kits. Grandma, in her own fantasy, is just as likely to be wearing our No. 9 shirt as some spindly-legged, two-foot-nothing toddler who might fancy his or her chances in goal.

Way back in the mists of time, four decades earlier, my aim was to be the people's chairman of the people's club. When I see fans of all ages, of both sexes, and from all walks of life togged up in our merchandise and purchasing their season tickets, I presume to hope that maybe, just maybe, some may feel as though that ambition has been achieved.

We exchange greetings at the main Villa Park reception desk, likewise with the other members of the office staff going about their business. My personal assistant, Marion Stringer, is busily looking after affairs in my outer office. I pass through there to my office, where I usually remain until long after normal office hours.

By now there is daily post to be dealt with, cheques to be signed – all of which are covered by a healthy bank balance – meetings to attend and immediate decisions to be made: all the daily cut and thrust of the job that I shall always enjoy. Football club finances are increasingly a topic of debate as escalating overheads eat into the admittedly high level of income. We have all read newspaper headlines of young players wanting £80,000 per week to sign new contracts; it is an indication of the enormous pressures placed on major clubs in pursuit of honours. While Aston Villa would not, in the foreseeable future at any rate, bow to such demands, this is the kind of world in which we compete, having once been operating while arguably insolvent.

Spending more than one earns can be a great temptation in any walk of life, but it will never happen at Aston Villa plc, not while I remain chairman. I make no apologies for being a six-days-a-week, hands-on chairman with sensible, prudent housekeeping my primary concern.

Not a single cheque leaves Villa Park without my personal signature on it. Each day, a tray-full of invoices with their appropriate cheques arrives on my desk. Signing them all can sometimes be a painful process, but it is rather like a footballer keeping his eye on the ball at necessary moments. Administering the affairs of a major Premiership club like ours is a full-time occupation, and more, for people who are experienced in dealing with vast amounts of money and who are not afraid of the enormity of the operation.

When I study today's costs, I can't help but compare them to the books I first studied back in 1968. Players' wages alone now tot up to £75,000 per day! Stadium maintenance adds up to £3,950 per day, youth development costs us £3,600 and rates, water, electric and gas, a combined £3,380. Our total daily commitment works out at about £125,000.

You could have bought a half-decent player for that amount thirty years ago. Now the top players are looking at such sums for their fortnightly wages and, in the last seven years, our turnover in transfer fees has been around £120 million.

When dealing with such astronomical figures, the process of being in daily touch with income and expenditure can prevent financial own goals from being scored. I can, and frequently do, pick up my internal telephone, dial our chief accountant,

Phil Longmore, and ask for an up-to-date balance on the club's deposit account.

Every penny of it is needed for team-building and the ground expansion plans that go on unceasingly, not to mention stage payments of transfer fees.

Thus, the figure in our account varies, naturally, but the principle does not: Aston Villa's affairs will remain healthy because it is the only way I know to run any business.

The one time in my life when I might have borrowed money was when I was first setting out on my own, and the bank granted me an overdraft facility of £2,500. That figure remained intact. I never touched it.

'Generate income before you spend it' is my business motto, though it is pertinent to draw attention to the help that Aston Villa gives to as many as a hundred charities and good causes each year – those in our own community as much as possible – under the umbrella of our own Charitable Trust.

These include, for example, a project with the Variety Club of Great Britain to supply electric wheelchairs for disabled children. They were accepted at Villa Park and driven around the track by the delighted recipients. We distribute many thousands of pounds every year to those who need it. Football does put an awful lot back into its local community, most of it going unnoticed, though some examples are of a higher profile like, for example, when we took several skips packed with aid to an orphanage in Romania with us when we played Steaua Bucharest in the UEFA Cup.

Several years before, when those deeply depressing pictures of the starving souls in Ethiopia tore at our heartstrings, we decided to charter an aircraft and dispatch some Villa-aid. A 707 cargo aircraft was located in Holland and flown to Birmingham airport at a hire charge of £40,000. The sum was covered by enlisting support from here and there, while we also appealed to major companies to chip in with foodstuffs and medicines. Our players packed the goods into the aircraft which was flown out to relieve just a little of the malnutrition, pain and suffering of these unfortunate people.

On that occasion, the *Blue Peter* programme took up the project to illustrate that football is not immune to the needs of the less fortunate. Valerie Singleton, her television crew and the local military were screened in Ethiopia moving the cargo up-country and supervising distribution to those who most needed it, the starving children.

More recently, on 10 January 2005 to be exact, together with the Aston Rotary Club, I invited 550 Aston Villa people to join me for a five-course dinner, free of charge, in our Holte Suite, on the condition that they each made a donation of at least £50 towards the Tsunami Disaster Fund for the Madras region. We raised £78,300 from that evening, and I personally added a further £10,000 and made it up to £100,000, for the purpose of purchasing food, medicine and water purifiers. I asked the regional commissioner in Madras to advise us and he organised transportation and hotel accommodation for four members of the Aston Rotary Club to journey there in February. The commissioner sent them to several villages 150–200 miles to the south of Madras. They found that while these people were not short of food, their fishing livelihood had been destroyed because all of their boats had been wrecked. We decided to use £80,000 to buy forty-five 30ft boats and they were allocated to two villages – twenty-seven to Ayyametta and eighteen to Themmanam. Each boat will provide a living for no less than nine families. They are all painted in claret and blue and each boat carries Aston Villa's name, together with the name of one of our current players. The people wanted me to go out and launch the boats, but I was not seeking the publicity and so declined. It was enough for me to see that Aston Villa FC can give something back to the community at large.

We do strive to maintain this balance of bankrolling a wage bill for highly paid professionals while also thinking of the underprivileged. Match days at Villa Park are always used to put something back into the public domain, before the match overwhelms all else and captures our attention for whatever emotions are to be stirred this time. My commercial and promotional staff have me dodging around in the hour or so before each kick-off, not to mention frequently throughout every week, meeting a most fascinating range of people, most of whom have some connection with a charity. I tend to regard this as a 'perk' of the job rather than as a chore.

I recall a ninety-year-old lady season ticket holder who was mugged in her own home and had her handbag stolen. 'Have they taken my season ticket?' was, bless her heart, her first question. When staff heard of her wretched experience, she was invited to join the directors for a special day out and I was delighted to greet her. Another elderly lady, only a couple of days short of her 100th birthday, also joined us for a match: it transpired that her father had been a Villa vice-chairman around the turn of the century. It was a lovely link with the club's great past.

Such visitors love the chance to mingle with the likes of Nigel Kennedy, Jasper Carrott, John Major, Michael Howard maybe, and a whole host of other top football personalities, both past and present. The mix can be quite a remarkable cross-section of society.

I am frequently introduced to young people at matches, who for one reason or another, have been invited as guests, often to take part in penalty shoot-outs or small-sided matches on the pitch for occasions they will not forget as long as they live.

Our football in the community scheme conducts fun coaching sessions in local schools and youth clubs on a daily and weekly basis throughout the entire year. When the holidays come, coaches run five-day courses for the children, of all ethnic groups, to keep them off the streets and away from the petty crime and drug culture that is becoming an increasing problem for parents.

Another incalculable transformation that has taken place during my time at the helm is the match-day operation on the hospitality and catering side. The normal full-time staff of more than 312, spread across all the various departments, not to mention some fifty-five players, is supplemented by 930 part-timers and, in an operation that would make the catering staff of a cruise liner blanch, we can serve up to 3,200 three-course match-day meals in our five restaurants, our banqueting suite and 120 private boxes. Wherever one ventures around the stadium there is the unspoken, but unmistakable, message that, whatever lies ahead, Aston Villa is up to the challenge. It wasn't always like that, however, not way back when first I drove into the club car park to take a look at what lay behind the scenes.

The transformation between Aston Villa FC, December 1968 and Aston Villa Plc, today, is as far reaching as the change that has taken place in the entire face of football in the intervening years.

Life has blessed me with a kaleidoscope of memories, ranging between building a business empire around the travel industry and getting the opportunity to help salvage one of the world's most famous football clubs, before steering it towards far more stable financial waters. If this sounds boastful, let me stress that I see no reason for being coy about factual progress any more than I will deny my mistakes – and I've made a few, as will be shown by the events I set out to describe as accurately as both memory and research allow.

I began my life in a poor, working-class family. I lost my father when I was three years old, later left the Fleet Air Arm after four years' war service, mostly in the Far East, with only a £300 gratuity and was a millionaire before I was forty. Now here I am in my eighties and find myself to be the proud, if rather amused, possessor of a Doctorate from the University of Central England, an OBE from the Queen and a 'deadly' reputation for sacking football managers: whether such a reputation is justified by the facts or whether it is simply a media interpretation of those facts, will be up to others to judge. I can quote the example of when Brian Little took me completely by surprise in tendering his resignation on the afternoon of Tuesday, 24 February 1998: one national newspaper quoted eleven managers over whom I had 'presided' and gave the impression that I had fired them all.

Indeed, I had not. The first one of these, Arthur Cox, was only in temporary charge before I became chairman. Another, Ron Saunders, left the club when I was not there; another, Graham Taylor, left to become England manager while, whatever else may have been said or written about Brian Little's departure, the fact is that he unexpectedly tendered his resignation, quite outside of my wishes, and left the club under no pressure to do so from myself. See what I mean about exaggeration?

However, how did I become involved in this chain of events in the first place? In a way it was inevitable that I would do so. Business and football have dominated my life for as long as I can remember, so I guess it was natural that these two pursuits should join forces. This first happened in a practical sense on Tuesday, 17 December 1968. We all know the well-worn cliché about remembering where we were when President John Kennedy was assassinated or when the Birmingham bombs went off. I remember just as vividly driving down the famous Carriage Drive at Villa Park on that wintry day, my first as a director and chairman-elect of Aston Villa Football Club. What I found there provided guidelines for the rest of my life in football. One of them is that when football managers try to interfere with the business side of football clubs, they are stepping out of their depth and are making a big mistake.

No football manager, whose professional life has been spent on the training ground and the playing pitch, would have been prepared for the immense financial balancing act that was required at Aston Villa FC Ltd at that critical time following years of neglect and decline. Not a Terry Venables, not a Gordon Taylor, not a Lawrie McMenemy, nor an 'old-fashioned' director with roots too far in the past.

Thus, my first lesson was: let modern businessmen run the business and football experts run the football. It is a concept I have put into practice ever since.

I knew that things must have been in a pretty bad way, otherwise I would not have been appointed the previous day to launch an immediate rescue operation. Aston Villa FC was known to be dying on its feet. One of the best-known names in world football, a club that had become an institution, was as near to being bankrupt as makes no matter. The former board of directors had finally given way to financial forces, as well as to the sheer weight of public and local press opinion.

Look at the stadium today and you see one of the finest in Europe. Back then, the Birmingham City fans joked that if visitors asked a bus conductor for the Hall of Memory they were taken to Villa Park. To be blunt, the club had become a joke in many people's eyes and the challenge to all of us involved was to give Aston Villa FC both a present and a future to add to the fine traditions of yesteryear. As a travel agent, my motto was always that first impressions are all-important because they stay in the mind of the observer.

I quickly discovered that 'first impressions' at Villa Park meant an antiquated front office, now long since knocked down, where a serving hatch masqueraded as a reception desk. In answer to my knock, the trap door slid open and a face appeared to ask: 'Yes?'

Not 'good morning', mark you. Not 'how can I help you?' Just 'Yes?' I was immediately appalled that this was how callers were greeted. It said all that I needed to know about the challenges that lay ahead beyond that crude serving hatch.

The whole atmosphere was more like that of an old-fashioned, out-in-the-sticks railway station than that of a big city football club. I know a little bit about that, as I will explain later.

On closer inspection, after climbing an old staircase, impressions did not improve. Quite the reverse, in fact. Time had stood still for years on end. You could write your name in the dust. Window frames were rotting, large areas of what should have been valuable space were unused and in decay, the smell of failure and imminent financial ruin hung in the air.

Long, bare corridors had paint peeling from walls, doors had cracked windows in them, bare light bulbs were commonplace. We've all seen the old Western films where the lone rider arrives in a ghost town with cobwebs and creaking doors hanging off their hinges. It was rather like that scenario. When I opened the door of the directors' guests' tea room, the doorknob came off in my hand. I particularly recall the so-called press room: it possessed an old-fashioned gas fire and had upright telephones with the separate ear piece on a hook.

There was just one item – in the old boardroom – that I made sure to keep. This was the handsome, large, solid table. If tables could talk then this one would have had a few tales to tell, believe me.

Perusing the accounts was even worse than touring the ground. The total assets of the club, that included the stadium, the land, staff houses and so on, were £203,770. The club's share capital was just £10,000.

More significantly, the overdraft had gone through the roof and the bank manager was calling it in. The last home gate, against Charlton in the old Second Division, was a mere 12,747; relegation was looming and the playing staff was, well let's just say 'inadequate'.

What's more, the backlog of unpaid bills was quite

unbelievable and the capacity to pay them was less than nil with resources haemorrhaging at an alarming rate and debts heading past a then-disastrous £20,000.

In retrospect, I realise now that, when I saw the true state of disrepair around the ground, the apathy among staff who had borne the brunt of the post-war slump and the insolvency of the accounts, for all my worldliness in life and in business, I was naive and inexperienced in the daunting scale of this perilous situation.

Although I had been an Aston Villa season ticket holder for many years, had almost become a director three years earlier and had followed the decline via the press, I was unprepared for the chaotic mess that landed in our lap.

If Aston Villa were to undertake a U-turn away from disaster, things had to change, and change very quickly. This would not be achieved, as maybe the dreamers imagined, by a snap of the fingers or a quick chat with the bank manager. In those days there was an unrealistic attitude that clubs in such a state, and Villa were not alone, had merely to appoint what was commonly known in the press as a 'Mr Big' with pots of money, who would wave a wand and all would be well.

Reality was very different and the most urgent priority was to stage our first board meeting, with two directors from the old board to give legal continuation of the company, namely Bob Mackay and Roy Ladbrooke, together with two new directors whom I had invited onto the board, Harry Kartz and Harry Parkes.

When I first set foot inside Villa Park as a new director, I knew we would set in motion some hard-headed business methods and appoint a new manager to replace Tommy Cummings who had been dismissed by the old board before the changes had taken place, with Arthur Cox in temporary charge of the team.

A few days earlier, having been approached by the club president, Sir Theodore Pritchett, to ascertain my willingness to consider becoming chairman, I had met up with the merchant banker, Pat Matthews, who had been appointed to organise the refinancing of the club and to select new directors who were prepared to invest £25,000 each for 5,000 shares at £5 each.

That meeting was another of those never-to-be-forgotten occasions that I will remember until the day I die. After lengthy and detailed talks at his London office, we shook hands on my appointment as a director and chairman-to-be when he pressed a button on his desk. This activated a hidden door in the panelling of his office, like the entrance to some secret corridor, and from the opening stepped a smiling Tommy Docherty.

To say I was stunned would be to put it mildly. I knew the Doc from my three-and-a-half years as a director of Birmingham City and was naturally aware of his chequered managerial career.

'Hello, Tommy,' I said. 'What are you doing here?' At the same time I thought: 'Heck, he's not a new director as well, is he?' Before he could answer, Pat Matthews replied: 'He's your new manager…'

New manager? For heaven's sake! I wasn't even chairman yet, not until it had been formally rubberstamped at a board meeting in accordance with the club's Articles of Association.

'Oh no he's not,' I replied. 'Pat, we had better get one thing straight from the start. I'll appoint the manager and if it's to be Tommy Docherty, he and I have a lot of talking to do.' In all honesty, though, the Doc would have been a good choice, bearing in mind his capacity to stir up the players, the crowd and the press.

On the one hand I resented the thought of a manager having been selected before I had even considered the situation but, realistically, his immediate availability to take the helm on the playing side was another point in his favour. If he were to become the first of the thirteen managers I have appointed, then the lines of decision-making had to be drawn up. Tommy Docherty was, in fact, appointed manager the day after I became chairman.

By now, though, there had been a subtle change. He had *not* been appointed by Pat Matthews; he had been appointed by myself and the other directors and it was to us that he was answerable.

One of the strict guidelines I put down with Tommy was that he would live, for a while, at my home so that I could see and hear what was going on. The club had no resources for any spending sprees, nor was I in any position, as virtually a trainee chairman, to risk letting his natural exuberance run away with him.

The Doc had a media reputation for being something of a free spirit, an impulsive individual who sometimes acted before he thought. I wanted to make sure that we *both* thought before *he* acted.

The flotation organised by Pat Matthews comprised an issue of new £5 shares and the upgrading of the original shares to 'special shares' which would carry fifteen votes each. A cash injection of £205,835 was raised by the flotation, less than was hoped, but it was nonetheless a lifeline sum compared to the total annual turnover to June 1968 of £150,720. To supplement our working capital, we later appealed for those who could not afford a £5 share to make a voluntary £1 donation and this raised a further useful couple of thousand pounds.

This was the situation undertaken by Doc as manager and myself as chairman as a slightly bemused, but relieved, public watched our every move. I believed then – and I believe even more so now – that the chairman-manager relationship has to be very close, with both of you pulling in the same direction. That same principle applied, to a degree, on the board of directors. I wanted no time to be wasted on personality clashes or destructive 'splits' on the board. I had suffered quite enough of that as a director of Birmingham City for three-and-a-half years. No way would I put up with it when I was chairman of Aston Villa.

One of my greatest strengths when I sat at the first Villa Park board meeting as chairman was that I had learned exactly how *not* to run a football club during my time at St Andrew's.

The Blues had taught me the wrong way. I wasn't to know it then, but ahead of me lay many years of battling to put into practice at Villa Park what I firmly believed to be the right way of doing things. Contrary to popular belief at that time, Aston Villa actually benefited from my experiences at the 'other' club, even though some insisted on calling me a turncoat. It was a cross I had to bear, but it wasn't always easy. What I obviously couldn't say then, in the explosive climate of the time, was that I had learned an awful lot about disharmony at Blues and not a lot else.

When I came to Birmingham in 1948, I immediately went to Villa Park to watch every match and, around 1952, I could afford to buy two season tickets and become a shareholder. It would be 1955 before I bought any shares in Birmingham City: the reason for that was that because I was a travel agent I had to do business on a Saturday and I could not go away with Villa so, because I was a lover of football, one week I went to Birmingham City's home games and the next I would go to Villa Park. It meant that I could leave the office at a quarter to three to get to both Villa or St Andrew's and still see a match a week.

I became a director of Birmingham City on Thursday, 25 November 1965, with the first of many bold statements: 'Football needs to be a big business from the boy who cleans the boots through to the directors. There is no room for losers in the modern world; I have no time for them.'

While some Villa fans frown on the fact that I was at the Blues for three-and-a-half years, it was a hugely valuable experience and one that has certainly helped Villa. In fact, the only reason I joined the Blues was because a directorship on the Villa board fell through.

I was invited to attend nine matches with the existing Villa board, mainly at the instigation of Bruce Normansell – the son of the former chairman – and Joe Heath – a well-known fish merchant – who were both directors, to attend home and away matches in the box on the understanding that they were going to invite me to become a director.

It was 1962. I had just received a lump sum of money for one of my companies from Sir Isaac Wolfson, so I had money available. I had agreed that I would put in neither a penny more nor a penny less, than any one of the existing Villa directors. The sum, suggested by Joe Heath, was only £30,000, but in those days, of course, that was quite a lot of money. The directors held a meeting after a reserves match at Stoke City. I wasted a couple of hours in the old boardroom here at Villa Park waiting for them to give me a decision, when Bruce Normansell came across and said: 'Sorry, I'll have to talk to you in the morning – we haven't come to an agreement.'

The following morning he phoned me, at half past eight, to say that a black ball had been put in; that meant that they hadn't got a unanimous decision. I would have to wait until after the 1966 World Cup when the chairman said that he would step down and I could take his position. Remember, I wasn't after the chairmanship, I only wanted to be a director, so I said: 'Ask the secretary to put that in writing.'

They wouldn't, of course, so on the Monday morning I had a phone call from Len Morris, the brother of the chairman of Birmingham City, to say he'd heard what had gone on across the other side of the city – it's surprising how the grapevine works in this city – and would I do the same for Birmingham City? I said: 'Not at all, of course, I'm sorry, I'm a Villa man through and through.' He said: 'Well, why don't you meet my brother and I? Come and have lunch with us – today.' I accepted his invitation.

We had a bite to eat in a pub in Small Heath one lunchtime. The following day, which was Tuesday, the chairman said: 'Look you haven't met our colleagues'. I agreed to meet them. 'We'll have a board meeting at 5.30 this evening. Come along about 6 o'clock, 6.30 and we'll just say hello.'

I couldn't believe it when I walked into the boardroom at Birmingham City that evening and they said: 'There's no black ball here, Mr Ellis. Unanimously, we welcome you'. I say again that that was not the reason that I went there, but there it is, that's what happened and, to some extent, I was so embarrassed that I didn't have the courage to say no.

My new board colleagues comprised Harry and Len Morris, David and Jack Wiseman, plumbers and builders, Harry Dare, a builder in a very big way, Bill Dare, who was a brewer, and the former Birmingham Lord Mayor, Neville Bosworth, a solicitor and near-neighbour of mine, who later became Sir Neville.

Little did I know the extent of the politics into which I had been drawn. Another millionaire Birmingham businessman, Clifford Coombs, owner of a large credit drapery store, had previously loaned the club £80,000, but had not been able to acquire a directorship.

My arrival, it seemed, prompted the giant Welshman to demand either a return of his very significant loan or a directorship. The outcome was that Clifford Coombs, who had two sons Derek and Keith, took over as chairman. Without going too deeply into my spell at St Andrew's, suffice it to say that I found that the various families pulled in different directions and board meetings usually ended with no measure of agreement on key issues. The club didn't even have a youth team coach.

The first time I went to the Elmdon training ground, there were young players like Garry Pendrey and others who were to become well-known names, just kicking a ball about on their own. I put on a tracksuit and joined in. I do recall once, when I was attempting to get some scheme or another through, that I was told by one of the other directors to leave football alone and stick to being a travel agent. I found that a bit rich, coming from a builder.

The one person I did learn from was Stan Cullis, the manager at that time. Stan used to ask me to travel around with him looking at players; a job that was right up my street.

Stan enjoyed being chauffeured around in my Rolls Royce, while I enjoyed going to matches with him and watching the extent that Stan and his chief scout, Don Dorman, went to in checking out a player's character and lifestyle.

I well recall once that Stan was told that a particular player he was keen to sign had been witnessed going out to the pictures with his landlady, sitting in the back row, and switching on the lights in only one bedroom upon their return. Stan was aghast. Even in the so-called Swinging Sixties, Stan was not going to sign a young player who might just have shared a bedroom with his landlady.

At the time Stan Cullis was the manager from whom I learnt a lot when we went scouting together in England, Scotland and Ireland.

Another thing I remember about Stan: he seemed to know the best fish and chip shop on the route back from any ground in the UK. Sometimes we would divert about ten miles to get there and, when we arrived, scouts from other clubs would be sitting outside eating their supper from an open newspaper... a valuable part of my footballing education, I guess.

After three-and-a-half years, though, not a lot had happened, despite the board changes, to undermine my true allegiances which were claret and blue, not royal blue and white.

When Pat Matthews approached me to consider playing a part in the newly reconstructed Aston Villa, this time with no boardroom 'black ball' possible, I was more than happy to be transferred from Small Heath to Aston.

In any organisation or family, firm direction has to come from the top with everyone pulling in the same direction. I hadn't seen much of that at Birmingham City.

# CHAPTER TWO

# LEARNING THE HARD WAY

By the time I took over the role of Aston Villa's chairman, my various business activities were in a very healthy state. Had that not been the case, I could not have thrown myself, body and soul, into the prodigious job of rescuing the club from insolvency. I savoured every single moment of the all-consuming challenge. That's the way my life had always been. Long working hours have never bothered me.

Some are born with silver spoons in their mouths. Maybe, in a funny sort of way, I was luckier than that. I was born on 3 January 1924, the son of two wonderful parents who could never have afforded a silver spoon. We lived in the village of Hooton, on the Wirral, halfway between Chester and Birkenhead. My father Herbert was one of the men who returned from the trenches of the First World War, his health wrecked by gas attacks and all the other horrors they had encountered.

I have always thought that my natural instinct for 'good housekeeping' came from Cheshire farming stock. My mother Jane's family was made up of farmers and while my father's family were also farmers, my father had completed an articled apprenticeship as a motor mechanic.

At age of nineteen, he was the first young man from Hooton to respond to the call that 'Your Country Needs You' in 1914. They also say that he was the first man to march back to the village, wearing a battle-scarred uniform and with French mud still on his puttees.

He died nine years later, at the age of twenty-seven, having earlier married my mother and set about starting his own garage business in the village to earn a living in difficult post-First World War England and to bring up his family. The gassing he had received left him unable to fight back after suffering an attack of pneumonia and pleurisy. The business premises near Hooton station where my father had started his garage a couple of years before his death, is still there today and even though the embryonic business was broken up after his death, and sold, my mother was left with nothing.

I was three when he died and my baby sister, Doreen, was only eight weeks old. Like other ladies of that era – after a generation of menfolk had been ravaged by the Great War – my mother had no alternative but to get on with her life as best she could and to bring up her two children with all the love and dedication she could muster, which was plenty.

Obviously, I have no personal recollections of my father, though I do have an old-fashioned, bromide photograph of him showing me how to kick a ball not long before his death.

He was a keen footballer who had been on Tranmere's books. One of my most touching moments in later years was when, having had a trial at Tranmere, the club's kit man pulled out a picture of Herbert Ellis, my dad.

Although a good footballer, he was better known locally as a promising athlete. I remember the small, rented, semi-detached house we lived in contained many awards for his sprinting feats up to schools, county and inter-county level in the North-West.

I like to think that I have inherited some of his qualities, but the fact is that I was brought up by my mother and she has had a tremendous influence on my entire life. As a widow with little or no income with two young children to support, my mum had to find ways of earning a living. No doubt that is how I unwittingly acquired a business sense myself.

I was very fond of my mother, who never married again, and I was heartbroken when she died, in 1988, at the age of eighty-three in Good Hope Hospital, Sutton Coldfield. Fortunately, I had long since helped her to buy and then sell the house in Hooton and move to a nice bungalow near to myself in Four Oaks. My mother worked her knuckles to the bone for something like fifty years of her life after which I looked after her completely for the last thirty-three years.

As for my own first attempts at earning a living, I believe this began when, along with my pals, I discovered that the peewit's egg was regarded as a delicacy by race-goers at the Chester racecourse on the Roodee, a large park and playing field area where our school team used to play. We used to find the eggs in open fields, as kids did in those days, and sell them to the punters: it was a nice little earner then. We'd sell them for three pence and they sold them for nine pence – and they'd crack them open and just swallow them like on oyster. I thought it was horrible, but I made a profit.

I attended the little village school at Willaston, near Hooton, and later passed an eleven-plus-type examination to move to secondary school in Chester. Even that was a big drain on my mother, who used to have to find me the rail fare; a sum that she could ill-afford.

When I was twelve, I got myself a milk round at Jones', the local village store-cum-dairy, earning six shillings for a seven-day week, delivering forty-eight bottles of milk to both our village and the neighbouring one from 6.30 to 8am before catching the

8.25am train to Chester to go to school. I would arrive at Chester station at about five to nine and would then have to run like blazes down the street to reach the school. I passed five bob of my princely wages on to my mum.

Later, I started going for evening classes at a school in Ellesmere Port where the headmaster was Bill Roberts, the driving force and chairman of the English Schools FA.

Officially, I was studying shorthand and typing, but at the back of my mind I wanted to catch the headmaster's eye on the football pitch and see if I was good enough to progress! I hate to admit it, but I guess I wasn't.

I had played for Chester schoolboys, and I knew that Joe Mercer and Stan Cullis had both been spotted by Bill Roberts by attending his school. Sadly I was never going to be in their exalted class, so some other career would have to be my lot in life, not football I'm afraid.

Bill Roberts had so much authority that if you wanted to be a professional footballer he could allocate you to different clubs. He persuaded Wolves to take Stan Cullis, for example. He persuaded Everton to take Joe Mercer and he got me trials and I spent – what – two years with Tranmere Rovers, but only as a schoolboy going on a bike nine miles every Tuesday and every Thursday to train a Prenton Park. In the end, although I did play for another couple of clubs during my wartime days, I had to recognise that I wasn't good enough.

By the time I was fourteen and preparing to leave school, I was already getting into the swing of earning money, my appetite whetted, no doubt, by those peewit eggs deals. My Uncle Fred, a farmer, once said to me: 'An apple well bought is half sold,' and that's a lesson I have never forgotten.

Armed with my Civil Service pass, I found that there was a long waiting list to get an opening, so I took a job on the railway when I left school that required me to pass a joint LMS-GWR exam.

# LEARNING THE HARD WAY

Off I went to work as a booking clerk at Little Sutton station, starting at 6.30am to supply tickets to the workers travelling to Ellesmere Port. I finished at 2.30pm, when I would then endeavour to make money in any other way I could think of. Starting life with nothing and having watched my mother struggle as she undoubtedly did, motivated me to pledge that I would never suffer poverty like that as I grew up. From an early age my goal was to provide her with a better standard of living, something that, thankfully, I eventually managed to do. From 1953 to 1988, a thirty-five-year stretch, she had a far superior lifestyle than she could ever have dreamed possible in her struggling early years. It wasn't long after starting work that I learned that while a routine booking clerk earned 12s 6d a week, you could get 30 shillings as a relief clerk working unsociable hours at whichever station you were sent.

A relief clerk? That's going up the coast of Wales, for example, very often leaving home at 5 o'clock in the morning by cycle to go to Chester to pick up the trains to go round to Rhyl and Prestatyn and places like that – I'd get 30 shillings a week. And kids today won't realise how little that was, but it was a lot to me then.

Off I would go, any old time, to Welsh coast stations such as Rhyl, Prestatyn, Colwyn Bay and around the Wirral peninsula to Heswall, New Brighton, West Kirby, Ellesmere Port and the like. I did those eight-hour shifts for eighteen months and enjoyed the work, largely because I was dealing with the public. It certainly stood me in good stead for what was to follow.

On 30 November 1941, just before I was eighteen, and with the Second World War in full swing, I volunteered to join the forces, as many young men did, and found myself in the Fleet Air Arm.

A year or so before that, fate had smiled on me. And saved my life...

At the age of sixteen, while I was doing the rounds as a booking clerk on the railway, a job came up that truly appealed to me. George Capstick, a friend of the family from nearby, was the third engineer on a Blue Star merchant vessel and he recommended me for a job as an assistant purser on its next trip to the United States.

I was interviewed in Liverpool and was accepted for the post. I saw it as a chance to open up new horizons. However, as the departure date loomed, I went down with a bad attack of flu, with complications. My mother would not hear of me going and what an uncannily wise decision it proved to be. My mother rang up the office and said that I couldn't go and they said: 'That's alright. You can go on the next trip.' The Blue Star vessel sailed from Liverpool bound for New York without the young Doug Ellis on board and was sunk in the mid-North Atlantic by U-boats, if I recall correctly, with all hands lost, including our friend, eighteen-year-old George. Here again we find my mother's positive influence on my life.

It is not difficult to imagine what that generation of womenfolk went through. Having either lost or seen their husbands, boyfriends or sons scarred for life by the First World War, history was about to repeat itself some twenty-eight years or so on with the Second World War.

My mother had lost her husband through the ravages of war. Would she now lose her only son?

I went to a base near Warrington for six weeks' square-bashing and then joined HMS *Daedalus* at Lee-on-Solent. From there I went to HMS *St Vincent* at Gosport and completed my training as a Leading Seaman, Electrical.

Then came the really scary part: I was sent to Burscough in Lancashire, which was a new Fleet Air Arm base to prepare ships' crews to man the Russian convoys to Murmansk and, hopefully, back.

The Fleet Air Arm pilots were trained there to do what was

known as 'circuits' and 'bumps' for landing on aircraft carriers. Nerve and precision were essential.

These Russian convoy duties were recognised as being among the most chilling of the war. While at Burscough, as a raw nineteen-year-old remember, I was constantly in contact with the survivors of these notorious voyages.

The tales they told were absolutely horrific, as were the injuries they displayed: the horrendous scars, the lost limbs, the signs of being shellshocked or frostbitten, or both.

Their war was carried out in temperatures so cold that their breath froze and formed an icicle to the upturned collars of their coats. They were continually being dive-bombed by the notorious Junkers 88s, which were based on Norwegian airfields and were queuing up to blow them out of the water.

I was ready to join one of the aircraft carriers on its trip to Murmansk and, unfortunately, was struck down with appendicitis. I say unfortunately – I say that with a capital 'U' now – because it saved my life. I went into hospital, a naval hospital in Liverpool, and the ship I was going on went off to Murmansk – not that I knew very much about what happened afterwards – but when I came back off leave after the operation, I was sent up to Rosyth to join another ship which, in fact, took me out to the Far East and that's where I stayed for two-and-a-half years, in sunny Ceylon, or Sri Lanka as it later became.

It was there that two further significant seeds were sown towards the creation of a successful business after the war.

The first of these was the opportunity I received to put some management skills into operation. The second was in hearing servicemen, many of whom were seeing the world outside of Britain for the first time, saying how much they would like to travel with their wives and families when the hostilities were over.

If they wanted to travel, I knew an ex-railway booking clerk who could help them to do so. But first, an introduction to transport.

Ashore in Ceylon, I was given the responsibility by Lieutenant Canavelli – who was from Wallasey – to start our own transport section, a stores division of the Fleet Air Arm.

I was a 'gash hand' – that's someone who hasn't got a specific responsibility. The reason for that was because I put ashore in Trincomalee with 'dengue', a mild form of malaria. I went into hospital and when I came out I just hadn't got a job.

Lieutenant Maurice Canavelli, a very good friend of mine, played in the same Navy football team that I was playing in. He was playing full-back and I was playing inside-forward and he said: 'Do you know anything about transport?' I said: 'Yes, I can strip an Austin Ruby,' a small Austin car, an Austin 7 as you know it. And he said: 'No I don't mean that – I'm talking about organising transport.' I said: 'Well, you know, I've been organising as a railway clerk and I'm thinking about becoming a travel agent, or trying to become one, when I get out of this lot.' And he said: 'Well, I want you to assist me in the transportation of stores that are sent in with the merchant vessels to Colombo and distributed across the island to the three Fleet Air Arm bases, plus the ships in Trincomalee,' which was about 200 miles away.

There was a chap named Slater there – he was a CPO. When he went off, I was left on my own, in charge of around fifty vehicles and eighty staff. I worked twelve hours a day and put in a lot of time making sure that those stores were delivered on time and collected from the merchant vessels down at the harbour in Colombo.

Because of the job, I had my own staff car and was eventually given a room in a bungalow on the beach of Mount Lavinia with two other CPOs. One of them was in charge of the NAAFI: it was a wonderful situation, because we had the best of food, the best of whisky – whatever else it was – and I had a staff car, which proved invaluable. I took the sister who had nursed me in the hospital out one evening in it. We went to Negombo and had prawns and chips on the beach at midnight. When we came home, we got married!

My demob number came up for December 1945 and Civvy Street beckoned, but I was asked to stay on in charge of the Fleet Air Arm transport until an Admiralty civilian came out from the UK to take over my job. I wasn't exactly sure where I was heading career-wise, but when I left Ceylon, in March 1946, I knew that I wouldn't be going back to be a railway clerk.

Football, even had I been good enough, was a non-starter because of a serious knee injury I had sustained while playing in a naval trial match when I was in the Portsmouth area. However, I'm sure I knew even then that the person I most wanted to work for was Doug Ellis. The problem was, all I had was my £300 gratuity in my pocket and a demob suit.

# CHAPTER THREE

# DOWN TO BUSINESS

As I mentioned, it was in Ceylon that I met my first wife, a beautiful, blonde nursing sister named Audrey Slater.

There were only about fifty white women on the island at that time and I reckon that Audrey was the best looking of them all. As for myself, I won't claim to have been the best-looking guy, but I did have a certain 'pulling power' in the shape of my staff car: that was a considerable attraction at a time of limited transport, believe me.

My meeting with Audrey, with whom my second wife Heidi and myself remain close friends to this day, came about through my being admitted to the St Joseph's Hospital at the area called the Galle Face in Colombo with a mild form of malaria.

Ceylon at that time was the HQ of South-East Naval Command under the late Lord Louis Mountbatten, whose offices were in the Galle Face Hotel. Because of the tight security arrangements on the island, as I struck up a relationship with Audrey Slater, I used to have to go and sign her out of the hospital and then sign her back in again.

Back in Civvy Street, in 1946, we married and settled in

Preston, where I took a job with Frames Travel Agency. By chance we rented a third-floor flat about a couple of hundred yards from where Tom Finney, of Preston North End, had built himself a bungalow.

He was already a famous England international footballer then, as interest in post-war football rocketed but, like me, he presumably couldn't afford to run a car at that time and sometimes we used to meet up at the local bus stop. One day he asked me how we were settled in the flat and I mentioned that, because we were on the top floor, rainwater was coming in through the roof where a slate was loose.

I arrived home from work one evening soon after and Audrey said to me: 'You'll never believe who's been out on our roof today… Tom Finney!'

A builder and plumber by trade, this legendary footballer, who went on to play seventy-six times for England, had got himself up on top of the three-storey building and repaired the roof, free of charge and without being asked. Tom was knighted in the New Year's Honours List of 1998, long overdue in my opinion, and not merely because he mended my roof for nothing all those years ago.

We've been mates ever since those early post-war days. He was one of the many surprise guests at my seventieth birthday party. So, too, was my first wife, and they no doubt recalled that first meeting. It was a great thrill to me that Tom spoke to the 472 guests and presented me with a life-sized oil-painting – it was the first I knew about it. It was done secretly by my other directors in appreciation of twelve months of hard work converting Witton Lane stand into what it is today; a torturous procedure, particularly after asbestos was found within the stand and, with half a dozen chaps in white coats going round, we had to have a site meeting every week. I swore I'd never do it again!

Significantly, bearing in mind what was to follow later, Frames Travel of Preston handled all the travel for the Football League and it became part of my duties to deal with the secretary of the day, Fred Howarth.

This included travel and hotel arrangements for representative matches, including their annual fixtures against the Scottish, Welsh and Irish leagues. One thing I shall never forget is the dinner menu, which they insisted upon and which never changed... soup followed by boiled fish and potatoes. It was always the same.

Players such as Stanley Matthews, Stan Mortensen, Tom Finney and the giants of the day were all weaned on boiled fish.

However, I soon became disenchanted with the drop in pay I had taken from my Fleet Air Arm pay to six pounds and ten shillings a week at Frames. I told the owner of the business, Wallace Frame, that I wanted more or I would move on.

Audrey was expecting our son, Peter, who was born in 1948, and I was far too ambitious to stand still. Wallace Frame then invited me to open a second branch of the business in Birmingham (there was already one in Small Heath). I arrived at New Street Station on Monday, 5 April 1948 and I've been an adopted Brummie ever since.

On board ship during the war, there were a number of Brummies in my mess and I used to think that it was a horrible accent. After telling Wallace Frame that I'd resign unless he gave me my own management and hearing that he was going to send me to Birmingham, I thought: 'Oh not Birmingham! Oh, no!' Anyhow, when I got there, I recognised how nice Birmingham people were – so kind, so helpful. I would say that in the last fifty-seven years, I've probably become the best public relations officer in the city of Birmingham, because I firmly believe that it's an excellent place to live: within fifteen or twenty minutes you're out in the country and the lifestyle today, and I give great credit to the councillors and the City of Birmingham hierarchy for what has taken place, for the city has become a very, very lively place at night and when I compare it with Soho, I would say it's better.

With my own part of the Frames operation now to tackle, at the age of twenty-four, I took an empty shop at 30 Hockley Hill, next to the post office, near the library and on the edge of the Jewellery Quarter. My basic pay was only £8 per week, but the attraction was a commission of one percent on my branch turnover. Now there were no bounds to what I could earn, provided I was prepared to put in long hours, which I did.

That little travel agency office proved to be a goldmine. I always tell people that life presents you with little windows of opportunity and that you must take them when they are open to you. Correct timing is everything, of course, and this was early post-war Britain, a time of expansion and of changing social habits.

I quickly found that jewellers or their staff would come to the post office next door to send off their precious parcels and would pop into the travel agent to see what was on offer. 'Going abroad' was becoming in vogue and I was both ready and eager to provide the means. We did a huge amount of business in the Jewellery Quarter in the late 1940s and early 1950s and, remember, one percent of it was mine.

I was soon running executive, champagne-style, sporting excursion trains or so-called 'deluxe' rail coaches with tables, a new idea, to various venues, including football, boxing and speedway.

I developed a business relationship with the famous post-war supremo of boxing promoters, Jack Solomons, and covered every major fight he staged with ringside seats included.

One very famous championship fight for which I recall arranging a trip was the World Middleweight contest between Randolph Turpin and Sugar Ray Robinson in New York.

The businessmen from the Jewellery Quarter and elsewhere would travel with us to Wembley for big football games, to championship fights and to speedway matches.

I later took the post of treasurer at Birmingham Speedway and got deeply involved in the sport during its boom years. We took parties to the likes of Belle Vue and Odsall stadiums, when Birmingham's glamour boy and superstar of the day was Graham Warren.

Graham went on to settle in Australia, but he still comes back to this country sometimes and was my guest at Villa Park for a match during 1996. During his golden years at Perry Barr, attendances reached around 40,000 and there were similar gates elsewhere.

Eventually, I took the opportunity to go half-shares with the famous former Birmingham rider, Phil 'Tiger' Hart, to run the Perry Barr track. My little office was right next to the pits, where the bikes were roaring and sending out their acrid fumes – it was a little uncomfortable, but the pay wasn't bad! I looked after the admin side of things there, which included collecting the gate money.

The punters used to pay two-bob a head and 'Tiger' and I would leave the track, after paying the riders and all the other expenses, with a bag of silver florins to be banked on Monday morning.

Phil had also opened up a second-hand car sales business on a former bomb site in Aldridge Road. One day, I saw him sending prospective buyers off to get their hire purchase and insurance sorted out elsewhere and I said: 'Eh, why don't you provide those services yourself?'

He said he daren't take the risk, so I said that I would. This led to us jointly setting up a car insurance and finance business in Kingstanding, around 1955, with a shareholding of £12,500 each.

We would advertise 'Cheaper Car Insurance than Anyone Else' and 'Cover Notes for £10'.

Business was brisk and the enterprise lasted for twenty years, making us quite a few bob each before it was eventually closed down. Phil died a few years ago at the age of eighty-six.

Several years before my involvement in speedway, a major development came my way. It had the dramatic dual-effect of breaking up both my relationship with Frames and my first marriage.

A Canadian gentleman called into my office. He turned out to be a Canadian immigration officer who was looking for a travel agency to feed his country's drive to attract immigrants.

A deal of £2.10s per successful applicant was on offer and so, in next to no time, we were offering interviews to those who wished to emigrate to Canada – from 6pm to 10pm, after normal office hours, every weekday. There would be queues stretching outside the office and down Hockley Hill. My only staff member there was an excellent young lady called Hazel Brookes. We were both working something like a thirteen-hour day throughout the week.

Within a year or two I was earning around £30 a week, a lot of money then, higher than any of the other Frames branch managers and even more than the general manager. This caused some annoyance among the others and a meeting was called by Wallace Frame at which the threshold for earning commission was raised; the result was that my income was reduced by about a tenner a week.

I wasn't standing for that, so I left Frames, taking the Canadian immigration contract with me, since I was the one with whom they had always dealt. They wished to carry on that way and I wasn't arguing.

An empty office in Cannon Street, near the old Birmingham Post and Mail building and the Windsor public house, proved ideal. Ellis Travel Agency was duly launched on a grand outlay of £2,500.

Once established as a travel agent in my own right, with minimal capital on which to draw, the more difficult process was in obtaining the various necessary licences to, quite literally, spread my wings.

# DOWN TO BUSINESS

To obtain commissions on the sale of airline tickets, an International Air Transport Association (IATA) licence is required. Believe me, they are granted neither quickly nor easily.

It actually took nine months for Ellis Travel to gain IATA recognition, nine months during which I operated without a penny of commission on the tickets I was passing on to customers, though admittedly the commissions were eventually paid retrospectively once the licence was forthcoming.

Fortunately, soon after I started as branch manager of Frames, around 1949, I had become the founder Midland secretary of the Association of British Travel Agents (ABTA). In those days, I carried out a good deal of work for ABTA in getting the Midland-based agencies to join and all this had been solid experience for me in the travel business.

I was consequently aware of the benefits in becoming licensed for the shipping lines. This I achieved for the North Atlantic (which included Canadian Pacific and Cunard) and for the South-East (for companies such as P&O, Union Castle and British India).

During my time at Frames, I had enabled them to become the Midlands' largest agents for P&O Cruises, mainly by courtesy of the jewellery fraternity who regarded a cruise as *the* way to enjoy the fruits of their post-war affluence.

Far be it from me to draw any false or unfair conclusions from methods of payment, but those jewellers did seem to pay more with the old 'white fivers' than they did with cheques or credit cards! Some days that little Hockley Hill office would be stacked with them.

Subsequently, when I started up on my own, due to the restrictions Frames had placed upon me, a lot of those jewellery dealers and manufacturers were happy to travel the little extra distance into the city centre for all of their business and holiday requirements.

Now those 'white fivers' were transferred to Ellis Travel, as business blossomed. That was Frames' problem, not mine. I was far too occupied in moving forward to bother to get involved in any recriminations with my former employers about the past. The Canadian immigration contract was also going well and this, of course, included all of the travel business involved, as well as the £2.10s per head paid by the Canadian government for actually securing those immigrants.

In the first year we had helped 1,250 people to emigrate to a new life. Today, near to Toronto, there is a whole community based on the families we sent over in those early post-war days.

There was a company called Lucas Rotax at Scarborough Bluffs just outside Toronto, which was largely staffed by our emigrants.

(Later, from 1963 to 1976 to be precise, I responded to an invitation to open an Ellis Travel branch in Toronto, largely to look after the requirements of the people I had sent out there.)

One of the conditions that arose in taking the Canadian contract was that I would cross the Atlantic myself to observe the industries offering jobs and the available accommodation. I was required to travel right across Canada for a month and this necessitated my taking two years' full holiday entitlement.

I was to spend most of my time in Ontario, but I also went to Saskatchewan, to Edmonton and to Calgary in Alberta.

Frames agreed to it and they put in a temporary manager at Hockley Hill while I was away, but my wife, Audrey, was not in the least impressed with the idea. Subsequently, our marriage failed.

Well, I suppose, whatever I'm accused of now, I didn't employ too many people – one to start with – I was earning, in total, more, by 1950, than the general manager of Frames with fifty-odd offices!

The Canadian government paid for me to see Canada – industry, commerce, agriculture – and I travelled all across the country, but it did pay and I learned a lot. I subsequently bought a travel agency in Toronto – Sharp's Travel – and then, having done that, I expanded again in 1963, when I started tour operating there. I'm the founder of the package-tour industry – I began tour operating when I was the first in Canada as I had been the first from Birmingham. I was the first from: Manchester, Glasgow, Belfast and Dublin – Belfast was my tour operation known a Midlands Air Tour Operators to start with, then Sunlight then Global and several more. But from Canada it was known as CTAL – Canadian Travel Advisers Limited – and had five flights a week to the Caribbean.

Eventually, I formed an alliance with three other travel agents and suddenly I was able to take people to Spain and Majorca.

We were operating with a thirty-six-seat Dakota and to get to Palma, which was a five-and-three-quarter-hour trip, we had to stop at Toulouse to refuel. Because of the weight, we also had to position people in the aircraft. A male was considered to be 70 kilos and a female 60 kilos, so you couldn't necessarily place a male and a female next to one another on the aircraft. To begin with, I weighed all of the passengers on my bathroom scales before they checked in. After one year, I could afford to pay for other people to do it.

Meanwhile, expansion simply continued unchecked as holidays abroad became more and more fashionable. This, I suppose, led to one of the major turning points in my business career.

Although some ten years had passed, I had never forgotten those servicemen back in the days near the end of the Second World War who, in seeing parts of the world that they thought they would never see, vowed to return there with their families one day, and to travel to other exotic locations around the globe.

Making such complicated arrangements I knew would be beyond many of them and, in 1956, aware of the huge potential market, I introduced pioneering 'package-deal' holidays. All of this took place at much the same time as similar services were being offered by Sky Tours and Horizon in London. As a result, we had an agreement that we would not trespass on each other's territory.

In order to gain a broad customer base, I initiated an alliance with four other Midland-based travel agents: Joe Schutz of Transglobe in New Street, Birmingham; Laurie Bloxham of Dillinghams in Church Street, also in the centre of Birmingham; Arthur Godfrey with Godfreys of Coventry; and Stan Banks of Winwoods in Worcester.

We were launched as Midland Air Tour Operators (MATO), with myself as managing director, and new horizons were opened up for the masses. Instead of the old 'bucket-and-spade' holidays in places like Blackpool and Bournemouth, or a caravan in Skegness or Weston-super-Mare, ordinary families, many on moderate incomes, were suddenly transported to the sunshine of Majorca, Spain and elsewhere.

MATO chartered Dakotas from Derby Aviation (now British Midland), two flights each week, one to Perpignan, for the Costa Brava and one to Palma, Majorca.

In the early days, the cost was about thirty guineas for two weeks, full board, in the sunshine on the Med, inclusive of coach transfer from airport to hotel. When these wide-eyed travellers got there, they discovered that they received hundreds of pesetas to the pound and that wine or brandy cost the equivalent of a few pence per litre.

Meals in the beach restaurants or foodstuffs in the stores were equally inexpensive and, what's more, the sun shone for about sixteen hours every day. It was a world they had previously only dreamed of in their wildest fantasies.

As those holidaymakers returned, starry-eyed, suntanned, packing duty-free booze and large Spanish dolls, they were already mentally booking up for next year.

One crucial component was that of keeping the cost down, which meant that we had to make everything at our end of the project cost-effective. Here again my mother, who now lived in Birmingham and looked after Peter, was an enormous help.

Our catering consisted of my purchasing large hams and turkeys, some of which came from Billy Walker senior, licensee of the Malt Shovel hotel at Stonebridge, and my mother cut the sandwiches to provide packed meals for on-flight consumption.

# CHAPTER FOUR

# MAKING A MILLION

In our first year of sending cut-price holidaymakers to Majorca and the Costa Brava, the sandwiches, covered in wet lettuce to keep them moist and cut by my mother the night before, were delivered to the aircraft in biscuit tins prior to in-flight distribution.

We would take our own tea, coffee, milk and sugar with us and, on the way to the airport, I would stop off and purchase a supply of alcoholic drinks to sell en route, since there was no duty-free facility at Birmingham Airport at that time.

The passengers used to be supplied with a cushion on which to rest their carton of sandwiches. Not very sophisticated I will admit but, remember, we were pioneers feeling our way and better catering was to follow as we developed.

I well remember that one of our regular captains was named Eric Lines and his wife, Audrey, was the hostess. Tom Pike was another of our captains. My involvement, in addition to getting the business in the first place, was simply to provide anything that was required at any time, including helping to hand out the sandwiches. Sometimes, for various reasons during the flight, I would disappear into the flight deck area.

On one occasion, we had an Income Tax inspector travelling with us, one whom I recognised because I had booked him in at Cannon Street – although I didn't know his job at the time. He was sitting at the front of the aircraft with his wife, watching everything that went on as I was busying myself around, helping out and, on this occasion, I must have disappeared onto the flight deck for a considerable amount of time.

Some time afterwards, a colleague of the tax inspector, who also went on one of our trips, told me that when he got back to the office he had told them: 'This guy Ellis, he books you in, brings the drinks, hands out the sandwiches, and what's more, he flies the f*****g thing as well…'

That 'slightly' exaggerated summing up confirmed that the package-deal holiday had arrived and, in 1962, when I sold Sunflight, another business I had started, to Sir Isaac Wolfsen, the *Evening Mail* in Birmingham ran a story declaring that the deal had made Doug Ellis a millionaire.

Since then I have learned that not every story you read in the press is true but, to be fair, I had no cause to deny that particular one. In 1956, without business partners, I began operating, from Manchester, a new company which I named Sunflight, with twin-engined Vikings. For the next twenty years I expanded with flights from Glasgow, Edinburgh, Belfast and Dublin. Together with MATO, which I had now bought from my original partners, this became the largest air tour operator outside London, flying to France, Italy, Spain, Morocco, Yugoslavia and Tunisia with four-engined Viscounts, a DC4 and a DC6B.

I sold Sunflight to Sir Isaac Wolfson, chairman of Great Universal Stores, but retained MATO. By this time I also had twelve retail travel agencies in different cities throughout the UK and Canada, booking passengers by air, sea and land.

Meanwhile, in the course of constantly travelling back and forth to Majorca and Spain in connection with block bookings for the package-deal holidays, I inevitably forged strong contacts with several hotels. This led, ultimately, to my having five of my own, all of which amounted to a total of 600 bedrooms, which we constantly filled with our own holidaymakers.

Just outside Palma, Majorca, there was the Rosamar in Terreno, the Mar Azul in Cala Ratjada on the northern coast, the Grand Sol in Cala Bona, the Albatross and the Clara Mar on the Costa Brava, all constantly occupied by the guests whom we had booked in at one of our offices. Alongside the travel business other interests also developed over a period of years, including farming, construction and a chain of various retail shops, notably butchers, cafes and shoes.

Ellmanton Construction was another of my companies. For years Ellmanton built leasehold dwellings around the area and though the building activities ceased a few years ago, the company is still in existence and receives income from the houses, shops and flats it created.

For a number of years Harry Kartz, who was also to become a Villa director and chairman for a year, and myself jointly owned a number of racehorses, which were based on my stud farm near Lichfield where we bred and raced thoroughbred horses on the flat.

At our peak in racing, I owned or shared in twenty-three bloodstock, including the fine mare Julie Andrews, and the colt, Ellkar. With Tom Taylor as my private trainer at Aldershawe, I persuaded a few friends to place their horses with Tom and, in one outstanding season, he produced nine winners. Throughout it all, though, I have to say that my main sporting love outside of football has been salmon fishing.

During the same period, when my business policy was one of diversification, or Vertical Integration as it is termed, we also ran our own coach company for the convenience of our holidaymakers.

My purpose in dwelling on all these aspects of my business affairs is to illustrate the grounding that it gave me when it came to working to get all possible essential services supplied under your own roof. This principle has been a main plank of our thinking at Villa Park.

With this approach one has to be constantly watching the market and being ready to meet public demand. For instance, when it emerged that a trend towards self-catering holidays was developing, our travel agency responded.

In order to meet this demand we built, in conjunction with a Spanish builder, our own block of self-catering apartments named Ronda in Fuengirola, near Marbella, consisting of a lounge, a kitchen and two or three bedrooms. When completed, we had 234 apartments with 720 beds and found that Mr and Mrs Joe Public were ready to fill them. I well remember a photograph being published in the Birmingham *Mail* of our passengers setting off from the airport, armed with their kettles, all ready to make a nice English cuppa on arrival at their destination.

Shoes were another commodity that found their way into our multi-purpose organisation for a year or two when I financed, on behalf of a friend of mine, a shoe shop in Erdington. This outlet provided the opportunity to take up vacant storage capacity in the hold of our chartered aircraft to bring back supplies of highly fashionable shoes from both Spain and Italy to be sold in the Erdington shoe shop.

When I reached the peak of my business diversification in the 1960s, I also had financial interests in three butchers' shops, two cafes, an electronics factory in Nuneaton and a couple of farms, one of them for stud and bloodstock purposes.

Car hire was yet another activity in which we were involved for a while, based at 117 Grafton Street, Dublin. This was to meet the needs of American travel agencies who sent tourists over to Ireland who needed motorcars to get around.

We purchased a fleet of 15 Morris Minors in the late 1950s and although it proved not to be a major profit-maker, it did add to our all-round services. For a period of time in the 1960s, there was also an Ellis Staff Agency Ltd with three offices in Birmingham, Dudley and Wolverhampton and this unwittingly led to my being advised by the chief constable of Birmingham, Sir Derek Capper, that I could be quite wrongly suspected of starting a very dubious business indeed.

At that time there was a dire shortage of shorthand typists in the Midlands, so with the old maxim 'where there is a shortage, find the supply and you are in business', I set about making plans. The bizarre episode began at my office in Cannon Street, Birmingham, where we had a staff of fifty on three floors, including some thirty girls on various shorthand and typing duties. On stopping to chat to any newcomers as I passed through, it came to my notice that the staff agency was being used by our department managers for recruitment purposes. The revelation didn't please me one bit. Employing staff in this way was an expensive exercise, so I hit upon what I thought was an original and novel way of starting up our own agency.

I knew that, whereas in Birmingham at that time, there were more jobs than typists, in Hong Kong the reverse was the case.

Off I flew to Hong Kong where I had an hotelier friend who confirmed my belief that there would be a big response from local girls, with both the necessary qualifications and a British passport, seeking secretarial work in England. To test the theory, he advertised in the local newspaper and quickly received about 200 replies. It was instantly clear that we could obtain a supply of such girls to work either in our travel agency or to be offered work by Ellis Staff Agency.

Two practical problems remained. How were we to get them over here and where were they to live? Simple. Or so I thought. Another friend of mine, Harold Bamberg, who ran Eagle Aviation, had regular flights to the Far East and readily agreed to bring girls over when he had vacant seats on return journeys.

As for the accommodation, I had an apartment block in

Moseley, which was virtually empty at that time. It was an ideal place for the Staff Agency girls to reside while they were working over here as shorthand typists.

Soon our plans were progressing encouragingly. We designed a smart blue uniform with nice white blouses and a split skirt, the fashion of the day, so that the girls would look the part.

My hotelier friend chose tall, elegant young ladies who would look good when we launched the agency and arrangements were in hand for the first group to arrive a few weeks hence.

I had in mind a nice picture opportunity for the press at Birmingham Airport where the girls would disembark, wearing their uniforms and line up wing-tip to wing-tip as the pioneering recruits for Ellis Staff Agency.

When all was in hand I was chatting to Sir Derek, a regular at our Villa Park matches when he was chief constable, and asked him whether he needed shorthand typists at the police headquarters in Steelhouse Lane. Indeed he did. At that I proudly outlined my scheme to him and off he went looking slightly quizzical. Early on the following Monday, a lady police officer rang my office to say that Sir Derek wished her to talk to me. Along she came with, to my amazement, a special request from him to abandon the idea, which he reckoned was fraught with danger. 'What you plan to do is not illegal,' I was told. 'But groups of girls living in a block of flats in Moseley will attract kerb crawlers and other unsavoury characters who assume that the girls would be available for far more lucrative services than shorthand typing.' To use a modern expression, I was gobsmacked. Such an interpretation of an innocent business initiative had never occurred to me. So, although frustrated at having what seemed a good idea denied in this way, I could only accept the chief constable's advice, though my staff agency ran for some years and earned a small fortune.

Recruiting clerical staff was one thing. Being accused of taking on a team of streetwalkers was not the name of the game I wanted to be involved in at all and, to be fair, I didn't need any further growth in my activities!

Success in business had enabled me to purchase a villa near Palma and a boat down in the harbour to add cruising as another enjoyable pastime. I also dabbled in sports car racing for a time, driving an Alfa Romeo, but back trouble and the awkward seating position put paid to that and a more comfortable and less adventurous Rolls Royce took over.

During the 1950s and 1960s, my business involvement grew and prospered in several different directions including, somewhat to my surprise, as a wine dealer.

One of my closest associates in Spain came to me and asked whether I would consider taking quantities of wine from his parents, who had a small vineyard in the hills and were producing far more wine than the Valencia co-operative would take from them.

This, remember, was back in the days when there was only a fraction of the demand for wine that there is today and, through limited demand, all this couple's surplus was seemingly going to waste.

A deal was quickly struck with them and they were delighted to be paid the equivalent of five old pence per litre for all the Spanish Red that would presumably otherwise have disappeared down the drain.

I soon had a bottling plant in the cellar of one of my hotels and we were able to supply our bars and restaurants amply with our own vintage.

It was not, I suppose, a Rioja to delight the expert palate, but it was certainly a more-than-acceptable Ellis Red to quaff and enjoy.

Some of it, you will not be surprised to read, would naturally end up at my home in Four Oaks, where guests would be quite impressed to be served wine with a personalised label, which they assumed to be an expensive choice especially for the connoisseur.

I would cheerfully allow them to wax lyrical about its rich fruitiness and pleasant bouquet before informing them that my 'vintage' wine actually cost five pence a litre. It was none the worse for that, though, I can assure you.

Although I left Frames to set up my own business, it turned out that, in the end, my old employer was one of my biggest agents: I paid them ten percent on my package tours and Wallace Frame, my old boss, used to tell people in the industry around the country: 'Well, of course, Doug Ellis was one of my boys.' He was very proud of me! But that's life.

As my business blossomed, I had the opportunity to explore some other pastimes, notably boating, fishing and horseracing. As I mentioned before, I even tried my hand at racing sportscars. My cousin by marriage, Geoffrey Duke, was a five-time world champion motorcyclist, as many more mature people will well remember. On one occasion, I said to him: 'I'd love to have a go at racing cars – I'd like an Alfa Romeo,' and he said: 'Well, come down and meet the president of Alfa. He's with my boss,' which was Gilera, the type of Italian motorcycle he was riding at the time. I met them down at Santa Maria in Italy and the president said: 'Oh that's alright. We'll bore one out for you.' I immediately joined three car clubs and I could race at Oulton Park, Brands Hatch and Silverstone on Sundays and, after a year having done reasonably well – I'd been on the leaderboard a few times – I went mad and bought a Lotus and put a Climax-II engine in it. I would get in the region of three races on a Sunday and it was only when I frightened myself to death, probably at the age of about twenty-eight or twenty-nine, when youngsters of seventeen or eighteen were 'earholing' us and we said and did such stupid things that I said: 'Well, that's enough.'

By now I was happily remarried. Having ended my marriage with Audrey in 1954, I was eventually captivated by Heidi. She was a courier with Sky Tours and a very good one at that.

Among her talents, she spoke English, German, Spanish and French, fluently.

It took me some eighteen months to convince the lovely Heidi that she should marry me, but marry me she did in 1963.

We had a registry office ceremony in Birmingham and a far grander church wedding at her parents' home near Hamburg. We have two sons: Simon and Oliver.

She was the head courier for Sky Tours based in Benidorm. A single girl, stunning to look at, she lived in a very small, one-room flat, which was provided by her employers. There was a boyfriend in my way, as one would expect of such an attractive young lady.

From the start I was attracted to her working ability and the excellent job she did for her employers. But that wasn't all. I was also totally bewitched by her beauty and the sort of person she was. There was I, now her ardent suitor, divorced and unattached and, some ladies would no doubt have said, an eligible bachelor of considerable means. Yet, if Heidi noticed, she didn't let on. I tried all I knew to get her to go out with me, but to no avail. She simply kept me at arm's length. In due course I was able to persuade her to change jobs and to work for my company, rather than for Sky Tours in Benidorm and, in so doing, was able to provide her with a nicer and more spacious flat.

Professionally, at least, I had the power to tell her what to do, but she still kept our relationship on a strictly boss-employee basis for quite a considerable time.

Younger readers will probably scoff when I use the word 'courted', but this in fact was what I had to do to win Heidi's hand in marriage, even though I was based in Birmingham and she in Benidorm. The ace up my sleeve in pursuing my interest in her, quite apart from now being her boss, was in being an air tour operator.

Every week I flew abroad to somewhere or other, so I made it my business to visit Valencia as often as possible, every other week, maybe. When I did so, I would request that my head courier in Benidorm must jump into a taxi, take the two-hour journey to Valencia airport, pick me up, and transport me back to Benidorm and, the next day, return to Valencia. Those cunningly arranged taxi drives were a winner as far as I was concerned, because it meant that I could mix business with pleasure and do a spot of old-fashioned 'courting' during the journey – all strictly verbally, of course, but it was a start.

This 'romantic' recipe appeared to work because she gradually agreed to go out with me, socially.

One weekend, just to impress her – heavens I must have been in love! – I arranged for my brand-new Mercedes SL 190 sports coupè to be driven down to Benidorm while I was being flown in via Valencia. Now I was able to whisk her along the sea front in my sparkling, open-topped sports car where she could be the envy of her courier colleagues and friends; among them, I hoped, her former boyfriend. For a lad who used to be carted around on the back of his mum's bike as she took in washing to survive, I reckoned that wasn't bad!

When I saw how much Heidi loved the sports car, I left it with her in Benidorm and, to continue the wearing-down process, I provided her with a winter job in England, based in Manchester.

Once here, she was able to take part in the annual Christmas parties, which I staged for staff, plus those travel agents who worked on our behalf, and their wives. These functions went round five centres in turn: namely Birmingham, Manchester, Glasgow, Belfast and Dublin.

Eventually my courtship, spread over many thousands of air miles, not to mention those taxi drives, won me my bride and she became Mrs HD Ellis in March 1963.

Peter, my son from my first marriage, is co-director of Aston Villa and has been very successful in building up the Aston Manor Brewery, in which we purchased a substantial interest after it had been founded near the site of the former Ansells Brewery, not far from Villa Park.

Peter was captain and head boy of Repton School and was an outstanding young footballer. Stan Cullis saw him play in a trial match for Birmingham City when, as a young defender, one of his tackles put Bertie Auld, later to win a European Cup-winners' medal with Celtic, over the touchline.

Stan offered him a professional career but, to my total frustration, bearing in mind my own unsuccessful early aspirations, he turned it down, preferring to play football for fun. Peter later joined my travel business after leaving a firm of chartered accountants and subsequently became managing director of my building company, Ellmanton Construction, before taking the reins at Aston Manor Brewery Ltd, where he remains as managing director.

Having recounted the Hong Kong episode earlier, I'd like to recall another experience of police intervention in my business affairs that was far less amusing. 'Deeply disturbing' would be a better description, especially for Heidi. She was often, literally, on the receiving end of a distressing situation. In the early years at Villa Park, when results were not always to the supporters' liking, I started to receive abusive and threatening telephone calls at my home.

Quite often it was Heidi who took the wretched, cowardly calls and, as a result, she suffered from two nervous breakdowns, and no wonder, since the callous callers sometimes talked of kidnapping our sons.

It became so frequent and so bad that, when we had been out in the evening, we would return and leave the lights off in preparing to turn in for the night. This was because a pattern was established of the calls often arriving as soon as our house lights went on. The police felt that the culprit or culprits were parked in a van nearby with walkie-talkie equipment, keeping the house under surveillance prior to making the upsetting calls.

With the curse of hooliganism taking root, the verbal attacks were felt to be football- rather than business-related, although another even more disturbing incident occurred during the period when the IRA pub bombings and the like were in people's minds.

My telephone rang during the early hours of the morning and as I awoke sleepily to answer it I was mumbling about the 'yobbos' being up to their tricks again. This time, however, a voice announced that it was the assistant chief constable, Harry Robinson. Being dubious about its authenticity, I asked for a number so that I could ring back and, sure enough, it proved to be the police office at New Street Railway Station. The caller was, indeed, Harry Robinson.

'They've got you this time, Mr Ellis...' he said. 'They've blown up the front of your premises on the station concourse.' Suddenly I was wide awake.

My automatic reaction was that I would be there in half-an-hour, but he advised me to go back to bed and said that he would get the shop-front all boarded up before I arrived the next morning. The police are accustomed to such situations but, to Heidi and I, it was a profound trauma. I learned that a bomb had been placed at the door, blowing out the front of the premises and virtually wrecking the office inside.

It was an uncomfortable experience, I can tell you. No message was received from the perpetrators of the crime, nor was anyone ever apprehended. For a while afterwards, I felt the need to be 'looking over my shoulder' whenever, for instance, I walked from my office at 44 Cannon Street to the Birmingham Club in Ethel Street, where I would have a lunchtime snack and maybe a frame of snooker.

Heidi's nerves took a considerable time to recover from the ordeal and answering the telephone was not her favourite activity... such was one of the penalties of public life.

The bottom line to the details I have described about my upbringing and background is that by the time I became Aston Villa chairman for the first time, I had learned a thing or two about sport, football in particular, financial struggle, business development, making profits, life in general and, most of all, people.

I was going to need every scrap of that experience, enthusiasm and business instinct at my disposal...

# CHAPTER FIVE

# DOC'S ARRIVAL – AND DEPARTURE

Tommy Docherty was once described as being 'like a fire engine speeding to blaze after blaze with its blue lights flashing and its siren sounding non-stop'.

Sure, there's a hint of journalistic over-statement in the description, but it is not a bad analogy, as I was to discover. When Doc started what was to prove a fairly short, thirteen-month term as manager of Aston Villa FC, he had recently completed a mere twenty-eight-day spell in a similar capacity with Queen's Park Rangers. Tommy lived his life in the headlines and the public at large waited eagerly for their newspapers, to read avidly the next Villa story, and the next.

When he was appointed on Wednesday, 18 December 1968, Doc felt it was too late to take charge of events for the following Saturday's home game with Norwich. He left that to the acting management team of Arthur Cox and Peter Doherty, who had been in charge since the previous manager, Tommy Cummings, had been dismissed.

But, as Tommy Docherty eased his way into Villa Park, all sorts of things were going on behind the scenes. I had invited ex-

Birmingham *Evening Mail* writer, Eric Woodward, to return from his administrative post with the Atlanta Chiefs in the North American Soccer League to be appointed as one of the game's first commercial managers and our club public relations officer.

Eric was ready to return to his native Birmingham after two years of successfully helping to launch soccer in the United States along with the former Villa player, Welsh international and BSc, Phil Woosnam. I was well aware that Eric had been out selling this 'new' game to the American public. Now he could come back and help sell the 'new' Villa to the city of Birmingham and its surrounds.

In my first press conference, I stressed that my ultimate aim was to make Villa Park a multi-purpose stadium available for a whole range of activities, 365 days a year, if feasible. 'I want Aston Villa to be another Real Madrid,' I announced, a shade presumptuously for a club heading for the Third Division! But I meant it; Eric was going to be busy...

Also, I never tired of pointing out that working populations of major European cities rely heavily on the performance of their favourite team to provide moments of euphoria in their lives. As an example, I would cite the experience in Turin, where the huge Fiat workforce ebbed and flowed in productivity terms depending on the fortunes of their beloved Juventus.

It was my conviction that great changes were afoot in society at large and one of these changes would be that industry and commerce would become more closely linked to football clubs. This was the way ahead for Aston Villa, I had no doubt about that then and I've never altered my stance.

I intended to have a line of executive boxes created at the front of the main Trinity Road Stand as quickly as possible and to invite businesses to hire them out on lengthy contracts.

These match-day hospitality units are commonplace now, but it was pioneering progress then and it is amusing to note that our first suggested contract was £5,000 for a ten-year lease.

DOC'S ARRIVAL—AND DEPARTURE

Another local headline-grabber was our appeal for scores of volunteers to come along to Villa Park on Sunday mornings armed with their own paintbrushes to give the dreary, dilapidated old stadium a facelift with a series of huge communal paint-ins. The true Villans did come along too, bless 'em, and when we asked those in local industry to help us by providing gallons of paint, that was also forthcoming.

Basically, we appealed to bricklayers, electricians, plumbers, carpenters, carpet-layers and the like to come along and show their concern for the club by carrying out a necessary service, free of charge.

One of the early good souls to respond to our SOS was a local builder, by the name of Ted Small, who subsequently became our stadium manager and who played a leading role in making the stadium what it is today. The first businesses to respond to our appeal were BIP Reinforced Products of Streetly, and Paynes of Aston, who offered to replace all the smashed windows in the Holte End on a complimentary, goodwill basis. The magnificent gesture was accepted in the spirit with which it was offered and others followed.

Part of the flotation scheme was that Birmingham Industrial Trust purchased 699 shares from the previous directors at £60 each and that 'old' shares were to become 'special' shares worth fifteen of the £5 new shares, and the equivalent number of votes. I was reminded of this by the flotation of 1997 in which these £5 shares achieved a value of £1,600, making those 'special' shares increase pro rata. Back then, just as was the case more recently, searches were undertaken in Villa homes everywhere for those precious share certificates, which had suddenly escalated in value.

To help us get underway, Pat Matthews arranged a working overdraft of £50,000, which, even in those days, meant that we were constantly treading a financial tightrope without a safety net. Generously, the resigning director, Joe Heath, having sold some of his shares to Pat Matthews, loaned £30,000 of it back to the club at a low interest rate. It helped a lot, but we were still very hard up.

Those early days from the Christmas-New Year period of 1968–69 are recalled all these years later as a blur of activity, action, controversy, wisecracks and public expectation.

For that first match under the new regime, against Norwich on Saturday, 21 December 1968, 19,923 fans turned up on, remember, the worst-supported day of the season, 7,000 better than had attended the previous match.

The public hadn't quite taken it all in and the Doc had made it clear that, on this occasion, he was just watching and learning. There was an atmosphere of expectancy in the air but, as we won 2–1, it was only the calm before the storm of hysteria which was to hit Villa Park on Boxing Day when Jimmy Scoular's Cardiff were the visitors.

To be fair to Tommy, he set the ball rolling in ideal fashion by signing Brian Tiler, whom he had admired when he was manager at Rotherham before his brief stay at QPR, three days before his first game at the helm. On a sad note, Brian was tragically killed in a road accident in Italy during the 1990 World Cup.

Trying to sign Tiler from Rotherham had been the issue that caused Docherty's split with Queen's Park Rangers only three weeks earlier. According to reports, Rotherham's asking price was £100,000 and Rangers' chairman Jim Gregory wouldn't agree. Doc, being the Doc, emptied his desk and left.

Whatever the truth or otherwise of that account, we got Tiler in a quick, uncomplicated deal. He was signed for around half of the original asking price to skipper a team that had long since lost its way and thus we went into those opening games of the club's new era with a new captain, a new manager, a new board and a new chairman.

'My name is not Oliver, it's Tommy,' said Doc to the local papers in typically colourful fashion before the game. 'The 19,000 for Norwich was great, but please can I have some more...'

## DOC'S ARRIVAL—AND DEPARTURE

At that time, Apollo 8 was making its historic first orbit of the moon and blizzards were forecast around the country for a white Christmas, but Villa Park was suddenly the only focal point for Villa fans responding to the new era. An amazing crowd of 41,250 turned up at Villa Park for that Boxing Day game and Tommy Docherty and Arthur Cox were like jumping Jacks on the touchline, orchestrating the outpourings of support.

Had Doc stage-managed the whole affair, there couldn't have been a more spectacular kick-start for the new Aston Villa, when, although the white Christmas didn't arrive, the icy, slippery pitch was regarded by many as being 'unplayable'. The game was almost farcical, but Barry Hole gave us a first-half lead and then, in the second half, a Mike Ferguson corner curled in for new man Tiler to race in, leap up and sign in with a superb headed goal that ensured our second successive victory. The roar must have been heard right across the frost-bound city.

Two days later we were at Carlisle and that fixture was to mark our volatile manager's first big controversy. Because of the weather, many fixtures were postponed, so additional spotlight was focused on our game, helped, of course, by the Doc factor.

After a rugged, battling ninety minutes on a bone-hard surface, we emerged as 1–0 victors through a goal by Willie Anderson. Carlisle had previously moved up the Second Division with a thirteen-match unbeaten run under Bob Stokoe. To understate the case, Bob wasn't pleased about the defeat. He reckoned that Tommy's team had been negative, obstructive and more interested in time wasting than indulging in a free-flowing game. Bearing in mind our desperate position in the Second Division, maybe he was right.

'I would rather sweep the streets than play like that...' Bob told the larger-than-usual gathering of media at the end of the game.

Sure enough, his scathing words hit the headlines up and down the country and Doc's Villa were labelled as destroyers. To my knowledge, Tommy lost no sleep over the complaints. 'Stokoe had better watch what he says or I'll report him to the FA,' he coolly responded with just the follow-up the press wanted to produce more headlines the next day.

But there was an amusing sequel when next we played Carlisle, at Villa Park. Before the game, the visitors' dressing-room door was pushed open and a broom was tossed in by one of the Villa players, presumably to help the Carlisle manager to 'sweep the streets'.

Mr Stokoe distinctly did *not* see the joke, but we had more important issues on our mind.

For instance, on my first day at the club, the eve of Tommy Docherty's appointment, I had wanted to meet the players for the first time. They were at a sports ground in Cooksey Lane, where they trained as 'lodgers'.

Frustratingly, the previous board had sold an ideal training ground, near to Villa Park, which they had purchased and had subsequently sold, far too cheaply, for building development. Seeing our players training on a works ground reminded me of another urgent priority: we had to acquire our own facility in addition to all the other requirements.

Clearly, with so much finance required for so many projects, success on the field was an absolute must and things had got off to an encouraging start. In the first three weeks after the changes, a thousand new season ticket holders were signed up, thus attracting £4,500 of new revenue.

This may sound a derisory figure all these years on, but it was quite a significant amount in those days and, what's more, it gave the bank manager a modicum of renewed confidence. Another £2,000 was raised by an unusual £1 bond scheme.

The 'pound bond' was suggested by Frank Owens, the editor of the Birmingham *Evening Mail* at that time, to be run through the columns of his newspaper. Each person who sent a pound received a scroll, personally signed by me, acknowledging their financial support in Aston Villa's most critical hour of need.

# DOC'S ARRIVAL—AND DEPARTURE

Around 2,000 responded. Many of the scrolls were framed and hung on walls around this country and abroad, but one reaction to the scheme sticks vividly in my memory. An airmail-type letter arrived from a location in Germany from the *burgermeister* of a little town who had seen an item about our pound appeal on Eurovision.

Expressing regret that Aston Villa was in financial difficulties, he went on, in broken English, to explain his most moving affinity with the club.

He had been a prisoner of war at a camp on Cannock Chase where his one pleasure during captivity had been to get out secretly and make his way to our games and back without his absence being noticed.

This he achieved every other Saturday by getting his hands on a civilian raincoat to cover his immediately-obvious POW uniform, crawling under the barbed wire fence and walking the 'eight or ten miles' to Villa Park and back. Obviously I cannot remember his exact words all these years on but, in effect, he thanked Aston Villa for helping him through his internment and, though not a wealthy man, he was enclosing twenty Deutschmarks towards our appeal, wishing us every success with it.

It was another case of football cutting across the animosities of war and political strife to create lasting friendships. We gave this lovely story, as we saw it, to the Birmingham *Evening Mail* and suggested that if they were to fly the ex-POW over, we would give him VIP treatment at a match and they could have an exclusive picture-story to publish. They declined unless we were to pay the airfare, a trifle paltry of them we felt at the time.

By then we had made it our business to keep the local press supplied with stories every day, not too difficult a task with the volatile Tommy as manager, Eric Woodward as experienced press officer and myself as chairman. The *Mail* had done especially well, as anyone can check by digging out the files of the late

61

1960s – early 1970s, but there were times when I felt that the spirit of co-operation was a shade one-sided.

The limited strength of the squad was a problem, as were the social habits of some of its members. Before we took over, there had been Sunday newspaper reports of what one might call 'unprofessional behaviour' off the field, though it was Sunday School stuff compared to some of the excesses one reads of in the tabloids four decades on. Let's just say that a certain player, who shall remain nameless, attracted a Holte End chant that concluded: 'He's up, he's down, he's in the Rose and Crown.'

To be accurate, the Fox and Dog in Four Oaks, Sutton Coldfield – not far from my home, and thus Doc's too, at that time – was the place that the many anonymous callers specified as the meeting place for Friday night drinking sessions.

One particular Friday, before a match the following day, my telephone rang and a concerned supporter informed us that a group of our players were knocking back pints of ale in the bar of the Fox and Dog.

'Come on Tommy,' I said. 'We'll nail 'em red-handed.' Off we went in my Rolls and nipped into the lounge, from where we knew you could see through the serving hatch into the bar.

Sure enough, the known culprits were sitting around a table laden with pints of beer. 'We've got 'em…' we thought. However, we must have taken a little while to make our way through to the bar, maybe via the loo or whatever, because when Tommy and I walked into the bar to 'nail 'em red-handed', all you could see on the table were glasses of orange juice. How well they must have had the pub's grapevine sorted out!

There was never a dull moment with the Doc around. When there was an outbreak of hooliganism, for instance, he called for the culprits to be publicly birched. Not one for half measures, our Tom.

There was always plenty of mickey-taking going on in those

days and I have painful memories of being the victim of one incident when I unwittingly set myself up to be the fall guy. The old urge to kick a football myself had not yet burned itself out and I remember on one occasion being encouraged to join in a practice match at Villa Park.

All was going OK, although I was reminded in the opening moments that professionals play a quite different game to enthusiastic amateurs, especially those of advancing years. On a rare occasion when I managed to have the ball at my feet, I took a tackle on the ankle, which led to my being carried off in considerable pain for attention by the physio. It was the same ankle I had injured while playing football in the Fleet Air Arm.

After receiving treatment, I went into the dressing-room showers – which were in different cubicles – and while I was in one of them Brian Godfrey, the Welsh international, went into the adjoining one and must have assumed I had left. Amid all the banter he gave a wicked little chuckle and said in a loud voice to no one in particular: 'Did you see how I clobbered the f*****g chairman?' I could only imagine how his face must have looked when I replied from 'next door': 'I did, Brian. I can still feel it.' There was a pregnant pause before he replied: 'Sorry Mr Ellis. I didn't know you were there.' Obviously…

Doc and I got on very well as relegation was avoided and we set about creating a junior scouting scheme up and down the country. On a Sunday morning, for instance, we would fly up to Newcastle to see a boys' match at our nursery club and then on to Glasgow, where we would watch two boys' matches of different age groups before meeting their parents over a cup of tea and a bun.

Eric Woodward was getting things like catering, the club programme, fundraising and other commercial affairs on a businesslike footing and the club was edging further away from the brink of disaster.

But, unhappily, the on-field euphoria did not last, despite what we felt was a scoop in signing Bruce Rioch, along with his brother Neil, from Luton Town for £100,000 in July 1969. For us to be able to spend such an amount of money was progress in itself.

Bruce had scored twenty-four goals in forty-four league games for the Hatters when they won the old Fourth Division championship the previous season.

The Rioch signing, at such a high fee for a club still in dire financial difficulties, sent a message around the game that we truly meant business; oddly, it unwittingly also created intense hostility from a local newspaper editor. I recall the chain of events vividly. When our new administration moved in, I told local reporters from the national and provincial press that while Aston Villa would be 'reaching for the stars' we needed each-way co-operation to bring it about.

For our part, we would never withhold information in order to favour either the morning or the evening papers. News, such as transfers, would be released as soon as negotiations were completed, whatever the time of day or evening.

I particularly emphasised this point, because a number of morning newspaper journalists had privately made the point to me that the *Evening Mail* always seemed to get the information first.

Among the journalists voicing this concern were the late Alan Williams of the *Daily Express,* the late Mervyn Thomas of the *Daily Mail* and Ian Willars, then the *Birmingham Post* football correspondent. After I had made my pledge to the press, Ian came to see me to say how much his editor, David Hopkinson, appreciated the promise of a fair crack of the whip for all.

Here, perhaps, I should explain that any news announced before around 1pm could then get big 'splash' coverage in that evening's main edition. The longer the afternoon progresses, however, and certainly into the evening, then stories come up nice and fresh for the morning papers. Such news releases considerably influence sales and it was felt that, prior to our arrival, there had been a 'leak' from the old boardroom to the *Evening Mail*.

Unfortunately, due to pure circumstances, the process of news getting out first for the evening newspapers continued, as transfers always seemed to be completed before lunch.

It must be remembered here that we had Eric Woodward, who was himself an ex-*Evening Mail* chief football writer, as our commercial manager/public relations officer.

The suspicion seemed to be growing, quite wrongly but perfectly understandably, that we were continuing to favour the evening papers. Had I, they wondered, been dishonest in my promise of a fair crack of the whip for all? They could point to morning papers, including the *Birmingham Post*, which was still constantly only being left with 'follow-ups' to news announced the previous day.

Proof to the contrary was required and our bid for Bruce Rioch appeared to offer me the chance to balance the books. We could give the morning papers the first bite of Aston Villa's club record signing and my promise would be honoured. By three o'clock in the afternoon, the deal was more or less concluded. Tommy Docherty and I set off for Luton. Tommy knew Bruce's mother quite well and she was a major influence on the household. We simply felt that, on balance, it was better for us to be in Luton than to have Bruce travel to Villa Park.

The timing seemed perfect for the *Post*, although there was now a delay because Bruce's younger brother Neil, himself a promising player, had been introduced into the talks for a dual signing.

By around 6.30pm, as talks progressed, it seemed sensible to alert the *Post* to be prepared. There I made my big, big mistake in authorising that they be advised to leave their sports page headline and lead story open because, no names yet, but we had a big transfer story coming up for them. Tommy went off to the Rioch home. I remained at Kenilworth Road with their chairman. Time ticked away. The Rioch family drove a hard bargain in terms of our signing not now one, but the two, footballing sons. It all took longer than we expected.

As the *Post*'s deadline approached and passed, negotiations were not completed. It was nobody's fault, that's just how it happened, despite our best intentions. It was the following morning before it was all signed and sealed. In evening paper time again.

The *Post* felt very badly let down, as I quickly discovered. I had arrived home from Luton around midnight to be greeted by a person-to-person call from David Hopkinson, the editor who was in Berlin on business.

He was distinctly *not* pleased. 'Hoppy', as he was known by his staff, was hopping mad. He accused me of trying to wreck his newspaper. My protestations that we had been overtaken by events were rebuffed. Subsequently I attempted, each time I met him, to heal the wounds, but he was not approachable and he declined a couple of placatory lunch invitations. The fall out from this unfortunate event had far reaching repercussions especially when he became editor-in-chief of the Birmingham *Evening Mail* and *Birmingham Post*.

Later on, in times of political unrest at Villa Park, the anti-Doug Ellis publicity in his papers was such that I could easily have concluded that I was the centre of a campaign. He subsequently left the Birmingham newspapers and later took a senior post with *The Times* in London.

As a result of the Rioch signing, hopes were high in August 1969 when Tommy started his first full season as manager, though it proved an illusion. By mid-September we had lost seven and drawn two of our first nine games and we were back in an even more serious relegation fight than before.

Managers know that they live by results. If you win, you stay; if you lose – successively – you go down. We had been in a bad position when the Doc took the reins and we had saved ourselves. By Christmas time in the manager's second year in charge, it looked pretty hopeless. There was no money in the kitty worth talking about – I'd loaned £100,000 but, by and large, there wasn't big money available. We'd been out in Atlanta the previous May, at the end of the season, with Tommy and we'd met Vic Crowe, who was a manager out there and an ex-player at Villa, and we brought him back to England. He was just about to become Tommy's assistant when we sacked Tommy and the result is that Vic took over as manager and he brought in Ron Wylie, who's recently left us as the academic manager, and they worked very well. Unfortunately, we went down that year and it was two years before we came back up.

It was about this time that Tommy told his famous story about my having told him I was 'right behind him'. 'If it's OK by you chairman, I'll have you in front of me,' was his version. 'Then I can see what you're up to…' A joke's a joke, but Tommy wasn't daft. He knew the score. By the end of the year we had played twenty-five Second Division games and had won only four of them. Gates were not bad, still averaging more than 20,000, but fans were getting alarmed and some of them were now calling him 'Doctor Dolittle'.

He had to go. My first managerial sacking had arrived, and Tommy Docherty accepted it – and a relatively handsome cheque – with good grace. Some years later I was interested to note in one of his books, *Docherty,* written by Brian Clarke (Kingswood Press) that Tommy said of me: 'Ellis was a good man in many ways. He had a good side to him.' No doubt he recalled that when the moment came I wasn't behind him, I was facing him and looking him in the eye having honoured, to his satisfaction, the unexpired part of his three-year contract.

To my knowledge, he has never since uttered a seriously bad word against either Aston Villa or myself. Indeed, there remained a welcome for him at both Villa Park and my home, as he well knew.

The managerial upheaval was not the only factor, in those early years, to attract the sort of headlines that conflicted with our desire for stability and progress. Boardroom unrest, with constant disagreements and changes of directors, continued to undermine our efforts.

Harry Parkes and I had a number of disagreements before he eventually lost his place on the board, and there were other examples of directors pulling apart rather than working together.

In a three-year period between March 1969 and September 1972, the structure of the board changed again and again. Jim Hartley, head of Harmo Industries, was co-opted in March 1969 to be joined later by his friend, Dick Greenhalgh. In May 1971, Greenhalgh and Harry Kartz resigned over differences of opinion. More problems lay ahead.

The most acrimonious example was to come in the autumn of 1972 when, in an internal power struggle, I was unseated from the chairmanship and briefly replaced by Jim Hartley.

A month later, after calling an EGM to outline what had gone on, I was given a clear vote of confidence from the shareholders and there emerged, under my chairmanship, a reconstructed board.

Jim Hartley, Harry Parkes and Bob Mackay departed and the new board included Harry Kartz, Eric Houghton, the club's famous former England player and 1957 FA Cup-winning manager, along with Alan Smith, then Warwickshire CCC's captain and England wicketkeeper-batsman. For a while the atmosphere was better and, in April 1973, I invited Sir William Dugdale, a Villa Park regular, and Harry Cressman of Bristol Street Motors to join the board.

In the meantime, we were looking for a manager to replace the Doc.

# CHAPTER SIX

# CLOUGHIE'S BID FOR VILLA JOB

A whole variety of incidents have combined to form what I regard as an eventful life in football. One of these started off as a simple car drive to Manchester, but turned out to be some of the most significant hours in the history of the club.

When Tommy Docherty was dismissed, after a 5–3 home defeat by Portsmouth on 17 January 1970, we clearly needed an urgent replacement. Relegation to the Third Division loomed and a virtual clear-out of the coaching staff had left the reserve-team coach, Vic Crowe, a former captain of Aston Villa and Wales, as the only experienced member of the backroom staff. Vic had thus become the caretaker manager, while the board and myself undertook our first, slightly precarious, search for a new, permanent appointment.

To be realistic, we did not have too much to offer any established, big-name boss at that time. Just think about it: we were right at the bottom of the Second Division, with only seventeen points from twenty-six games, there was little cash available for new players and the previous manager had lasted for little more than a year.

Ominously, there was a danger that the initial lift-off that had taken place in December 1968 was only leading to a further crisis and the unpalatable truth was that Aston Villa was in the second worst plight of its entire ninety-six-year history. Though an immediate appointment was needed, there had never been any intention of offering it to Vic Crowe who, in both personality and image, was the exact opposite to the Doc.

I was sifting through what I now know to be the usual crop of applications from a few 'possibles', a host of no-hopers and the odd crank, when I travelled to Manchester with Vic to watch a player.

During what proved an enlightening drive, I got to talk to him seriously, at length, for perhaps the first time and, as we chatted, that scouting trip became a successful job interview.

Long before we arrived back, I realised that this Welsh-born, true Brummie was Aston Villa to the core, a very serious-minded professional and a man with an absolute desire to see Aston Villa on top of the football world. That was precisely what I wanted, too. Why look any further? Vic attended the next board meeting expecting, at best, to be asked to remain as caretaker manager for the rest of the season, but walked out as a permanent appointment.

History now reminds us that it was too late to avoid relegation to the Third Division, but it also reminds us that he was ultimately the man to complete the U-turn from disaster that Tommy Docherty had inherited and had then moved the team in the right direction.

As I said earlier, it would be difficult to imagine two more contrasting characters. Where Doc was volatile, controversial, the master of the quick quote, not too bothered about whom he upset, Vic thought before he spoke, thought twice before he acted, weighed everything up carefully and left others to make the shock-horror headlines.

In his first full season, now with former playing colleague Ron Wylie back as his assistant manager, we finished fourth in the

Third Division and took a huge following with us on the rounds to the tiny, dilapidated little grounds where our visits were greeted like cup-ties.

But Vic truly made his mark as a manager by reaching the Football League Cup final after a magnificent pre-Christmas, semi-final victory over Manchester United that middle-aged and older fans still recall with relish. Later, at Wembley, even the London-based press confirmed that we played better football than our distinguished First Division opponents, Spurs, who won with a couple of goals by Martin Chivers after being forced to chase us for much of the match.

We set new attendance records around the Third Division, while of the 100,000 gate at Wembley, 30,000 were Villa fans.

During his four years as manager, Vic Crowe bought selectively and shrewdly with such performers as Andy Lochhead, Jim Cumbes, Ray Graydon, Chris Nicholl, Ian Ross, John Gidman, Sammy Morgan and John Robson completely raising the standard of the team. A young player named Brian Little had begun to make his mark, with other juniors also progressing well. We had purchased our training ground at Bodymoor Heath and the club as a whole was moving forward.

The Third Division championship in 1971–72 was followed by a tantalising third place in Division Two and no one was sorrier than I when a disappointing final few weeks of the 1973–74 season saw us slip back to fourteenth in Division Two.

Vic Crowe, I know for certain, found it unsettling as manager to be aware that there was little unanimity at board level.

All of this was a great pity since we had made a trading profit of £35,000 in our first year, quite a turnaround from the £200,000-worth of debts and mounting losses we had inherited.

Even when we went into the Third Division, we took a record £50,000 in advance sales and, by the end of that Wembley season, we made a trading profit of £84,452, quite a handsome figure at that time.

Off-the-field activities were getting better, too, with *Aston Villa News and Record,* our match-day programme, winning awards and all-round facilities at the club were being gradually upgraded.

Soon after the 1968 changeover, the long-serving secretary, Fred Archer, had retired, to be replaced by Alan Bennett, who had been assistant secretary at Chelsea, and his more modern thinking also helped improve our administration. Coupled with that was my continual insistence in the philosophy of giving our supporters a much more personal service as valued customers and listening to their views.

Extensive efforts were being made on the commercial side to meet my aim – one that I publicly expressed when I took the chairmanship – to capitalise in every possible club-related way.

With Eric Woodward in charge of the commercial side, we were a pioneering outfit in this regard, using many of the principles that Eric and I had both witnessed in American sport.

In this country, advertising tended to be very restrained at that time, whereas the Americans would cleverly use television as an instant, visual means of catching the consumer's eye. We have caught up with them to a large extent, but at that time we were distinctly feeling our way at Villa Park.

I well remember an amusing episode that demonstrates the efforts we made to establish more firmly the advantages of advertisers using football and television as an ideal combined medium to display their wares and their company name.

Harry Cressman, chairman of Bristol Street Motors, was persuaded that he should have a pitch-side advertising board at the ground on the theory that, apart from being there on show before the live, captive audience at each home match, it would also get some national screen coverage when our games were televised. We asked him for a sum of £3,000 for the board on the 'television side' of the stadium opposite the set camera position. In reply, he wanted to know how much television time he could expect his advertisement to receive and we forecast about three minutes, i.e. £1,000 per minute, plus twenty-odd home games when it would be seen by thousands for a couple of hours or so as an added attraction.

Harry wasn't convinced. So we did a deal with him. He would have the Perimeter board with no down-payment, but he would owe us £3,000 if he got his three minutes on television, a situation that would have to be carefully monitored. As the season in question was approaching its conclusion, the board had been on screen for a total of some two minutes. Danger signs were flashing. Unless we helped the situation along a little we would miss out on that £3,000.

A big home fixture was coming up with planned television coverage, so we let it be known to the players that it would be in all of our interests if that particular advertisement were in camera shot for as long as possible.

Sure enough, in the nick of time, our winger Willie Anderson went down heavily under a challenge and his 'injury' was such that the physio had to run on to give him attention as the camera kept rolling.

To our delight, the episode went out on screen as the BSM board proclaimed the merits of Ford motorcars. By the final fixture, when a full count was carried out, the advertising board had received in excess of three minutes' exposure and a satisfied Harry Cressman sent us his cheque for £3,000. Willie Anderson survived his 'injury' and got his promised £100 and this form of advertising now brings the club a very substantial annual income.

However, I was always totally committed to the intention that Aston Villa would constantly move forward and not slip back. So, in the summer of 1974, we sadly, and with genuine appreciation of what they had done, dispensed with the services of Vic Crowe and Ron Wylie. Another phase of the campaign lay ahead. Another new manager was required.

At that time any top club had merely to say 'we need a new

manager' and the public would clamour, with ample justification, for Brian Clough. This was particularly the case with Aston Villa; though our supporters could never have known how close he was to becoming our manager, nor how keenly he told me that he wanted the job. My first indication came in December 1972, when Vic Crowe successfully negotiated with Clough to sign the England Under-21 full-back John Robson for £90,000 from Derby County.

The deal had been settled at the Baseball Ground, Vic had gone off with the player to his home and I found myself alone in the small Baseball Ground boardroom with Clough and his assistant, Peter Taylor.

Since then it has been written in Clough's autobiography by John Sadler, of how the pair had a 'wearing-down' technique when they wanted to get their own way, by each of them standing on a different side of their subject and talking to that person in turn to the total confusion of the victim. This was precisely the situation in which I quite unexpectedly found myself in. At first I wondered if I could believe the evidence of my own ears.

The Clough-Taylor partnership was then the most effective in club football with five years of headline-making progress behind them. Also, as it was to transpire, the First Division championship was on its way to the Baseball Ground the following May.

To the best of everyone's knowledge, outside of those closest to the club, their fiery relationship with the then-chairman Sam Longson would go on and on as long as Derby County were successful.

How wrong we all were. 'Shut the door...' said one.

'Shall I tell him or you?' replied the other.

'No, you tell him,' came the quick-fire, seemingly well-rehearsed rejoinder.

'Look, Mr Ellis... fetch us.'

By now I was feeling totally bemused. My only purpose in

being there, remember, was to support my manager in purchasing one of County's players.

'Fetch us?' I replied. 'What do you mean?'

'Fetch us... to Villa,' added one of them.

'That's right, Mr Ellis. Fetch us to Villa...' confirmed the other.

'We'll come and make you the most successful chairman in the country. We'll win some trophies for you,' the double-act went on.

My first reaction was to be stunned speechless. My second was to protest. Our manager, Vic Crowe, was serving us well and had only just walked out the very door that they had just closed behind him.

It's true that Vic was subsequently dismissed, but by then I felt he had been given a fair crack of the whip.

Needless to say I cut the conversation short, but it was not the only time Brian Clough made a strong play to become the manager of Aston Villa FC.

There was the time when he contacted me through an intermediary to say that he was available to become manager of Aston Villa, but that he could not officially apply. I sent a message back saying that, on this occasion, I was in a position to interview him, but his application had to be in writing before we could approach his club to request permission formally.

The intermediary came back to me and said that although Brian would not apply in writing, he wished to meet me for a chat and to offer his services verbally. His suggestion was that we meet at a restaurant in Derby.

Fat chance of that, I thought. It will be straight into the local papers the moment we are recognised.

In the event, I chose somewhere a shade more discreet, namely the Corn Exchange restaurant in Lichfield, owned by a salmon-fishing friend of mine, Maurice Nock, where we could be a little less obvious. How naïve I must have been. From the moment we arrived Brian put himself right on show, chatting to anyone who approached him, signing autographs, the lot. Discreet, my eye!

Perhaps he would also have wanted someone to ring the newspapers to get the rumour going nicely and sound the alarm bells at his club. I was never quite sure, but I had my suspicions. Maybe he wanted me to offer him the job so that he could put pressure on his own club before turning it down.

Again, I was never sure.

With so much uncertainty in my mind, the outcome of our meal and chat came with me telling him: 'Look, Brian. It would never work. There is only one boss at Aston Villa and that's me. You and I could never work together.'

After the meal I drove him in my Rolls to my farm in Lichfield, where we sat in the car with rain cascading down outside, as he attempted to persuade me to change my mind.

He didn't succeed but, give him his due, he apparently never gave up trying, though I continued to wonder whether he wanted a Villa approach to use as a lever at his own club. He left Derby County, remember, in a storm of controversy in 1973.

On a third occasion a writer named Jim Waters, now deceased, of the *Evening Mail* and *Sports Argus*, Birmingham, went to interview Cloughie in Majorca where he had gone on one of his famous breaks.

The journalist, who lived in Derby and who was a County fanatic, had correctly heard that all was not well between the manager and the club and felt that, if he turned up unexpectedly at the poolside for a general chat, the story would come out.

How right he was. As the poolside socialising flowed, so Cloughie opened up about how he would gladly leave Derby and join Aston Villa, a sentiment expressed in his own colourful and inimitable fashion.

It was even better than Jim Waters had expected. The next day, the *Mail* was able to carry a banner headline exclusive quoting Clough as saying: 'Come on Doug, I'm ready to crawl on broken glass to Aston Villa… if you've got the guts to come and get me,' or words to that effect.

The story was packed with the usual, forceful Clough observations, all aired in public, questioning my resolve and putting me in an impossible position. It killed off any hopes there might have been of forging a sensible chairman-manager relationship, which I continue to insist is absolutely essential for long-term, if not short-term, club success.

I still didn't think it would work and I've never changed my mind. There will be those who will believe that I was wrong and that I should have let him have his head. All I can suggest is that Nottingham Forest, for all their trophies during the best years of Brian Clough, have also had more than their fair share of problems, including a temporary loss of financial stability, a lengthy spell out of the FA Premiership and a change of ownership.

# CHAPTER SEVEN

# DOWNSIDE OF SAUNDERS

The selection of Ron Saunders to succeed Vic Crowe as manager in the summer of 1974 was not a universally popular move with either the public or the press, though he was to prove the most successful manager of the club's first century.

Because of his reputation as a stern-faced, sergeant-major type who was extremely selective with whom he co-operated, not everyone warmed to him. 'Image' apart, however, he had steered Norwich City to the Second Division championship in 1972 and to the League Cup final a year later before moving to Manchester City.

He reached another League Cup final in his first five months at Maine Road, but after losing to Wolves at Wembley he was dismissed.

It was not, of course, the League Cup final defeat that had cost him his job, but his uneasy relationship with big-name, star players who could not easily accept his military-style methods. 'Player Power' as it was described at the time.

Such well-established internationals as Mike Summerbee, Peter Barnes, Colin Bell, Joe Royle and the like were at the club at that time and there were reports of serious dressing-room disagreements with the new manager.

Consequently, when Aston Villa were looking for a successor to Vic Crowe, one with the experience to get the best out of the excellent squad of players left behind, Ron Saunders was readily available. He was recommended by Alf Ramsey; we had also interviewed him for the job, but he had made it clear that he would not move from his home in Ipswich, thus making his appointment a non-starter.

Let me say here that it has always been my way to ensure that new members of staff with specific duties are made aware from the start exactly where they stand with regard to responsibility and authority.

That principle set the tone of my ensuing relationship with Ron Saunders in the first few weeks of his reign as manager.

One night around 10pm during his first pre-season, he called me at home from the Penns Hall Hotel where he was staying, to say that he had signed Frank Carrodus from his former club, Manchester City, for £100,000. I had never even heard of the player's name, that's how little consultation there had been.

'Oh no you haven't,' I replied. 'You don't have the authority to commit the club to that amount of money.'

'Sorry, chairman,' he replied. 'The deal has been completed.'

'Stay where you are,' I said. 'I'm coming over...'

Penns Hall is only about a ten-minute drive from my home, so I was in his twin-bedded hotel room in a flash. I sat on one bed. He sat on the other.

Ron protested that it was too late to stop the deal so I insisted on telephoning Peter Swales, the Manchester City chairman, who was himself in bed by now. My call didn't please Ron, but it had to be made.

Swales insisted that our manager had shaken hands on the deal and that, therefore, it had been sealed and was still on. I replied: 'No way...' Peter called me at the crack of dawn next day and said that one of his directors was journeying to Villa Park to discuss the matter with me.

In the meantime, Ron had explained to me that Carrodus would be a big asset to our team inasmuch as, while not the classiest of players, he would run all day. He was a great workhorse, the sort of player that every team needs, Ron explained; it was the sort of consultation that ought to have taken place before, and not after, the deal was set up.

Subsequently, of course, we have had similar types in Des Bremner, from the League championship-European Cup-winning team and, more recently, Ian Taylor.

I was never in dispute with Ron Saunders about the team-building logic of signing Carrodus, merely his absence of consultation and lack of courtesy.

When the Manchester City director, Dr Rose, arrived next day, I sat down with him, reduced the fee from £100,000 to £90,000, a useful ten percent saving, and Frank Carrodus joined Aston Villa, the right way, and went on to give us excellent service. It could be said, however, that getting off on the wrong foot in that way soured the relationship between Ron Saunders and myself thereafter.

Ron then signed Welsh international Leighton Phillips from Cardiff soon after the start of the season and, following an indifferent run to Christmas, got the team's act together in outstanding fashion.

Our promotion aim was achieved, as runners-up behind Manchester United, and we also won the League Cup, against Saunders' former club Norwich at Wembley. At the end of the season, Ron Saunders was selected as Bell's Whisky Manager of the Year, ahead of Dave Mackay, who had succeeded Brian Clough at Derby County and who had led his team to the First Division championship.

It completed a remarkable first season with the club for Saunders, and perhaps it had been all the better to have established the demarcation lines. He did, however, have a rather strange sense of humour. By chance, the final match of his first season, when promotion was assured, was against Norwich, whom he had left amid forceful criticism of the then chairman, the eminent Sir Arthur South JP.

When we started the return journey home, we arrived at a roundabout adjacent to Sir Arthur's business premises, a furrier's shop.

Ron instructed the coach driver to go around that roundabout two or three times while all our players were asked to give the two-finger sign to Sir Arthur's place. He seemed to derive a good deal of amusement and satisfaction from this rather childish display.

However, any critical recollections that I have of Saunders are well-balanced by my admiration for him as a strict disciplinarian who made many excellent buys, built possibly three successful Villa teams and who had the knack of getting the best out of his players. I would never belittle or undermine these achievements in any way, because while Ron Saunders was manager, the club achieved the targets set at the time of the 1968 upheaval.

His team went on to win the League championship and the European Cup, the latter after he had resigned, and there are no higher club accolades than that and, therefore, no better confirmation of his managerial prowess.

He bought Dennis Mortimer and Andy Gray in his second season, excellent purchases both of them, as indeed were the majority of his signings.

On the other hand, it is fair to say that I found him a most difficult person to deal with; a manager who never appeared comfortable with any of the high-profile players who attracted publicity.

During those years, when the public were acutely aware of the tensions that existed between Ron Saunders and myself, individual players were also having an extremely rough ride with their manager, notably one particular club servant who simply did not deserve to be treated the way that he was.

I refer to Charles Aitken. The full extent of Charlie's experiences was only brought home to me in full detail later, when he became a much-respected club vice-president for a three-year period during my second spell as chairman.

Charlie's distinguished eighteen-year playing career was terminated – in what, to this day, was a manner I utterly regret– by Ron Saunders in 1976.

Just to put the matter into fair perspective, let us recall that Charlie had joined Villa as a boy from Edinburgh junior football in 1959, had made his debut as a teenager, had played non-stop first-team football until he was thirty-four and, in so doing, had set up a club record of 656 full appearances.

During that time, he had caused not so much as a ripple of dissent in the club as he went about his business with all the dedication of the ultimate model professional. Understandably, against such a background, the sense of injustice had lingered on in Charlie's memory when he later described to me how his distinguished Aston Villa career came to an end in what he called 'total degradation'.

One day in December 1975, while still in the first team, he was called into the manager's office and told that he could stay at Villa Park as long as he liked and whatever he did in the future would be his own decision. Charlie thanked him but, wanting to play on as long as possible, volunteered no observations about future retirement.

Yet, some three weeks after that meeting, he played his last game for the club, against QPR in January 1976. Without offering a reason, the manager stopped picking him for any of his teams, even though he remained one of the fittest players at the club, forced him to train on his own, banned him from the first-team dressing room and only spoke to him just once more.

This is Charlie Aitken's own description of how he was

discarded, and I have no cause to disbelieve him. A few minutes before the March transfer deadline, he was called in and told that he had been released on a 'free'. At some stage he could have a testimonial match. No further discussion. Goodbye.

This, I am assured, is how the club's longest-serving player was summarily discharged.

Fortunately he was snapped up by the New York Cosmos, Pele and all, and in that way his playing career did end on a high note, no thanks to Aston Villa. His sense of grievance was such that it was many years before he could bring himself to return to Villa Park. When he did bury the hatchet and make friends with the club again, he was welcomed back with open arms and was virtually given the run of the place. That is how highly we regarded him on his return.

Charlie has many stories to tell about Saunders, whose training methods, team coaching and trophy-winning achievements he still holds in the very highest esteem. 'One-hundred percent efficient' is how he has described his training routines and match-preparation schedules. Indeed, he found him 'friendly, chatty and agreeable' in his first season, despite the stories he had heard from his mate Mike Summerbee at Maine Road. Then he appeared to undergo a complete change of attitude after he had brought some success to the club.

Why, then, the contradiction between the man's unquestioned qualities and what appeared to be professionalism bordering on the ruthless? Aitken's theory is that Ron set himself very high standards against which he constantly had to prove himself.

He certainly left Aitken, an Aston Villa man to his core, with some remarkable memories. One story he tells is of an occasion when some of the players went to the PFA's televised annual dinner where Jasper Carrott was speaking.

In his own inimitable fashion, Jasper poked fun at just about everyone, including Ron Saunders. One comment he made caused widespread laughter and the camera panned onto the face of Jim Cumbes throwing his head back and having a good hearty laugh, just as he would have done had the wisecrack been about anyone, most of all himself, knowing Jim and his sense of humour.

It was all part of the lighter side of the game yet, apparently, at the next training session, Saunders accused Cumbes of being in league with Jasper to cause him public ridicule. Jim is the mildest of men, but he was annoyed at the ludicrous accusation, answered back sharply and, the two of them clashed.

No one suffered more from Ron's sharp tongue than his coach Roy McLaren. One day the manager asked for opinions on a particular point, Roy seemingly offered one and was instantly pounced on, verbally, by his boss. Saunders castigated him in front of the players for being 'completely wrong' and then added: 'Right. You are now a goal post.'

There then followed a practice match on an impromptu area and Roy McLaren, who later went to live in Australia, was instructed to stand for a considerable time doing the job of one of the goalposts. It was said to be a joke, but no one noticed Roy McLaren laughing.

Charles Aitken, like myself, believes that Ron Saunders would have remained at Villa Park as the club's greatest manager – which his outstanding record endorses – but for this inexplicable other side of his nature. Ron Saunders was also a manager who would involve himself in what might be termed 'club politics', 'running with the hare and hunting with hounds' as I called it. I knew for a fact that he would visit the homes of other directors for discussions aimed at undermining my position as chairman, a distinct policy of 'divide and conquer'.

He always responded well to financial incentives, but I was astonished by one incident. I vividly remember one occasion – during the time when I had handed over the chairmanship to Sir William Dugdale, due largely to the manager's involvement in board affairs and was serving just as a director – I recommended, at a board meeting in the manager's presence, that a £250 bonus should be paid to our youth coach Frank Upton and our chief scout Neville Briggs, in recognition of the achievements of the youth scheme.

The silence that greeted my proposal was deafening. To my amazement, Ron Saunders would not support the suggestion and, because of this, the chairman turned it down. In all my years in business and football I had never heard a head of department turn down a bonus that had been recommended by his directors for his or her staff who deserved it.

It may be that Ron had thought that it was his work that should be recognised and that if there were any bonuses to be had they should go to him.

Ron Saunders had huge qualities as a leader of footballers and a builder of football teams, but in my opinion he did not like anyone who had a high profile whom he thought might get more public attention than he did.

Because of the big turnaround in the club's situation since 1968, I tended to get a lot of publicity myself, and this he clearly did not like, any more than he liked individual players being in the headlines.

It led to a lot of tension between us and more than one intense disagreement.

The question of Saunders and his problems with the star names at Maine Road often sprang to my mind in his dealings at Villa Park.

To me, players such as John Gidman, Andy Gray, John Gregory, Chris Nicholl and others, were all sold too soon, even if it is true that trophies were subsequently won without them. All of these were players with strong views of their own.

There was the occasion in 1977, during Sir William's chairmanship, when Andy Gray was chosen by his peers for the Professional Footballers' Association's Player and Young Player Awards. Andy, rightly proud of the dual selection by playing colleagues, was required to attend the PFA's annual presentation dinner in London to collect his trophies. All he required was the formality of club approval.

The dinner was on a Sunday night, players from virtually every club in the League were in attendance, having chosen playing colleagues whom they admired and respected for annual awards. The concept had originally been put together by Eric Woodward, Villa's commercial manager, who, after all, was present and would have looked after Andy, if necessary.

But Ron Saunders said 'no, you can't go', because of the League Cup final replay against Everton at Hillsborough the following Wednesday. The PFA then offered a chauffeur-driven car each way, with a promise that Andy would be home in bed, stone cold sober, before midnight. Ron Saunders still said no. I firmly believe that Andy was too popular for him. Journalists have told me that if, at a post-match press conference, he was asked something like 'what did you think of Andy Gray's two goals', he would reply: 'Frank Carrodus was our best player...'

PFA officials were distraught that their function was being devalued in this way so, as a weak compromise, the trophy presentation was made by Chris Nicholl in Andy's garden, filmed in advance, and screened at the dinner.

I sometimes wonder if Andy ever forgave him. I have since been told that he accepted his manager's decision like the good pro he was, but realised afterwards that he had been denied what would have been an important hour or two in his life. Incidentally, I was thrilled when he won his well-deserved Commentator of the Year award in recognition of his effervescent work for Sky TV.

This approach by Ron Saunders players enjoying their moments of glory contrasted sharply with the situation when Ron was named as Bell's Manager of the Year, while we were on an end-of-season tour in the Caribbean in 1975 after our promotion and League Cup successes.

On this occasion, our manager was adamant about being flown back home, first class, with his wife who was on the trip, to receive his award and a cheque for £1,000 from Eric Morecambe at the Café Royal and then flown back to the Caribbean. I never understood how the manager could fly back and forth across the Atlantic for *his* award. In contrast, a star player was not allowed a chauffeur-driven return trip from Birmingham to London.

Strangely, although he had crossed the Atlantic three times by now, Ron's fear of flying caused us problems on that trip. We had just one match to play, in Barbados, in order to establish that this was a working trip and not just a mere holiday.

We had a week in St Lucia, a week of absolute luxury on the Cunard *Princess* cruising around the West Indies en route to Bridgetown, Barbados, until a fire in the engine room left us adrift and without power for twenty-six hours. We eventually docked in the Dutch East Indies, some 800 miles from our destination and without the necessary liner to complete the journey.

I hired two small aircraft to ferry our party, which included wives, to Bridgetown. Our manager and a director and a leading player were so nervous at the prospect that they wanted us to charter a KLM jet that was available to fly us to Amsterdam and return home without playing the fixture.

This we couldn't do, since we had already committed and eventually, under protest, Ron was persuaded to fly with the rest of us and the fixture was played. It was just as well that we made it, just in time, because when the news got through to Barbados that the fixture was in danger, there was a threat of serious unrest among disappointed supporters. There were riot police both in and around the ground.

In the event we received a terrific welcome. The Ambassador was waiting with tears in his eyes and said: 'Thanks, fellows. Thank God, you came. You have no idea what the radio and newspapers have been saying about the English.'

We won by about seven or eight goals and, subsequently, I received a letter of thanks from the Foreign Office for the efforts we had made. Twenty-six hours adrift at sea with no engines, no electricity and no air conditioning sorted the men out from the boys. And the babies. I'm not saying who was which, but I did vow that we would *not* take wives and girlfriends on club trips again, a rule that I have subsequently relaxed.

To be fair, out-of-season club tours over the years have provided a rich source of amusing episodes, as one would expect in a holiday atmosphere when all normal pressures have been temporarily left behind.

A couple of what were, to me anyway, hilarious examples of this came in the early days when we were in Dar es Salaam to play the Tanzanian national team.

During our visit, we were taken into the game park on safari to watch a whole variety of exotic beasts running wild at close quarters.

Our party was split into three or four suitably armoured vehicles, each with a port-hole large enough for a couple of people at a time to poke their heads out and either watch, perhaps through field glasses, or if the animals were close enough, to take still or moving pictures of lions, giraffes or whatever.

Our front truck contained half-a-dozen or so members of the playing staff and, players being players, there were three heads, instead of the maximum of two for which the aperture was safely designed, jammed in tight. Jimmy Cumbes, our goalkeeper-cricketer, was one. Charlie Aitken was another.

Suddenly a rhinoceros, possibly disturbed by the intrusion, decided to make a charge. In a flash, from being serene one moment, a couple of tons of angry rhino was then hurtling at breakneck speed towards the players' vehicle. One of the funniest things I have ever seen in my life was those three heads, with wide, panic-stricken eyes, all trying to pull out of the hole at the same time and being stuck there because the space was not really big enough for them. They made it. Just about. And the runaway rhino pulled up short. But the trio kept their heads well down after that.

The match itself also leaves an indelible memory of another player who thought his day of reckoning had arrived early.

The little national stadium only held about 25,000 people, but what seemed like 50,000 turned up. Some of them, we were told, had walked about a hundred miles just to watch a well-known English team in action. There were riot police everywhere and thousands of disappointed Tanzanians were locked outside when the match kicked off. Unknown to myself and my wife Heidi, sitting in the president's box with the country's dignitaries, large numbers were trying to climb into the ground.

To stop what might have become disastrous overcrowding, the police shot off tear-gas shells with a series of bangs that sounded like gunshots. To add to the pandemonium, the tear gas was caught by the breeze and wafted into the stand and across the pitch. The Tanzanian players had clearly experienced it all before and they simply fell flat onto their bellies to allow the gas to pass over them. To the inexperienced onlooker, however, it looked as though they had been shot.

At the time, I happened to be watching Neil Rioch, Bruce's brother, on the far side of the pitch. Poor young Neil thought that a war had broken out and that he was in the firing line. He set off for the safety of the tunnel and the dressing rooms like a startled rabbit and a group of people at the entrance to the tunnel scattered to let him through.

I'm sure he never ran as fast before or after those few moments as he feared for his life. In my mind's eye, to this day, I can still see his knees pumping up almost to his chin in his haste to reach cover.

Just as I could see the funny side of his plight, there is no doubt that he would have laughed like a drain had he been able to see his chairman crying like a baby as the tear gas drifted over us.

# DOWNSIDE OF SAUNDERS

As Heidi and I were guests of honour, nobody else in the president's box moved for a while, out of a sort of reluctant politeness. Then, when Heidi reached down to pick up her handbag in search of a handkerchief, they took this as a sign that we were leaving.

Quick as a flash, the president, the prime minister and all the other ministers fled off down the aisle, leaving the two of us crying, coughing and spluttering on our own. Anyone who has inhaled tear gas will understand how unpleasant an experience it was. I eventually got Heidi to the dressing room, along with the players, to help splash water on her eyes and face and relieve some of the discomfort. Not many matches have actually moved me to tears. This one certainly did...

Ron Saunders' determined style of management won us the League Cup for a second time when we beat Everton at the third attempt at Old Trafford after draws at Wembley and Hillsborough. By now he had added more excellent signings to the team in Alex Cropley from Arsenal and John Burridge from Blackpool, while Gordon Cowans and John Deehan had been schooled through the junior system, following Brian Little's lead. All of which reminds me of my smart, expensive Italian suit...

Through my business travels, I had come across a wonderful tailor in San Remo, Italy, from whom I had ordered a superb suit of the finest mohair cloth with an eye-catching sheen on it.

That particular period, when Ron's team was earning a fourth place in the First Division while also reaching the League Cup final, with three semi-final games against QPR and a final and two replays, with extra-time, against Everton, were just about as emotional as you could get.

Once the final whistle sounded at Old Trafford, and we had won 3–2 after extra-time, having drawn the first replay at Hillsborough, we were all on a tremendous high.

Normally I would not go into the dressing room until the manager and players had enjoyed say fifteen minutes of privacy and, bear in mind, I was not chairman at this time. On this occasion, though, I was so exhilarated that I made the mistake of rushing straight in as the bubbly corks were popping and the players were doing everything but turn somersaults.

As I appeared through the dressing-room door, about four pairs of arms reached out – I seem to recall that they belonged to Chris Nicholl, Ray Graydon, Chico Hamilton and Ian Ross, though my memory is a shade hazy – and into the bath I went. Head first. And wearing my shiny, expensive, San Remo, hand-tailored suit.

For a while, however, that was the last thing on my mind. As I splashed into the bath my head went backwards, under the water and, in the boisterous horse-play, it was being held there as water went into my mouth and up my nose. At the same time, Ray Graydon was tipping champagne all over me. It was a prank that nearly went badly wrong. I was half-drowning and very relieved when I eventually got out and was supplied with a tracksuit to travel home in on the coach while the soggy, crumpled Italian job went into the skip along with muddy shirts, shorts and socks.

One bizarre follow-up to my unscheduled, fully-clothed bath sticks in my mind. As I came out of the dressing room dripping wet I met one of the other directors, the American Harry Cressman, one of the brothers who had founded Bristol Street Motors Group.

He realised what had happened and, to my astonishment, he went into the dressing room and jumped into the bath, fully clothed, emerging later also to travel home in a tracksuit.

All the way down the M6 we were surrounded by a cavalcade of about a thousand motor cars escorting us all the way with horns sounding and their passengers waving scarves and the like.

On the surface all was well. Underneath? It was turmoil.

It was all rather unfortunate, bearing in mind how well things were progressing at the club, that unrest at board level persisted and this was to lead to my leaving Villa Park for three years, other than watching the games as a fan.

# CHAPTER EIGHT

# OUTFLANKED BY BENDALL

The most difficult task I have found in attempting to relive periods of club history from three decades ago is to put the boardroom unrest of the 1970s into a fair perspective.

I have unearthed among some old papers an actual account of it all, which I wrote during the 1979–82 period when I was in exile. I do believe that a picture emerges from it of an individual whose fairly brief involvement in Villa affairs played a significant role in those turbulent days of the 1970s.

During the season 1974–75, when Ron Saunders' team was winning promotion from the Second Division, I was invited by the late Trevor Gill, the chairman of the old Villa vice-presidents' lounge, to have lunch with an associate and himself. The third person concerned was a man of considerable means, already a club shareholder, who wished to invest more capital into the club. Trevor Gill was, among other things, an auctioneer, an immaculately dressed gentleman in a traditional sort of way. A person of precise manners and presentation, he specialised in the auction of goods from business liquidations, an activity that brought him into close contact with our lunch companion.

The three of us duly dined at the Plough and Harrow in Hagley Road, not far from Birmingham city centre. Trevor Gill's associate was the late Ron Bendall. None of us can rewrite history to our own design. Were it possible, I would remove that lunch date from my bygone diary. Little did I know it then, but Mr Bendall was probably already plotting to have me removed first from the chairmanship and then from the board of directors.

Ron Bendall was, to put it mildly, an unusual man. Exceedingly tall, broad and bulky, slightly stooping, not a handsome individual, he had bushy, prominent eyebrows above facial expressions one could not always fathom.

He was an accountant, the head of a firm specialising in receiverships, and a very successful one at that. Bankruptcies were part of his stock-in-trade, and one would assume that, six years earlier, Aston Villa FC would have interested him merely for that purpose were it not for the fact that his son, Donald, was a Villa fanatic and season-ticket holder. Ronald seemed to have little knowledge of or interest in football, or Aston Villa, other than the going rate of shares.

I had no reason to believe that Bendall senior had any hidden agenda at that time, especially since, ironically, he had signed an EGM requisition notice a couple of years earlier to support me in the removal of three warring directors from the board.

During the meal, it transpired that he wished to purchase more shares to add to those already held by his family and himself, and to become a director. I responded by informing him of the restriction that no director should own more than five percent of the company. This was to ensure that we all honoured an undertaking I had made to this effect at a gathering of 3,000 shareholders and potential shareholders at the flotation meeting at Villa Park on 5 April 1969.

However, under the club constitution, a vacancy existed on the board, so against this background and after our Plough and Harrow discussions, Ron Bendall was invited to join us on condition that his and his family's shareholding was a maximum of 5,000 at £5 each. With a maximum of seven directors, this would total a combined holding of not more than thirty-five percent, the remaining sixty-five percent being available to the public at large, should they choose to take it up.

In the interim period, to help the finances of the club, I had invested an interest-free loan of £100,000, taking up as security an option to convert the loan into 20,000 shares at £5 each. The understanding was that I would recover the loan as and when the club was back in the First Division with no debts and a sum of £500,000 in the bank. This situation was subsequently achieved and we were reminded by Harry Cressman that it was now appropriate for me to recover the loan while rescinding the option to take up the 20,000 shares.

The promise was duly honoured, but to the detriment of my own position. Within the next few months, at successive board meetings, Mr Bendall introduced the transfer of shares under the names of his two sons and himself, totalling 27.2 percent of the company's equity. Naturally, I reminded him of the stipulation he had accepted when he joined the board but, to this, Harry Cressman responded: 'Ten years have elapsed since you committed yourself to supporters and shareholders. There is now no need to cap individual holdings.'

I was stunned speechless by Harry's remarks because only a short time earlier I had relinquished my option somewhat reluctantly since it was at a distinct disadvantage to me. At that time, Harold Wilson's wealth tax left me with only a tiny proportion of my income, so I would have much preferred to leave the money invested in the club. However, I went along with the principle of keeping faith with the promise I had made to shareholders and supporters, yet here it was being overturned in favour of a newcomer to the board. So much for trust and unity.

It was around this time that another remarkable example of board disunity took place. Our youth set-up was keen on signing a player from Liverpool schools, Frank Pimblett, but it looked as though we would lose out to another club whom we suspected were bending the pay rules on signing such players.

In order to help us sign him, I visited the player's home in Liverpool where I found his family to be on hard times in the kind of stark conditions found there in the mid-1970s.

Pimblett's mother was asking for terms that were simply not permissible, so to meet what another club had agreed, I overcame this by promising to meet their requirements when he was eighteen, which would comply with the appropriate regulations.

One problem remained. The lad had no decent gear to wear to join other, better-off young professionals, so I arranged for a couple of new outfits to be purchased for him so that he could arrive at the club with his head held high.

The next thing I knew, I had been reported to the FA by my own board colleagues for breaking the regulations. I saw a copy of the letter sent from Villa Park, so I was left in no doubt as to who had 'reported' me. Would you believe it... my own board colleagues!

Down I had to go to Lancaster Gate, to answer charges of illegal inducement and I expected to have a fine imposed of about £1,000. When it was time to speak up on my own behalf, I explained how I had found the lad, in a very poor home, keen to join Aston Villa, but embarrassed at being unable to clothe himself adequately. I received a sympathetic hearing about my trivial offence and a fine of £500 was imposed. This, to the FA's surprise, I paid in full, on the spot, in banknotes, having taken the sum of £1,000 with me which I expected we would have to pay, thanks to this treachery from within.

In my account of that entire period, written back in 1979, I refer to myself as having been the victim of 'knife-in-the-back tactics and skullduggery' and outline the following scenario.

Following the AGM of 1975, a hugely successful one in the wake of the promotion-League Cup double, I returned from holiday in Norway to find that secret meetings had been taking place among the other directors. One meeting, I gleaned, had been at the bedside of Ron Bendall when he was in hospital for a spell.

Unknown to myself, they had decided that I should be relieved of the chairmanship and replaced by Sir William Dugdale, then Sheriff of the County of Warwickshire, with myself being demoted to a place on the board. My first reaction was one of extreme anger, to tell them to go to hell, but I quickly had second thoughts. The club is always bigger than the individual and badly needed a period of harmony. If I could continue to serve the club as a director while, after seven years at the helm, someone else took the ultimate responsibility, why not? During those seven years, without my daily attention, my own travel business had gone into serious decline, making a £250,000 loss on the last financial year, a significant amount of money at that time.

Taking everything into account, I agreed to take a back seat, serve under Bill Dugdale, head of a family of true Villa folk and still a friend, and hopefully continue to see the club progress from the dark days of pre-1968.

Bill was a good professional chairman of meetings, but he lacked the experience of being in charge of a football club. Having been 'born with a silver spoon in his mouth' he was unused to the Machiavellian politics associated with most top flight football clubs. Other directors and myself were sometimes left aghast at his lack of know-how in dealing with commercial enterprises or with architects and builders carrying out work around the stadium.

Thus, changes had been made at the top, but stability had not been achieved. Ron Saunders was being allowed to rule his staff with a strong hand and the atmosphere in club was very bad.

In 1978, Ron Bendall approached me and asked if I would support him in putting his son Donald, a friendly and seemingly well-meaning young man, up against Alan Smith, who was up for re-election at the next AGM. Bendall senior was a tax exile who spent most of his time in the Isle of Man. It would obviously suit him to have a foot in the boardroom back at Villa Park. I could see the sense of it, but declined to give an answer because I was not happy about the situation as a whole.

While I was hesitating, it came as a complete surprise to me to hear that Sir William, together with Harry Cressman and Alan Smith, had called a press conference to announce their resignation from the board a few days before the August AGM. Ron Bendall was putting up Harry Kartz as the next chairman, obviously as his front man, plus his son Donald, which left me isolated alongside Eric Houghton, who was now approaching his seventies.

I did not oppose the appointment of Harry as chairman. He was an old friend and racing associate of mine, but after the changes had been made, I was astonished to find that a new contract had already been agreed for the manager, Ron Saunders. More behind-the-scenes lobbying, no doubt.

They were awarding him a six-year contract with a three-year revolvement, quite unnecessarily I felt since his existing contract still had two years to run. I'm well aware that, here, it will be pointed out that in 1977 the League Cup had been won for the second time and that within that new six-year deal the First Division championship was on its way.

My response is that well before the six years had been completed Ron Saunders walked out on Aston Villa in the advanced stages of the European Cup-winning campaign. I wasn't with the club at that time, but there was enough publicity on the subject for everyone to be aware that by now he wanted his notorious 'roll-over' contract.

By this time, the Bendall family held some twenty-seven percent of the club's issued share capital in direct contravention of our earlier principles. To cut a long story short, I decided to call an EGM with the objective of getting Ronald and Donald

Bendall, along with Harry Kartz, removed from the board. On the night, the voting figures, as compared to the proxies, were interesting. When the formalities were completed, it emerged that he had taken his 27.2 percent to forty-four percent of the votes, while I took my five percent to forty-two percent and lost out narrowly, despite getting a large majority of ordinary shareholders on my side at the actual meeting before it became a ballot.

After that, my place on the board became untenable and I eventually resigned and sold my stake to Ron Bendall with an agreement that should he ever sell, it would be to me at par, namely £5 each.

Subsequently, in 1982, after more wheeling and dealing, he honoured that promise, though at considerably more than £5 each and after craftily getting one over on me, yet again. That's another story. First I had to learn to endure life without Aston Villa as the club enjoyed its finest hours with a set-up I had done so much to bring about, largely through the youth policy we had introduced and which had borne fruit with some magnificent home produce.

# CHAPTER NINE

# 'DEADLY' — MORE LIKE 'GONE FISHING'

I'm 'Deadly' with my fishing rod, not at sacking managers! I might well have created the impression that I have been a workaholic with little interest in social or leisure pursuits.

An escape route from daily pressures is essential for everyone, including myself. Among the many pursuits at various times, my get-away-from-it-all passion has been salmon fishing.

A consuming interest evolved from adversity. In 1960, I suffered a duodenal ulcer, the classic danger for live-on-your-nerves professional people. The ulcer burst and I ended up in hospital having five days of blood transfusions to make me strong enough to undergo an operation at the hands of a very fine surgeon, Victor Brookes. I was 'between marriages' at that time and my mother would visit me constantly; she was driven to the Queen Elizabeth Hospital by a friend, Sid Newey who, incidentally, had won a bronze medal for the steeplechase in the 1924 Olympics. On one visit, Sid expressed the view that, to ease some of the pressures in my life, I should accompany him to his salmon-fishing beat on the River Wye. Sure enough, when I was convalescing, he kept his promise. On the first two occasions, I caught absolutely nothing; on the third visit to the lovely stretch of the River Wye in Herefordshire, I landed a 16lb salmon. In those few minutes, just like the fish, I was hooked. I was soon renting a stretch of the river myself at The Carrotts Beat near Hereford for two days, on Sundays and Mondays.

Later, I had two days at Holme Lacey, still on the Wye. It was there that both my son Peter and myself landed 30-pounders, though he claims to this day that his was a quarter of a pound heavier than mine. Well, you've all heard these fisherman's tales!

From there I was a guest of Eric Haines, the well-known Birmingham butcher, who owned, at one time, about twenty-three shops. An All-England coarse angler, he also owned the angling rights on a mile stretch of the Wye to which he gave me an open-ended invitation.

One day I was in my office in Toronto, when I was invited to join a syndicate of twelve who were to contribute 1,000 Canadian dollars each to finance the searching of rivers in Newfoundland and Labrador for salmon spawning beds. About a year later, we went on our first of what was to be a series of memorable salmon-fishing trips to the far north of the country. We flew to Montreal and then on a further 1,000 miles to Goose Bay, where we changed to a single-engine Otter seaplane and flew another 300 miles north-east.

We touched down at the mouth of the Eagle River in an area between two massive icebergs where we were met by Jack, our Eskimo-Indian ghillie.

For the uninitiated a 'ghillie' is your guide, fishing expert and general factotum. At first we had employed him to help us to build a cabin in which we would live.

It was all a shade rugged on that first trip, believe me. The cabin was a bare structure with no heating and, while there was unlimited summer sunshine by day, the night temperatures were below freezing. Our shower was a suspended bucket of water with a pull cord. We were, remember, 120 miles from the nearest other dwelling and 300 miles from the 'corner shop' which was back in Goose Bay.

We undertook this annual pilgrimage for ten years and each year the accommodation, which eventually had six bedrooms, became more and more civilised. Jack married the maid, Claudette, setting up home in the annex and they proved a marvellous asset in making our yearly breaks so beneficial.

As for the salmon fishing, it was simply idyllic. During the course of our seven-day trip, our six rods would land about 250 grilse, namely young salmon returning from the sea to freshwater for the first time. The largest fish caught was about 16lb, but on average they were about 6lb. To make it an 'even playing field', we all fished with 3oz, one-piece rods – which meant that every catch was a little battle all of its own – with a small imitation fly on a single hook. We fished beneath one of the biggest waterfalls in Canada and to see the thousands of salmon congregating there to 'jump the rapids' was a sight to behold.

One laughable little cameo sticks in mind. I was fishing on my own, up to my waders in the cold, clear water of a separate pool I had found, when a noise from the bank of crashing undergrowth broke the silence. My first, rather scary reaction was that it must be a roaming brown bear which one saw occasionally. They would rear up on their hind legs to pick berries off the trees and, when they did, they stood about 6ft tall. I had encountered one that had come along and stolen the fish I had left on the bank. They were not to be treated lightly. On this occasion, however, when I looked over my shoulder, I saw this character wearing plus-fours and a deerstalker hat, extremely red of face, angrily informing me that I was fishing in his private water. How he got there, in that gear, and in such a remote area I had no idea. I said: 'My name's Doug Ellis, I'm from England, and I do apologise if I'm trespassing. There seemed to be no one for miles around.'

He introduced himself as Dickie Hull and made it very clear

that he was not at all pleased at his privacy being invaded in this way. Off I went to find myself another pool and I subsequently found out more about him.

The military-looking gentleman who had so invaded my isolation and solitude transpired to be very high-ranking 'military' indeed. Dickie Hull was the British Army Defence General who had made a wager with the Canadian Air Force Air Marshall that the River Dee in Scotland was more salmon-prolific than the Eagle River in Labrador. Dickie's peace-shattering appearance at 'my' pool was in pursuit of his attempt to prove his point. I can only add that, whatever his wager was, he lost it due to the sheer abundance of the Labrador species.

During these marvellous trips we each had a special role to play. I had volunteered to look after our necessary food supplies. These we purchased at Goose Bay before flying out to the cabin and I always included a bottle or two of scotch and gin. Well, as I explained, it was a little chilly at night!

We did, of course, live pretty much on the fish we caught, including trout. When Claudette was doing the cooking, she would reprimand us for handing her fish that were far too big to get into the pan.

Lunchtimes used to be, to me, something resembling heaven on earth.

We would assemble on a little sandy bank in the middle of the river and Jack would come along in his boat to join us, bringing the drinks and a supply of ice, which was always in ready supply from the roof of the cabin.

He would light a fire of bracken and branches and inquire which were the most recent of the large fish to be landed. This could have been only about twenty minutes earlier. He would cut the selected specimen into large steaks, which he cooked on the open fire in tin foil and the fresh fish oil, having rubbed in salt to enhance the taste.

We would be waiting at the fireside armed with large chunks

of fresh bread, which Claudette had baked. Believe me, when you've been fishing in paradise all morning, and have teased the appetite with a couple of gin and tonics, the sensation of eating the freshly cooked salmon or trout al fresco, while dipping fresh, home-baked bread in the juices all added up to the finest meal anyone could eat. I was blessed to do so many, many times.

Eventually, however, that particular annual trip ran its course and simultaneously the beats on the River Wye were badly affected by salmon disease. The time had come to fish new waters so, in more recent years, I have been a member of a syndicate which took out a timeshare for one week each year for ninety-nine years on the Waulkmill and Goldcastle beats on the River Tay in Scotland, where I go annually to this day.

My companions include my son Peter, Maurice Nock, ex-proprietor of the Corn Exchange restaurant in Lichfield, a Yorkshireman named John Gill and Barney Barnett. During our week, we reckon to catch in excess of a hundred salmon having once, in the late 1980s, caught a record 188 between us. One individual who enjoyed a trip to Scotland with me was Graham Taylor, subsequently to become manager of Aston Villa and then England. When he came up to try his hand at the sport, I gave him a little tuition and off he went in a boat for the day with our ghillie. He was a total beginner, remember.

This would usually result in a rather disappointing nil return. But not for Graham. He came in with an amazing *five* salmon, all of which he had caught himself. When you consider that thousands of fishermen go for years without landing that many in total, it was some feat. Naturally, as one would expect, he claimed that it was a result of pure skill. Me? I just reckon he was a lucky beggar.

Graeme Souness was another to try his hand with us, when he was manager of Rangers in Glasgow. Graeme had never caught a fish in his life, but confessed to having seen his father poach one, not an unusual occurrence in Scotland. Like Graham Taylor, he was given some basic tuition, having been roused at 6.30am, and sent off in the boat with the ghillie to a favourable spot.

Less than half-an-hour later they were back, with Graeme having caught a 17-pounder. He was white as a sheet and dripping in perspiration. It turned out that his exhausted appearance was more down to euphoria than to fatigue, though he could not believe the strength of the fish in 'resisting arrest'.

The local press was informed of the Rangers manager's catch and one of the reporters inquired of his greatest sporting moment. Was it scoring a goal for Scotland or landing his salmon? 'Catching that bloody fish...' he told them, or words to that effect.

Jimmy Greaves also joined me on a salmon-fishing expedition in Scotland, though he came to make a television programme. We took him to a rock about 4ft square in the middle of the river, with water raging around him, but as we were pulling away in our boat so that he could be filmed in isolation he was pleading in a frightened voice: 'Don't leave me. I can't swim...'

Anyway, after a while, with a little help, he hooked a fish and was handed The Priest, which is a special truncheon to kill the salmon quickly and avoid any suffering. He simply looked aghast at the suggestion. 'I couldn't do that,' he insisted as I took The Priest from him to deliver the fatal, stunning blow. There is a lovely moment, on the film, where he is looking at me out of the corner of his eye and saying to the others: 'See, I told you Doug was deadly.'

Salmon fishing in Ireland, where I got to enjoy the company of Jackie Charlton, has also provided rich memories, though a horseracing episode springs strongly to mind. Back in 1958, I had taken out a twenty-one-year lease on the travel agency office in Grafton Street, Dublin, operating package-deal holidays under the banner of Sunflight and Global. I later opened another in North Street, Belfast, for similar purposes.

On one occasion, around 1962–63, when I visited the Irish

Derby at the Curragh with the trainer Aubrey Brabazon, I was accommodated in the Jockey Hall; it was very basic and open-ended, like stables. Anyone who has visited the Irish Derby will confirm that the party goes on nearly all night.

I gave in around 2am and was awakened at about 7.30 when a face appeared above the half-door and said in that lovely Irish lilt: 'Your horse is ready for you to see, Mr Ellis.'

'Horse? What flippin' horse?'

'The one you bought last night, Mr Ellis.'

'I never bought a horse last night. Did I...?'

Anyway, I scrambled up and took a look at the horse, liked it very much and agreed to buy it for £2,000. A spot of kidology on their part had turned out for real and though they offered me a get-out, I was sold on the idea. The two-year-old was renamed 'Sunflight' and we ran it in claret-and-blue colours, sadly without winning a bean, in five races. It should have been an expensive hobby, but I was receiving no bills from Aubrey Brabazon in the entire five months of ownership. Then I received a telephone call from him. He had found some Malaysians who were interested in buying the horse and was advising me to sell and to leave the details to him.

I agreed, and when I eventually did receive an invoice, it was a little Irish classic in its own right. On one side were the registration fee, the vet's bills, the training fees and so on. On the other side was the income from the sale... and I ended up out of pocket, by one shilling, on the entire deal. I don't imagine that the Irish lads 'lost' much, either.

Although I didn't win a single race in Ireland or didn't catch many salmon for that matter, we did OK when it came to footballers from the Emerald Isle, with players such as Steve Staunton, Paul McGrath, Andy Townsend, Ray Houghton, Gareth Farrelly and the like all making their mark in claret and blue.

We also have an active Villa fan club out there. If Villa Park is my second home, I would readily adopt Ireland as my second country.

While salmon fishing has been a source of great pleasure and relaxation in my life, another pursuit I have tried, namely skiing, proved only to be a pain in the neck.

As a family we would sometimes visit the famous resort of Kitzbühel for winter sports, but while Heidi, Simon and Oliver became excellent skiers, life on the slopes proved difficult for me. In contrast to their being perfectly competent for the more difficult black route, I would confine myself to the far safer blue route and I well remember my last descent.

The day before we were due to return home, our two sons, teenagers as they were then, persuaded me to try the black route on the assurance that they would stay with me and safely escort me down. Off we went and I was managing OK for a while when Simon and Oliver, in typical teenager fashion, forgot their undertaking and left me trailing behind in order to display their own expertise. There had been a particularly heavy frost overnight and the surface of the slope was even more treacherous than usual.

Try as I might, I just could not get any grip once my speed had picked up. I was soon more or less out of control and heading downhill, fast. Alberto Tomba I was not. Heaven knows how fast it was, probably very slow by skiing standards, but to me it felt about 70mph. In order to feel safer, I was crouched on my haunches negotiating my own version of the slalom, when I noticed a little hollow ahead of me with a rising slope behind it. If I could steer into that hollow then the slope at the back would pull me up. Or so I thought. Wrongly, as it transpired.

Into the hollow I went… and straight over the top of the rising slope, as though in some comedy film, to end up headfirst in a tangled heap and momentarily unconscious; I was found there by an Austrian lady skier, who kindly helped me down the blue route, where I ought to have been in the first place. The outcome of that little episode was seventeen days in the Priory Hospital with a cracked vertebra in my neck. That ended any passing fancy I'd ever had for skiing. Even recalling this story is a pain in the neck.

Because of the neck injury I was warned to avoid certain activities, like diving into the water, though I have to confess that, when out on my boat, the temptation to do so has sometimes been too great. Medical advice has been ignored on more than one occasion.

Talking of boats, I recall spending a particular day with the England party anchored in the Mediterranean off Sardinia during Italia '90. The players were skylarking on the deck and Paul Gascoigne, being Gazza, decided that since we had a Bull (namely Steve) in the party, he would complete the scenario by acting out the role of matador. Gazza had Bully charging at him, head down, as they gave a mock display of bull fighting. Gazza would playfully take the head-down charges on his body.

However, as Bully warmed to his impersonation of a beast of the same name, Gazza waited for him to make his most ferocious charge yet, before executing a true matador's side-step, to see Bully's rush take him headlong into the sea, to howls of approval from their England colleagues.

# CHAPTER TEN

# BUYING BACK
# FROM BENDALL

Every professional person has a profit-and-loss account in their career and I am well aware that one of the 'debits' against my name, in the eyes of some observers, has always been that the greatest trophies were won during my absence.

Historically and factually this is perfectly accurate. In the three years between 1979 and 1982, when I had little connection with Aston Villa FC other than as a continuing supporter, both the championship and the European Cup were won. The Super Cup was won after my return in 1982–83.

I do not attempt to gloss over these details, which are there in the record books. Indeed, in one way, and without attempting to steal anyone else's glory, I remain rather proud of them.

To appreciate why I feel pride rather than embarrassment in the reality that these momentous achievements came during my absence, one merely has to recall the state of the club at the time of what has been called the '1968 Revolution' and the transformation which had gradually taken place since that time. Only by that rescue act of 1968, and all the progress made in the following ten years or so, could Aston Villa FC have become champions both of their country and their continent.

Also, I categorically maintain, that these major successes were brought about with the very club set-up and managerial staff that had been initiated by the board during that period.

What better example of this could there have been than the influential role played in those successes by the young players Gordon Cowans and Gary Shaw from the youth scheme we had set up? The captain, Dennis Mortimer, was also from those earlier years.

To the day I die, it will remain my firm conviction that Aston Villa would still have won those trophies had I been allowed to remain as chairman or simply on the board. What's more, I humbly submit, the club would have continued in a far more stable financial state than it did during my three-year absence and for a while afterwards.

Another firm conviction of mine is that had Ron Saunders concentrated on his outstanding strength, that of building trophy-winning football teams, we could have achieved much of what Alex Ferguson and a supportive board have since achieved for Manchester United.

Instead, Ron played an instrumental role in my departure from the club and, during that time remember, success on the field went side-by-side with a lack of continuity behind the scenes.

There were several changes of chairman and other directors in a period of less than ten years, mostly during Saunders' term as manager from 1974–82: I was not the only one who had difficulty with him, believe me.

Even during the successful European Cup campaign, there were ongoing problems between the manager and the board, notably the rollover contract dispute which finally led to his own sensational walk-out.

That particular episode remains etched in my mind for the amusing way in which I first got wind of it.

## BUYING BACK FROM BENDALL

Not far from where I live on the Four Oaks estate was the original home of Keith Coombs, the chairman of Birmingham City, who by then had moved to Knowle, Solihull.

Before he changed residence, his gardener and my own were friends and, like all staff anywhere the world over, would have their little chats about their job and the household for which they worked.

When Keith moved both house and district, he retained the services of his gardener, who thus travelled from his home in Sutton Coldfield and back each day and kept in contact with his mate who was employed by me.

One day during this period, my gardener was able to inform me that, while Ron Saunders was still at Villa Park, he had been seen entering Keith Coombs' residence in Knowle.

Consequently, when the shock-horror of his departure from Villa Park and the 'surprise' of his joining Birmingham City as a replacement for Jim Smith hit the headlines, I must have been one of the very few football enthusiasts who was not in the least bit surprised. My gardener had kept me well posted!

However, soon afterwards, a newspaper headline that not only did surprise me, but also annoyed me intensely, appeared in a local newspaper, stating that Ron Bendall, the then Aston Villa chairman, was to sell his shares in the club to Harry Parkes. Over my dead body!

In next to no time, the lines from Four Oaks to the Isle of Man, where the Bendall family lived, were humming loud and clear.

'What about our agreement when you purchased my shares three years ago,' I asked him. 'You promised that you would give me first refusal to buy them back at par and we shook hands on it...'

To give him his due, he accepted that we did have such a gentleman's agreement though, typical of the shrewd financial operator he was, he pulled a fast one on me despite 'honouring' that agreement.

'You can have them if you pay the same as Mr Parkes has agreed to pay,' he replied. 'If you do that I will honour my commitment to you.' 'You're on,' I said, and was on the next flight to the Isle of Man, where I booked into a hotel not far from where he lived.

The shareholding involved was just less than forty percent of the total share capital of the club, namely the controlling element. When Ron Bendall and I met next day, he told me the price that Harry Parkes had offered to pay him. In return, I offered him £1 more, which he accepted and, with professional witnesses whom I insisted should be present, the deal was done.

Bearing in mind the manner of my departure in 1979, I took a measure of satisfaction from the belief that I had out-negotiated one of my previous rivals by the princely sum of £1. Incidentally, I suggested to Ron Bendall that this banknote ought to be framed and displayed by him as a reminder of the day that he sold Aston Villa to the highest bidder, by £1.

Little did I know that there was still a twist to come in this particular story: it was only when I met Harry Parkes later, and we discussed what had taken place, that I discovered that Mr Bendall had over-quoted the actual figure to me by £80,000. Harry produced copies of three cheques comprising his total offer, with two associates, to prove that I had been duped by a canny financial operator.

There was I believing that I had outbid my rival for the club by a mere £1 only for it to turn out to be £80,001. To be fair, though, I had re-secured approximately forty percent of Aston Villa FC and I was certainly not complaining about the cost.

The one thing I had wanted, professionally, since my departure, was to get back to Villa Park and carry on the all-round development of one of the greatest names in football. Now the door was open for this to be achieved. In this context, a sum of £80,000 was incidental.

However, the biggest 'plus' of all was that in my second term I could bring into being the principles I had learned at St Andrew's; namely that a board of directors all pulling in the same direction is essential for a club's on-going progress. Things would be very, very different in my second term. There has been no more wrangling and no more destructive disputes, thanks in the main to colleagues who keep any differences of opinion – and there are some – at the boardroom table.

At the start of the story, I described the state of Villa's affairs in December 1968. In 1982, I returned to a ground which now had a North Stand replacing the old Witton terraces – a project that I had been instrumental in starting before my departure – while, on the field of course, the team had been champions of both England and Europe.

Sounds cosy all round, doesn't it? The reality, it is sad to say, was slightly different. There is a figure burned deep into my brain of £1.8 million debts that existed at the club. A whole pile of bills were in the in-tray still to be settled on the new stand, firms who had supplied services had not been paid, I will not dwell on this unhappy state of affairs – the subject is covered in detail in the book *Villa Park – 100 Years* – other than to observe that Aston Villa FC did not possess the feeling that one would expect in a club that has been well-managed behind the scenes, bearing in mind the outstanding success it had achieved on the field.

Sadly, by now, playing affairs were also not as healthy as one would have expected, either. It seemed to me that the opportunity to use the trophy successes as a springboard to further glories had already been wasted.

The manager when I returned to the club was Tony Barton, who had been Ron Saunders' assistant, largely with 'chief scout' duties.

Tony was a very nice, well-meaning and professional man who had been an absolutely first-class talent-spotter at first-team level. Many of the excellent signings made during Saunders' reign were down to Tony. Anyone who knew Ron at the time will tell you that he hardly ever went to watch players himself. Just as

Saunders' strength was in turning sets of players into well-prepared teams, so Tony's was in finding the players with the necessary qualities.

Tony sadly died later from heart trouble and I will simply say of him that I did not feel that he was the right person to take the club forward in the long term. I received a good deal of criticism over his dismissal but, like all those people in executive positions, I had to do what I thought was right at the time.

Looking back now, I guess it was in that period – between May 1984 and May 1987 – that I acquired the nickname 'Deadly', pinned upon me in jocular fashion by Jimmy Greaves because of these managerial changes, or maybe it was just because of my expertise in stunning a salmon!

Three managers were dismissed during this extremely mediocre spell for the club, namely Tony Barton, Graham Turner and Billy McNeill MBE. From being champions in 1981, Villa had slipped to eleventh, sixth and tenth and average gates had declined from 33,000 to 21,000. We felt that a new direction was required and I have to confess, in retrospect, for those first three years we did not get it right.

In order to replace Tony Barton, we advertised for applicants, a short-list was drawn up and Graham Turner was appointed. I had admired his work as player-manager of Shrewsbury Town, on a shoestring budget, and the board was impressed with the man when we interviewed him.

My feelings were that we had found someone who could develop into a top name, in the same way as previous young managers had emerged around the country. Finding the next great manager while that individual is still in his embryonic stage is like discovering a rough diamond; one of the greatest services any board of directors could provide for its club.

We tried to do so, with the best of intentions, in appointing Graham Turner, but unfortunately his weakness proved to be a lack of First Division experience and know-how. This almost certainly worked against him in the eyes of some of his experienced players.

Graham did an honest, hard-working job for the club, but without making the necessary breakthrough he required into the big league. He finished tenth in his first season, then sixteenth and was struggling when he departed in the September of his third season. Consequently, we were back to square one in terms of finding a manager of the necessary calibre to take the club forward.

This time we were deeply conscious of the fact that lack of experience in the major leagues had worked against Graham Turner. Now supporters were calling for someone who possessed this experience in abundance.

Again we advertised and this time Billy McNeill, the then manager of Manchester City, appeared to be the ideal person. Billy, like Graham Turner before him, was an amiable individual, but the important difference was that he had won a record number of medals in Scottish football with Celtic, was an ex-Scottish international centre-half and a European Cup winner.

His contribution to Scottish football had been honoured with an MBE in the Queen's Birthday Honours List in 1974 and he recognised the huge opportunity of the job at Villa Park. Once again, however, practice did not match the theory and he was unable to check the slide initiated under his predecessor and we were relegated in 22nd place at the end of 1986–87.

It is only fair to point out here that, while we attempted to fund the purchase of players, attendances had been at a poor level and the club was not in a good state financially, despite the successes of the early-1980s. Resources for massive purchasing in the transfer market were simply not there.

A look at the annual profit or losses on trading during this period is revealing: 1979 (loss) £150,000; 1980 (loss) £679,000; 1981 (profit) £203,000; 1982 (profit) £311,000; 1983 (loss) £53,251; 1984 (11 months to May, profit) £263,426.

These figures show that finances had been heading in a downward spiral after the two major trophy successes; thus the first priority had been to reverse that trend: memories of 1968 and all that were still fairly fresh in my mind!

By now I had truly been through the mill in football, both as a director and as a chairman, 'helped' in a strange way by a fleeting connection with Wolverhampton Wanderers during my three-year absence from Villa Park. Quite candidly, it would have been better had I not allowed myself to get involved in any way. Hindsight is a wonderful science...!

Basically, I was invited by the late John Wardle, the senior partner in the solicitors' firm of Edge and Ellison, to have lunch with him and Sydney Shore, a high-ranking executive of Lloyds Bank whom he had also invited. When we reached the coffee stage, Mr Shore asked whether, since I was no longer on the board of Aston Villa, would I be interested in taking over at Wolves?

At that stage not only had I no idea of the extent of the financial problems at Molineux, but I had also been approached to one extent or another by five football clubs who were seeking new directors who were able to make cash injections. I will not name the clubs concerned, since the talks were strictly confidential and possibly some of those involved are still connected with those clubs, but I did visit three of them, purely in an advisory capacity.

My first reaction to the Lloyds Bank approach was similar to the other five, namely that my allegiance still lay with Aston Villa FC and that I was quite reluctant to consider joining any other club. That's where the matter seemed to have ended until, a few weeks later, I received another call from John Wardle saying that Sydney Shore wished to return his lunch invitation, at the bank boardroom in Colmore Row, Birmingham, and that again I was included. This time the topic of Wolves arrived at the 'second' stage and, in a weak moment I guess, I agreed to visit the Lloyds branch in Wolverhampton with Mr Shore.

*Above left*: I was brought up in the aftermath of World War I following the death of my father while I was only a toddler.

*Above right*: When I turned eighteen, I volunteered to join the forces. During World War II, I served in the Fleet Air Arm.

*Below left*: A portrait taken when I was in my twenties.

*Below right*: The happy day that I married my beautiful wife, Heidi.

*Above*: I built a successful business empire around the travel industry. Our travel agency is pictured, *right*.

*Below*: My dear mother Jane and my two sons, Oliver and Simon.

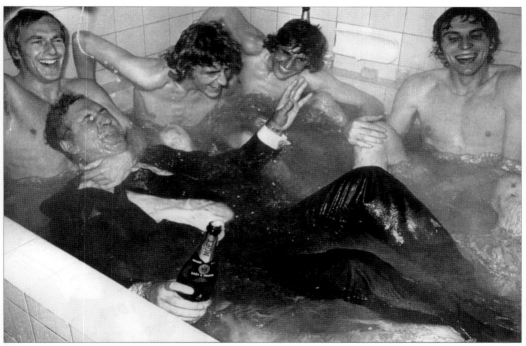

*Above left*: My football career has always been in the boardroom but I'd have loved to have played at Villa Park!

*Above right*: It was footballer and top pundit, Jimmy Greaves who was cheekily responsible for my nickname 'Deadly'.

*Below*: After the Football League Cup Final went to a second replay, Villa beat Everton to win the trophy. As Ray Graydon showers me with bubbly, the team celebrate their victory.

*Above*: Aside from football, another love of mine is fishing. These are a few of my prize catches.

*Below*: Setting sail aboard my boat 'Deadly' in Palma, Majorca.

*Above left*: Meeting one of my football heroes, Tom 'Pongo' Waring, the great pre-war Villa goalscorer.

*Above right*: Watching a match with one of the greatest football legends, Sir Stanley Matthews.

*Below*: Paul 'Macca' McGrath, one of our greatest signings at Aston Villa.

My wife Heidi always
keeps me smiling.

# 1O DOWNING STREET

### LONDON SW1A 2AA

THE PRIME MINISTER

It can be said of few people that they have left an indelible impression on their chosen walk of life. There is no question that Doug Ellis is one of those few. He joined Aston Villa when memories of England's success in the 1966 World Cup were still fresh in our minds. Our national team's fortunes may have waned since then, but Doug has helped take Villa from success to success in the years since then. Today it is in the first rank of professional soccer teams in Britain.

His many friends, and all the supporters of Aston Villa everywhere, will want to join me in wishing Doug many happy returns for his 70th birthday, and congratulations on reaching his quarter century at the helm of "the Villans".

*John Major*

It was an honour to receive such warm birthday wishes from John Major on my 70th. My meeting with the ex-Prime Minister is pictured, *inset*.

My beloved Villa shirt – I would have loved to have been a top Villa goalscorer!

By now the position had emerged that Wolves were in a state bordering on bankruptcy and that their affairs were in the hands of the bank. The 'financial rescue' experiences I had gleaned at Aston Villa in 1968 were clearly regarded as the necessary qualifications for some sort of similar salvage operation at Molineux.

Things were certainly very bad. The team was sliding towards relegation from the First Division and debts were mounting.

The reason for Lloyds Bank's persistence in wishing to appoint a new chairman and to strengthen the board was to avoid the other alternative. This would have been for the bank to call in the receivers to close the club down, a move which would have alienated supporters; not a move they relished, bearing in mind the affection for the club in the region and the number of prestige customers on their books who would have been mortified by such a turn of events.

When I arrived for the meeting in Wolverhampton, Mr Shore had also invited two Wolverhampton Wanderers directors. I accepted the chairmanship of the club at this meeting on the understanding that my friend Malcolm Finlayson was also brought in as a director.

Malcolm, a former fine Scottish-born goalkeeper for the club, had made more than 200 appearances for Wolves between 1956 and 1964 and, after his playing days, he had become a successful businessman and multimillionaire, owning several factories in the Black Country.

Another condition I made was that I brought in my own chartered accountants, with all costs being met by Lloyds Bank. On 10 June 1982, the then chairman, Harry Marshall, resigned and I replaced him.

In the event, our new regime at Molineux survived for only about ten days, as I recall. The figures produced by my accountants revealed Wolverhampton Wanderers to be hopelessly and irretrievably bankrupt.

I note in an official club history that debts were said to be £2.5

million, a huge figure in those days and £500,000 more than was originally believed. 'The cost of the new Molineux Stand had become a millstone' it adds. It is also interesting to recall that, before Ian Greaves took the ill-fated Wolves managerial job, a certain Alex Ferguson, the then manager of Aberdeen, had been approached, but in vain. In retrospect, Alex wasn't a bad judge in waiting for the Manchester United offer to arrive.

By company law, directors cannot continue to run a company that is insolvent, so we had no alternative but to put the proud club, which had been founded in 1877, into receivership. Now remember, it was not Lloyds Bank who were 'responsible' for this, but the new board under Doug Ellis.

By this move the club was saved from extinction by just twenty-four hours (again as reported in the club's official history) and subsequently a survival package was accepted from the Bhatti brothers-backed Derek Dougan consortium and a new company was formed.

All this confirms that, by the time I returned as chairman of Aston Villa, I had learned a thing or three about the necessity of keeping a football club's finances in good order, though the component parts did not begin to bear fruit until we appointed Graham Taylor to succeed Billy McNeill in July 1987.

# CHAPTER ELEVEN

# HOW WE NEARLY LOST DAVID PLATT

Let's get back to this nickname of mine, 'Deadly Doug', that, oddly, took on a new lease of life when Brian Little, against my wishes, decided that he would resign for reasons of his own and under no pressure whatsoever to do so.

I'm not resentful about the nickname 'Deadly', having explained that it was partly down, anyway, to my ability to stun a salmon. Nor am I reluctant to discuss it. Likewise, to complete the picture, I am not filled with remorse that I have been responsible for firing seven managers during my time as chairman. I have no qualms at all about the principle that if a manager fails, he pays the price with his job.

One aspect of it that does irritate me rather, though, is that newspapers come up with a list of a dozen managers over whom I have 'presided', leaving the impression that I have fired all the others which, of course, is not the case. The reality is that seven have been dismissed in my term of more than forty years. Arthur Cox was no more than a caretaker manager and this was before I became chairman; Ron Saunders, whom I had appointed, left the club of his own free will when I wasn't there; two others,

Graham Taylor and Brian Little, have left voluntarily; while a third, Jo Venglos, had expressed himself as more than willing to resign before we mutually agreed to his leaving.

The departure of any manager from a major club is, naturally, a news item of great public interest, but it does occur to me that the newspapers who make the procedure all sound so heartless have probably fired more top executives in twelve months than I have dismissed in all my years as chairman, and with a lesser cheque in their hand, than we have frequently provided to soften the blow.

The fact is that managers know the name of the game when they accept a managerial appointment. The rules are clear enough. They *must* bring about progress in playing affairs during the period of their contract. If such progress is not being made after a respectable period of time, then an agreement is reached over the unexpired portion of their contract, and they leave.

Generally speaking, a manager gets the praise for success. A chairman gets the flak for failure. He is left with one option if he wants to improve things. Basically, the board's job is to oversee the welfare and financial health of the club and to keep its facilities up to scratch; the manager's responsibility lies in the results; the supporter remains as the most important cog of all. I never forget these guidelines.

I have frequently been accused of dwelling too much on balancing the books, a charge that I find unacceptable. Anyone wishing to play Fantasy Football can do so in the newspapers. In the real world, you only get what you pay for in real money, not make-believe.

All I ask is for my record as the head of what is after all a football-business enterprise to be judged by the official figures published at the time of the 1997 flotation. I will happily be assessed in this way if managers agree to be judged equally on their own results.

I never, ever interfere with training, fitness, tactics, team selection or a manager's relationship with the media. On the other hand, I never hesitate to give my opinion on players whom we might sign to strengthen our squad. Whenever I see a player whom I consider to be of the right quality, then I make it known to the manager for his consideration.

A case in point was when Brazil played Sweden at Villa Park in the Umbro Cup competition in the summer of 1995. I was so impressed with Juninho and Roberto Carlos that I sounded out the Brazilian president about them and he expressed the view that Carlos could be available. I invited the player to the boardroom and, though rather nervous, he said he was very impressed with the club and the facilities of the stadium and would be interested in joining us. The Brazilian president acted as interpreter for us, and it emerged that the player would accept a contract with us, paid in American dollars, at a rate that was no higher than our highest-paid players of that time. He indicated that he would be interested in having a further meeting with us back home in Brazil but, unfortunately, Brian Little was less enthusiastic than myself and thus we did not pursue the deal.

Since then I have watched his wonderful displays for Real Madrid with interest, and whenever I see Roberto Carlos on television, bending free-kicks around walls of defenders and scoring sensational goals for the Spanish club, I must confess to reminiscing about that meeting in our boardroom and thinking, 'If only I had insisted...'

However, I would always respect the manager's right to make his own player selections, while managers in turn have to accept board decisions on finance.

To the best of my knowledge, top managers have never been poorly paid and, in the increasingly lucrative world of the FA Premiership, they receive up to ten times that of the prime minister.

No, I do not object to being called 'Deadly Doug' when I dismiss a manager, especially since contracts are carefully honoured.

However, at this point, I readily hold up my hands and confess that neither of the first two appointments I had made during my second term as chairman had been successful. I take some of the responsibility for having selected them in the first place.

To be fair to Graham Turner and Billy McNeill, they served the club during a period when it was necessary to exert the most prudent financial policies, because I would never preside over any organisation that was allowing itself to fall deeper and deeper into debt.

The bottom line in all this was that, in the summer of 1987, it was absolutely essential that we appointed a manage with proven experience who could steer the club back into the First Division quickly and while so doing point the way towards further steady improvements.

One name that found favour with a section of the public was Ron Atkinson, who by then had been dismissed by Manchester United despite winning the FA Cup twice for them. Ron was one of the possibles I had in mind myself but then, among the has-beens, up-and-comers and no-chance merchants who apply for every managerial vacancy that arises, I opened an unexpected letter that changed everything.

It was from a gentleman named Dick Taylor, himself a former Aston Villa manager, who originally came to the club as Joe Mercer's assistant in December 1958 and succeeded Joe as boss in May 1967 when affairs at Villa Park were heading for an all-time low. After leaving Villa Park, Dick, who is now deceased, started a sports outfitters business not far from the ground and soon took over the role of equipment supplier to the club.

Dick's ever-smiling face could frequently be seen at Bodymoor Heath or Villa Park as he became friendly with the successive managers, players and staff who could always rely on a generous discount on his goods. I feel sure that he performed the excellent service for the club at a minimal profit for himself.

During his playing days, at Scunthorpe and Grimsby, Dick had been a friend of Graham Taylor's sports writer father, Tom, who covered Scunthorpe for the local *Evening Telegraph*. True to Dick's caring manner, he had always kept an eye on Tommy's lad's career and was thus in regular contact with Graham, who was then manager at Watford.

The football world at large would probably have believed that Graham, having put down some fairly deep roots at the club over ten years of magnificent progress, would stay at Vicarage Road for life.

Not so. The letter I opened from Dick Taylor said that his mate Tommy Taylor's lad was ready to move on and that the challenge of managing a major club like Aston Villa was just what he was seeking.

As soon as I read Dick's letter my reaction was: 'Yes, yes, yes…'

To be totally fair to the previous two managers, it had not been easy for them as transfer resources had been limited. To some degree, they had needed to help generate their own team-rebuilding resources by wheeling and dealing.

A kick-start was required to get the club's playing affairs moving forward. They had not been able to provide it. Now I felt I knew a man who could: Graham Taylor.

He became my one and only candidate and although it took a good deal of negotiation through his representative, who meticulously formulated the nuts and bolts of his contract, he was appointed manager in July 1987. By comparison with what Graham had been earning at Watford, it was a very good deal. The attention to detail by Graham's representatives also told me a lot about him. This proved one of his great strengths, in that nothing was knowingly left to chance. His organisational ability was absolutely excellent.

Obviously Graham's was a very high-profile appointment, announced to a packed press conference at Villa Park. Certainly, there was no hiding the reality that Graham's brief, if possible, was to get the club back into the First Division at the first attempt. A tough assignment, indeed, and the players had to know he meant business. Graham's first meeting with the players, after I had introduced them to him, sticks in my mind for a particular reason.

One of the first things he did was to ask them collectively if any of them had any problems, any complaints or any desire to leave the club, anything at all they wished to discuss with him, because his policy as a manager would be that of honest relationships. Everything had to be out in the open.

There was complete silence from the group. So Graham asked again, with a similar negative response. Then, turning to Tony Dorigo, he said: 'Well I understand that Chelsea want to sign you and that you want to go...' Everyone knew it was true. Dorigo could only meekly agree that this was the case.

Thus, within minutes, Graham had got his message across. 'Don't try to pull the wool over my eyes lads, because I know the score...' This 'don't-mess-me-about' attitude and his attention to detail quickly saw him become highly respected by his players. I recall that he had a notice on his desk saying: 'Thank you for not smoking in my office.' Nobody ever did. He hated the habit. At one time managers would allow smoking on the team coach. Graham jumped on that straight away.

However, Dorigo was sold to Chelsea and, in that first season, the fee helped to fund relatively inexpensive signings such as Kevin Gage, Steve Sims, Alan McInally, Stuart Gray and Andy Gray. This was, of course, the 'other' Andy Gray, but mention of the name reminds me of when we resigned the original one, now the BSkyB analyst, from Everton in 1985. That was an experience in itself. Graham Turner, then the manager, was on holiday, so he asked me to complete the signing, a task that proved far less simple than it sounded. The process necessitated finding Andy, who was also on holiday, somewhere along Portugal's Algarve – somewhere, but where?

Despite inquiries among all his friends, we were unable to

obtain either a holiday address or a telephone number for him. All we knew was that he was in a private bungalow with his ex-Wolves playing colleague, Kenny Hibbitt, and their respective wives. I flew down to Faro with his friend, and subsequently his agent, Dave Ismay, and being in the travel industry, I commissioned former staff who were resident on the Algarve to check Andy's whereabouts with each hotel and travel agent along the famous eighty-mile stretch of coastline.

As a result of the search, and within forty-eight hours, Dave and I were able to arrive, quite unannounced, at a particular villa on the edge of the beach. I can still picture the expressions on the faces of the little party who were enjoying themselves around their private swimming pool when Dave and I appeared around the corner of the building. They just couldn't believe how anyone could have tracked them down to such an isolated hideaway when they had left no forwarding address with anyone.

However, I had taken a blank contract with me and, after a brief negotiation, Andy agreed to return to Villa Park, whereupon we all adjourned for an excellent meal at a fish restaurant near the beach. The next day, I understand, the president and manager of the Dutch club Feyenoord wanted to sign him and were standing by with a private jet, but they were twenty-fours too late. That's if they could have found him... However, back to Graham Taylor's reign as manager.

Our start under him in the Second Division, with a rather fragmented squad, was not encouraging: namely draw, defeat, defeat, draw. In fact, looking back at the records now, I see we won only one of our opening seven Second Division matches.

No one doubted that Graham Taylor had a big job to do as the football fraternity watched to see whether he truly could operate at a major club in the same way as he had done when he took Watford from the lower reaches to Wembley and into Europe. The answer gradually unfolded positively as the results improved. However, as they did, another 'star' player problem arrived, as it became clear that Mark Walters wanted to move on.

Mark, an outstanding local lad who was born close to Villa Park, was firmly on the England international ladder as one of the most naturally talented young players in the country. We suspected that Everton, who under Howard Kendall had won the championship in the 1986–87 season, were interested in signing Mark.

Sure enough an approach arrived, followed by an offer and negotiations for a fee of £550,000, which I felt was too low for such a player.

What followed was a chain of events which Everton knew nothing about and which resulted in Mark Walters joining a different club for a fee £50,000 higher.

I made a telephone call to Graeme Souness, then manager of Rangers in Glasgow and someone whom I knew socially, having salmon fished with him.

'Do us a little favour, Graeme,' I asked him, knowing that as an ex-Liverpool player he would not mind us putting a little pressure on Everton. 'Make it known in the Glasgow press that you are interested in signing Mark Walters for £650,000.'

The reason for this, I explained, was that Everton were getting the player a touch too cheaply.

Graeme agreed and then telephoned me back to ask: 'Who is this player, Mark Walters? Do I know him?' When I filled him in with a rundown on Mark, Graeme remarked: 'We're looking for a player like that. Can we talk to him?' Sure, they could!

My next task was to get Mark's agent to make sure that, before the player signed at Goodison Park, that he was made aware that Graeme Souness wanted to talk to him at Ibrox. This we succeeded in doing and Mark told Everton that he would think over their offer, but that he also intended to talk to Rangers. In the meantime, Graeme Souness did his homework on Walters, realised what a quality player he was and made him a contract offer he couldn't refuse. That left the small matter of the fee.

'How much do you want?', Graeme asked me.

'You know the price,' I replied. 'It's £650,000...'

There was a disbelieving pause.

'Surely you're not holding me to that price,' he remonstrated. 'Everton were only paying £550,000. You rang me to do you a favour.'

I couldn't argue with that, so we compromised on £600,000. Mark Walters went to Ibrox Park instead of Goodison and Aston Villa banked another £50,000 to assist Graham Taylor's team-rebuilding plans.

And very successful they were, too. To confirm this I have merely to think of the name David Platt and to recall another episode that remains etched in my mind. First, let me say that Graham Taylor was always cheerful in his manner, extremely calm and courteous in all his dealings and careful about what he said. He was an even-tempered sort of person. With this description in mind, you can imagine the impact when, one day, he burst into my office like a totally different individual to the one I had come to know.

He was absolutely incensed. 'That bastard Steve Harrison,' he blurted out. 'He's stabbed me in the back over David Platt...'

Steve Harrison had been Graham's number two at Villa Park, but had left to become manager at Watford. Steve, according to Graham, had been privy to the knowledge that Villa wanted to sign Platt from Crewe, and were intending to do so.

Graham had been systematically watching Platt and doing his homework on his character. As a result, he was convinced that he had found a ripe plum in the transfer market, waiting to be plucked from a club who would not be able to refuse a reasonable offer.

I could understand this simmering anger in Graham that I had not witnessed before. His feelings were that he had looked after

Steve as a player, helped him into the coaching side, brought him to an outstanding job at Villa Park and then released him from his contract so that he could return to Watford as manager.

Yet here he was, trying to step in and make a signing which was to be one of the most inspired made by any manager at any time. Graham had naturally confided in Steve about the conversations he'd had with the manager of Crewe, Dario Gradi, thus putting him in an ideal position to make a bid himself.

Before this outburst took place, I had been quietly advised by contacts in the directors' guest room at a match to 'go and get this boy, Platt', so I had personal confirmation that the proposed signing was a sensible one.

'He [Steve Harrison] knew all about my talks with Crewe,' added Graham. 'I had offered £175,000 and he has gone in behind my back and agreed a deal at £200,000.'

My obvious reaction to Graham's annoyance was to ask him what he intended to do about it.

'Nothing,' he said. 'If that's the way they want to work, they can get on with it.'

Fortunately, without having suffered the irritation that had so got to Graham, I was able to see the situation a little differently.

'Look,' I said. 'You've done your homework, you've had all the recommendations, I've had a recommendation myself. Don't give up on him. Get in your car, get up the M6, go in and offer £225,000.'

If I recall correctly, Graham's words to me were: 'Do you really mean that, chairman. I don't like it. It's against my principles.'

He felt he had done a deal at £175,000 and didn't feel inclined to be gazumped by his own mate into offering more. I have never seen Graham Taylor so agitated as he was on that occasion, even when he was prowling the touchline in the famous film of the World Cup qualifier that ended his career as England manager.

In contrast, I had no such reservations about upping the price for such a promising young player.

## HOW WE NEARLY LOST DAVID PLATT

'Go and sign him,' I said. And he did.

Had I been Steve Harrison's chairman, I would probably have been equally enthusiastic about his enterprise in attempting to sign such a bargain! Strange how football works out. Steve was, of course, John Gregory's choice as his first-team coach to return to Villa Park from Preston where he worked at that time. We were more than pleased to welcome him back. There were no hard feelings about his trying to 'sign' David Platt from under our nose. Football is a competitive business.

Platt, whom Graham declined to pigeon hole when the press quizzed him about the type of role he would play, went on to appear in eleven of the final twelve matches of our promotion campaign and played a most valuable part in our return to the First Division in one season. Graham always insisted that Platt wasn't just a midfield player or a striker or a forward, he was simply a footballer, full stop.

When you consider that David Platt was subsequently sold by us to Bari for £5.5 million, that extra £50,000, which you could say was actually provided by Rangers when they paid the extra on Mark Walters, was small change, indeed. You will also see what I mean when I say that Graham Taylor performed a magnificent team-building job for Aston Villa FC in that the fee when Platt was sold was used to underwrite Ron Atkinson's signings in 1991–92.

Likewise, those critics who, over the years, have written that 'Doug Ellis won't cough up the transfer money' don't know the half. No one has heard any of the club's ex-managers make such a claim.

Actually, there has been one, though it was said tongue in cheek. I once read in a newspaper that the shares Tommy Docherty had purchased in Aston Villa for a few pounds in 1968 had gone up in value to £25,000 as a result of the 1997 flotation, and that this, the Doc said, was 'more than Doug Ellis ever gave me to buy new players'.

Another of his witty one-liners. All I can say in reply is that, if it were true, which it wasn't, then when he told me that he had paid Luton Town £100,000 for Bruce Rioch and his brother, Neil, all those years ago he must have done OK with the £75,000 'surplus'. My turn for a wisecrack now, Doc...

However, the signing of Platt was to prove a masterstroke, as he scored five goals in the final eleven Second Division fixtures, leading up to the tense 0–0 draw at Swindon which took us into second place and promotion by a heartbeat.

In my mind's eye, I can still see Graham's face down in the dressing room area at the County Ground and the warm embrace that signalled our mutual mixed feelings of relief, triumph and respect.

Back in the First Division in 1988–89, that first season predictably proved hard work as we struggled to a precarious seventeenth position and Platt began to make a name for himself.

It was during a summer tour before the following season that another signing took place under Graham's reign that would ultimately prove even more inspired than that of Platt.

We were in the West Indies playing in Trinidad and Tobago against the island team in a stadium without stands. Graham and I were side-by-side on a bench beside what was little better than a park pitch and I remember after about ten minutes into the game nudging Graham and saying: 'Eh, what do you think about this boy up front?'

Graham said: 'I like him.'

We didn't even know his name, but I was excited enough about what I saw to go to the other bench twenty yards away where the manager of the national side was sitting with his coaches.

He told me that the player in question was named Dwight Yorke. I asked him if the lad had any honours and he told me he had seventeen caps. I asked his age and was told 'sixteen' (although it later transpired that he was seventeen).

I said: 'You mean Under-18 caps.'

He said: 'No.'

I said: 'You mean Under-23 caps.'

He said: 'No.'

He meant full caps. I couldn't believe it. Seventeen full caps by the age of sixteen, as we understood at that time.

All this convinced me that I should suggest to Graham that we invite this young Dwight Yorke over, with his local club manager in Tobago, to Villa Park with a view to signing him. Shortly after our return home, we sent three air tickets and Dwight travelled to Villa Park with his manager and his aunt, a very attractive lady barrister, who acted for him and his club. His club was delighted to accept a sum of £10,000 for a seventeen-year-old unknown and Dwight's aunt was equally delighted to advise Dwight to accept the contract we offered. The transaction was amicably settled in our boardroom. We were confident we had done a good deal, though we probably couldn't have predicted that, eight years later, we would sell him for £12 million.

Looking back, I feel as though Graham and I forged a sound working relationship and, certainly, we have remained friends. We all have our qualities and shortcomings and, to me, Graham sometimes seemed a little precious. He liked to be loved, admired, praised and never took kindly to criticism. I suspected he was jealous of the high profile that I have always had and would have preferred a chairman with no public profile at all.

Strange that, really. I never did wear funny spectacles and shiny suits while playing the piano and singing to millions of people all over the world, like his previous chairman!

The average football fan never gets to hear of many of the negotiating situations that evolve behind the scenes in any football club. There was, for instance, the sale by Graham Taylor of the Scottish international striker Alan McInally to Bayern Munich in 1989 for £1.2 million.

We also had a gentleman's agreement with the German club, with whom we had links dating back to when we beat them in the European Cup final of 1982, that we would play a friendly game at Villa Park for which we would retain the proceeds as part of the fee, less their expenses.

Sadly that game has still to be played; whenever we have contacted them on the subject, which has been frequently over the years, they have never had an available 'convenient' date.

On more than one occasion, I have raised the issue with 'The Kaiser' himself, Franz Beckenbauer. This included the time when I found myself, at the England-Germany semi-final of the European Championships at Wembley in the summer of 1996, with Beckenbauer next to me on my left and Pele on my right.

Strange, really, the sort of stunts that life can pull on you. As a lad I would probably have dreamed of being between two of the world's greatest-ever footballers, though we would have been out on the pitch wearing football boots and not sitting in the stand wearing suits.

However, I took the opportunity to ask Beckenbauer when Bayern Munich were coming to Villa Park to honour that agreement. I'm still waiting for the answer.

It reminded me of the time, I believe it was after Graham Taylor had left, that I made an attempt to offer Franz the job of manager of Aston Villa. He has a house just outside Kitzbühel in Austria and, by chance, we both sometimes went skiing at the nearby resort. We had also spent some time together when, with our wives, we once had a meal in the McGregor Suite at Villa Park. Heidi is German, remember, while Franz speaks fluent English.

Consequently I felt I knew them, as a couple, when I attempted to speak to him to establish if he would be interested in joining Aston Villa. Having rung his number, a lady answered the telephone and I chatted to her for a moment or two on the basis that, as she would no doubt recall, we had dined together in our foursome and had also met at the ski resort. After a while she broke in and said: 'I'm sorry, I think you must have the wrong wife...'

How was I to know that, in the interim, he had changed partners? However, I passed on the message that he could ring me if he were interested in being Aston Villa's manager, but he never did take up the option. That, of course, could depend on whether 'the wrong wife' ever passed on my message. One interesting conversation I do recall holding with him, when he was a player, was on the question of the excessive number of matches clubs sometimes play. When I said that we had played fifty-five he shrugged and said: 'So what? We play seventy-five.'

I said that I couldn't believe that figure because the German Bundesliga was smaller than our then First Division with only eighteen clubs.

His reply was that they flew somewhere or other around the world every week to play a cash-raising, prestige, friendly game 'otherwise we don't earn our money'.

'We play in Hong Kong one week, maybe South America soon after, with league games in between,' he said. He also reckoned that they had asked their coach for an increase in terms and had been told: 'Fine. We'll play another five friendlies each year to pay for it...' I don't think I dare try that approach the next time a Villa player's contract comes up for renewal!

However, to return to the Graham Taylor era, he proved his merit as a team builder, planner and motivator by steering us into that runners'-up place in the 1989–90 season when David Platt scored nineteen goals in thirty-seven First Division games and earned his place in Bobby Robson's World Cup squad for Italy '90.

When taking an overview of Graham Taylor's contribution to the club, the obvious conclusions would be that David Platt and Dwight Yorke were his pre-eminent captures. There would be, however, an unforgivable omission. Let us never forget one other signing which rates among Aston Villa's, and certainly Graham's, best ever.

The decision to enlist Paul McGrath from an unhappy situation in which he found himself at Old Trafford, in August 1989, was, in my view, as enlightened as any managerial move in my memory.

Macca, as he became known, was simply a joy to watch on the field of play and a delightful person to have around the club. His personal problems have been well documented already and I don't propose to rake over them, other than to say that there were times of potential trouble when he seemed to regard me as a father figure and it was a role I was more than happy to play.

One problem any memoir writer must encounter when outlining successes, as compared to being self-deprecatory about failures, is that it can come across as a case of glory seeking. Thus, rather than use my own description of Paul's experiences at Villa Park, I reproduce here an extract from his own life story: *Ooh Aah Paul McGrath* (Mainstream Publishing). In a passage concerning his move to Aston Villa he wrote:

> I couldn't help but be impressed when I first sat down to talk serious business (with Aston Villa)... there were no agents involved. Just me, my wife, Graham and his chairman, Doug Ellis. They laid it on the line. They wanted me to be part of the new Aston Villa. They wanted to build a team that would challenge for the title. They felt I was cheap at £450,000 from a United only too willing to get rid of me at any price... To this day, I do not believe there is a crooked bone in Aston Villa. The manager and chairman were first class.

Could there be a better testimonial than this, from a more popular and talented footballer, to endorse my favourite principle of players, manager and chairman working together for the benefit of any club?

Here Graham sensibly accepted the merit of the principle along with an experienced, world-class player and Aston Villa went on to enjoy seven wonderful years of Paul McGrath's services.

Ironically, by proving for the first time that he could operate successfully as the manager of a major club, as distinct from leading a smaller one from obscurity, Graham became the Football Association's choice as the man to replace Bobby Robson.

The approach duly came to me from the FA and the then president Bert Millichip, a long-time associate of mine through his original status as chairman of West Bromwich Albion even before his elevation to the figurehead at Lancaster Gate.

Naturally, we didn't want to lose our manager at such a crucial time but, obviously, being offered the job of managing your country is a very exceptional case. There was no special clause in Graham's contract to meet this eventuality, but what were we to do? When Graham came to me and told me that he wished to accept the appointment because it was what he had wanted since he was about nine years of age, it was a case of Hobson's Choice.

Well, almost. Graham had about two years of his contract to run, a contract that he had undertaken with a total commitment to Aston Villa Football Club. Fours years earlier, remember, when given permission by Manchester City to approach Billy McNeill, the understanding was that Villa would 'buy up' his contract in full if he were to join us, which we did.

The feelings of the Villa board as a whole, therefore, were that if Graham were to leave us managerless after leading us to the runners'-up place, then the Football Association would have to pay up his contract as we had done with Manchester City.

Once that principle had been accepted and established, the negotiations were between Bert Millichip and myself and they came to a head when we met at the Football Association's summer conference.

We had asked for the full salary value of the unexpired period of the contract, which was around £250,000, to be paid to Aston

Villa. The FA wanted to pay £200,000, hence that eventual get-together of Bert and I at the summer conference.

Bert took me aside and said: 'Look Doug, let's settle at £225,000.' It was an offer I could not refuse and so I duly said 'goodbye' to manager number seven.

# CHAPTER TWELVE

# 'SACK ME' INVITED
# GENTLEMAN JO

The loss of Graham Taylor, who went off to attempt to help England qualify for the 1994 World Cup in the USA, vainly as it turned out, left Villa, yet again, having to seek a new manager. We quickly discovered, if we didn't already suspect it, that there were not too many around.

I did, however, come up with one intriguing personality, not a familiar one in this country outside of those who follow the European game closely, but someone whom I met during the World Cup in Italy.

History now confirms that it was Dr Jozef Venglos, a hugely respected national team coach from the former Czechoslovakia, now split into the Czech Republic and Slovakia. Jo was one of the most respected coaches in the Eastern bloc, a highly intelligent man and a fine former Slovan Bratislava player who spoke fluent English along with six other languages and was a PhD graduate from Bratislava University. As manager of the club for whom he had played with distinction, he won two Czech championships and also helped lead his country, as assistant coach, to becoming European champions in 1976.

Later as Czech national coach, he led them to third place in the 1980 European Championships and to the World Cup finals in Spain in 1982. Also, he had held coaching appointments all around the world and was an official adviser to FIFA and one of their coaching instructors. With this wealth of knowledge and expertise, I felt that he could bring a new perspective to the English game because of his grasp of continental coaching methods. Bear in mind that, despite reaching the semi-final of the World Cup that year, our players were widely regarded as being well behind the best of the foreigners. Perhaps coaches like Jo Venglos could help us improve on that reputation? This was our theory, anyway, when we introduced him to a Villa Park press conference on a Saturday in July 1990.

I have been teased since about having kicked off by saying 'This man needs no introduction' to local press guys who hadn't the faintest idea who he was! They soon found out when we distributed his lengthy CV.

Jo actually took up his duties in earnest in August and his arrival at our Bodymoor Heath training ground coincided with a temperature of about 105 degrees Fahrenheit, the hottest English day since records began.

Jo was a lovely man, gentle, respectful, sincere and anxious to prove himself to the English, whom he clearly held in very high esteem. Despite the unbearable heat wave, the fifty-one-year-old dived into a practice game, dashing around in the sweltering heat like a teenager, giving and accepting passes, making tackles, the lot. By now there were batteries of local and national media with television cameras, microphones and the usual paraphernalia.

Another press conference was set up in our gym, which was several degrees hotter and even more humid than it had been outside. They all wanted to show him in his sweat-soaked training gear and were puzzled as to why they had to wait a considerable time for his appearance into the television arc lights.

When he arrived, Jo, bless his heart, was dressed in a suit and tie, but with beads of perspiration streaming down his face, determined not to let the club down by appearing in his role as manager 'improperly dressed'. He was correct and proper at all times and, in that regard alone, set an example to everyone. He was accustomed to working on the Continent, where coaches are mainly just that, employees who carry out the club's policies, unlike in this country where the manager expects to be, and often is, all powerful.

Jo had never before enjoyed the kind of status he had at Villa Park, but he could not come to terms with the sums of money that were being paid for signing new players in this country, a fact which probably explains why he did not strengthen the team as it needed in order to build on Graham Taylor's foundations. He did sign Gary Penrice from Bristol Rovers, though the player he really liked at that time was Vinny Samways.

It was a great shame that his reign at Villa Park did not work out as we would have liked. The players were gobsmacked by some of his modern methods of preparation, by his knowledge of all aspects of an athlete's requirements and by his courteous manner.

They were taught warming-up and warming-down procedures they had never encountered before, with different stretching exercises for all the various muscles, all things that have now become more common in our games, but which were very half-hearted at that time.

In retrospect, I'm not sure that some of the English club managers were too happy about his being here and taking, as they perhaps thought, one of 'their' top jobs. I sometimes had cause to wonder.

He remained a very modest man who, while he was here, resided in one of the club's houses along with his charming wife and two sons, one of whom is a barrister.

The bottom line, however sad to recall, was that it didn't work out, for whatever reason. By the end of December, we had won but four of our opening nineteen First Division games. I do recall appointing Peter Withe as his assistant to introduce some English-style communication and we just about avoided losing the First Division status we cherished so much, finishing in seventeenth place.

Give Jozef Venglos his due, as I always would. He was so honest in his self-assessment that he came to me about a month before the end of the season to say that if I was dissatisfied with his efforts then he would stand down voluntarily. That was something new, I can assure you, having a manager questioning whether he was earning his keep.

I recall him saying: 'I love it here and you have always been very good to me, but if you feel, for the sake of the club, that you ought to appoint someone else, it will not be a problem.'

Although he had signed a two-year contract, there was a 'break' clause in it to the effect that he would leave before the end of the term subject to proper compensation being paid. This was the arrangement we implemented, most amicably, at the end of one season in the mutual knowledge that an idea that seemed a perfectly good one when undertaken had not been successful.

There was no animosity whatsoever. In fact, we have been in touch from time to time and, when we played Slovan Bratislava in the UEFA Cup in September 1993, Jo was there waiting for us and was visibly delighted to renew acquaintances. It was an education to walk around the beautiful city of Prague with him – as I did on one occasion in company with our secretary Steve Stride – he was such a popular person. They simply idolise him. Wherever we walked, at whatever time of the day, there would be people of all ages recognising him and wanting to shake his hand, sometimes crossing the thoroughfare to do so. In return, he had that wonderful capacity and willingness to respond courteously and give a little of his time to chat to them.

His relationship with the club was never less than totally cordial, but I can state categorically and with total honesty that I have been able to settle satisfactorily, on the very day of departure, with every dismissed manager except one, and they have gone away with a suitable cheque in their pocket.

And so the hunt was on for a replacement for Jo Venglos. This time, however, I did not have to look very far. Waiting in the wings was a certain former Aston Villa player who still lived in the Midlands and who had always wanted to manage Aston Villa Football Club.

# CHAPTER THIRTEEN

# LIFE WITH BIG RON

Once Jozef Venglos had left Villa Park, it proved easier than we expected to appoint a successor in July 1991. Just as Graham Taylor had made himself available four years earlier so, this time, it was Ron Atkinson who tossed his hat into the ring virtually from day one. Ron had led Sheffield Wednesday from relegation the season before, straight back into the First Division. Only a matter of weeks earlier, his leadership had taken the League Cup to Hillsborough.

Reflecting on his situation as it must have been at that time, one could only imagine his psychological dilemma. Although born in Liverpool, he was brought up in Birmingham as a Villa supporter who achieved his childhood dream of being signed by the club as an apprentice.

Once his playing days were over, his ambition was to be manager of Aston Villa and, four years earlier, had been a 'possible', until Graham Taylor made it known that he was available.

Now the job was vacant just at a time when he was established as a folk hero at Hillsborough. What should he do? Presumably the temptation was too strong to resist. He telephoned our then secretary, now director-secretary Steve Stride, to make it known that he was interested in joining Villa if we were interested in discussing the possibility.

Yes, indeed we were, but first he would have to sort out his own situation at Sheffield Wednesday. That wouldn't be easy for obvious reasons and Ron was presumably left with deeply mixed emotions and a great deal of soul searching. One part of the equation, and very much in our favour, quite apart from his ambition to manage Aston Villa, was that, while he wanted to continue to live in the Midlands, he was genuinely tired of commuting each day from his home near Birmingham to Sheffield.

Jo Venglos left 'by mutual consent' on 29 May and the usual media guessing game began. One interesting name included in the speculation proved later to have been inspired crystal-ball gazing, namely Brian Little. Others were Kenny Dalglish, who had left Liverpool, but who had not yet joined Blackburn Rovers, Bruce Rioch and Arthur Cox. At that stage no one so much as suggested Ron Atkinson, simply because he was being offered a new two-year contract by the Sheffield Wednesday chairman, David Richards. Within a couple of days, however, Ron resigned from Hillsborough and, as a result of his phone call to Steve Stride, we were confidently able to announce his readiness to join Villa. It all seemed straightforward enough at the time. In reality, his appointment proved anything but.

Ron went back to Sheffield to attend an end-of-the-season celebration of the club's dual success and being back in that environment and meeting up with his chairman prompted a change of heart. I received a telephone call from him on around 1 June to say that he was staying at Hillsborough after all, a decision I felt I reluctantly had to accept.

Thus, our search was on again and this time the name of Joe Royle appeared in newspapers as the new favourite. Alongside the renewed speculation, Atkinson was being quoted as saying that, when he walked into his Hillsborough office and sat down, he realised that he would be 'barmy' to think of leaving. We understood that, but we also knew that he would regard himself as 'barmy' if he turned down the Villa job, the very one he had always wanted. In this lingering air of uncertainty, all was quiet for about a week as the headlines gradually subsided.

Unknown possibly to Ron, since the well-being of Aston Villa was as imperative to us as his relationship with Sheffield Wednesday was to him, by now we had another name available as Plan B if Plan A broke down.

That name must remain secret to avoid any embarrassment, but I do recall Steve Stride coming to me to say: 'Chairman, we have either got to appoint Ron Atkinson this week or reject the idea and go for our second choice. Why don't we sort it out by going and knocking on Ron's door?'

I could hardly argue with such logic, so this is what we did. Steve and I sat and talked to Ron and his charming wife Maggie at their home for at least an hour and when we left he had accepted the job and an excellent contractual deal, which he had firmly negotiated for himself.

I was delighted to have him, no argument about that, because one could only admire the fact that he had won the FA Cup twice with Manchester United and had more recently won promotion and the League Cup for Sheffield Wednesday.

Much earlier in his career, it had not escaped my notice that he had learned the managerial ropes successfully with Non-League Kettering Town before taking Cambridge United to promotion from the Fourth Division to the Second Division in successive seasons. He had also led West Bromwich Albion to an FA Cup semi-final and into the UEFA Cup, sharing in the development of Bryan Robson, before moving to Old Trafford. Even over and above all this, one admired the kind of entertaining attacking football his teams always played, his relationship with the media and the attention he attracted to his club with his television personality.

My first contacts with Ron, years before, were in his Kettering Town days when I was still running my MATO package-deal trips to Spain and elsewhere. I used to make it known to the Professional Footballers' Association that free flights were available to their members during the month of May, subject to availability. This was a facility I could offer to fill empty seats on any of my twenty-seven weekly flights to various locations. Ron would ring me, remind me that he was an ex-Aston Villa player and would take advantage of the offer.

Later, after he joined West Bromwich Albion, we had quite a deal of social contact at, for instance, the old regular monthly luncheons staged by the Midland Soccer Writers. I used to pull his leg that his brother Graham, a very nice, quiet chap who played with him at Oxford United, was a better player than him. I liked Graham and Ron's late father, Fred, an ex-wartime Royal Navy man like myself. Consequently, Ron and I knew each other quite well when he became our manager, just at the time when the club needed someone with his experience, expertise and crowd-pulling charisma.

Big Ron's appointment put Aston Villa firmly in the national limelight, no doubt about that. Television cameras, still cameras, microphones and football writers packed into our North Stand banqueting suite as never before for the press conference to confirm his arrival.

I well remember sitting with him in my office waiting to meet the media. Our mood was one of cheerful celebration and optimism. He sank a brandy or two while we were waiting to go into the press conference. Once there, he was his usual wisecracking self 'on stage' and the whole buoyant feeling was that exciting times were ahead.

I seem to recall a moment when I interrupted something he was saying and Ron responded by saying: 'See, he's interfering already...' to big laughs all round from the assembled media. In retrospect, I sense that there was a barely-concealed message in that comment.

From the point of view of available transfer resources, his timing was spot on. His arrival more or less coincided with the Italian club Bari making repeated bids for David Platt who, a year earlier, had become a world star along with Paul Gascoigne because of their displays for England in Italia '90.

We had rejected two Bari approaches at £5.5 million before Ron was appointed, but the situation was still boiling up when he joined us. Life can and does continually throw up some unpredictable situations and this was one of them. During his Manchester United days, with a playing staff packed with good players at all levels, Ron had released a young Platt on a free transfer to Crewe Alexandra. Now, some six years later, he was taking over at Villa Park just as Platt was leaving, having, in the meantime, become one of the most expensive players in the world. I seem to recall reading somewhere a classic comment from Ron that he had had David Platt on his books at two different clubs and had never so much as picked him for his first team.

There were delays in the Platt transfer for several reasons. David was on an England tour of Australia and Malaysia, Ron had some summer holiday organised and I was abroad for a while myself. Eventually, on Thursday, 18 July, the Bari president and owner Vincenzo Mattarese came to Birmingham and met Ron Atkinson and Platt, while I was out of the country.

The name 'Mattarese' is big, powerful and influential in Italy. Vincenzo had a huge business in the construction industry and is said to have supplied the cement for half of the nation's motorways, a fact that was later to inspire one of Big Ron's classic wisecracks. One of Vincenzo's brothers was a cardinal in the Vatican and another, Antonio, was president of the Italian Football Federation. They are the sort of family who tend to get their way.

After this visit, the player was satisfied with the terms offered, but Ron, give him his due, was asking for £6 million, about £1.5 million more than Bari's original offer. At that meeting an appointment was made for Bari representatives to come back to Birmingham on the Saturday morning to meet me at Villa Park. We had had previous dealings with the ambitious club from the south of Italy some years before, when we sold them Gordon Cowans and Paul Rideout. One slightly unusual feature of our dealings this time was that David Platt's representative was Tony Stephens, who had learned the ropes as Aston Villa's own commercial manager.

Tony had helped Platt to a magnificent contract, which was reported in the press as being worth some £4 million over three years. The whole story was very big news indeed, because it was a record deal and the forerunner of others that were to follow as transfer fees escalated each season.

I recall looking out of my Villa Park office window on that July Saturday morning onto a scene teeming with a large press entourage from both countries. I gather that they had been at Birmingham airport to meet the Italians coming in and the scene had now shifted to our car park. When you deal with the Italians on footballing matters, everything seems a shade larger than life.

By now I had received a fax message from Bari with a written offer of £5.5 million, a compromise between their first offers and Ron Atkinson's demand. Signor Mattarese was not on this trip, having already done the spadework. His big, impressive general manager, Franco Janich, was his representative with the authority to complete a deal. Mattarese's club vice-president and a commercial director were with Signor Janich, ready and authorised to set a new UK transfer record.

After lengthy discussions, with the media circus still camped outside, I sensed that £5.5 million was their final offer, which I accepted, while carefully imposing one condition, namely that Aston Villa would be entitled to fifty percent of any profit from a subsequent sell-on. Such a future deal was a distinct possibility, since Juventus had already made it known that they admired Platt's work in Italia '90 and his progress with Aston Villa ever since. The sale of Platt and also of Tony Cascarino to Glasgow Rangers gave Ron considerable resources with which to fund the building of his own team.

Once that first season got underway, fate stage-managed another ironical situation when Ron Atkinson's first match as manager of Aston Villa was away to, of all clubs, Sheffield Wednesday, whom he had left amid so much acrimony. Trevor Francis was now their manager, on Big Ron's recommendation.

Such was the ill-feeling on the part of the minority idiot fringe that can give every club a bad name, there was talk of death threats and of Ron needing a police escort. None of this seemed to bother him one jot and, moreover, he strode through it all untroubled before heading home with a satisfying record of played one, won one.

Atkinson's early signings included such players as Dalian Atkinson, Kevin Richardson, Steve Staunton, Shaun Teale, Garry Parker, Cyrille Regis, Earl Barrett and others as he completely rebuilt the squad. Some of these acquisitions reflected the undoubted managerial skills for which we had appointed him. Kevin Richardson was seen, rightly it transpired, as a player who could help Villa to honours, just as he had done with both Everton and Arsenal, whom he had assisted to the championship. He was Ron's skipper and a very dedicated one, too.

Shaun Teale was an unsung player with Bournemouth when Ron signed him for a mere £300,000 fee and the player became one of the most effective defenders in the First Division. Steve Staunton, a very shrewd capture from Liverpool, gave Aston Villa superb service and Liverpool, I'm sure, must regard him as one of the sales they most regret.

In that first season, with his restructured squad, Ron Atkinson took the club ten places up the old First Division from Jo

Venglos' seventeenth and also reached the sixth-round of the FA Cup.

A good team was taking shape and the quality of the passing football was also an encouraging sign. It would be nice to reflect that everything was going according to plan yet, the truth was, that it did not take long for me to realise that the kind of chairman-manager relationship I have referred to earlier, and would have liked to have had with him, was not going to evolve. He did his job and I did mine, but often we were, let's say, 'distant'.

Ron remained just a big boy at heart, in my observations, and I suspect that he would not have argued had you referred to him as a frustrated player sitting in the manager's chair as the best alternative to being 'one of the lads'. In his wisecracking way, he sometimes used to refer to himself as 'the player-manager'.

Never a day went by without him being out at Bodymoor Heath, playing in a six-a-side match and seeing himself as either Pele, or Cruyff or Matthews or whatever legendary name took his fancy.

The fans loved this Jack-the-Lad image and the players responded well to his imposing presence among them. I had no argument against all of this. Indeed, one of the qualities that attracted me to him as a potential manager was that he was very much a 'player's manager'.

From my perspective, however, cracks in his image soon appeared. Being at the training ground playing football every morning was fine, up to a point. What I found hard to accept was that, although he had an office at Villa Park, we never saw him, even after training was completed, unless he had a very specific reason to meet someone there. It was as though, for the most part, he saw his job as beginning and ending at the training ground.

When he accepted the appointment, it was agreed that he could continue his television work as long as it did not interfere with his Aston Villa duties. Naïvely, I guess, I imagined that he would inform me when he was undertaking such work. Not so, I'm afraid.

There was a classic example, early in 1993, of how this lack of contact between us seriously affected the running of the club and the possible loss of an important signing at the right price. The player in question was Andy Cole, when he was at Bristol City. I knew Ron Atkinson fancied him, because he had told me as much in one of our discussions.

When I was at the FA offices at Lancaster Gate one day for a meeting, I was in the foyer, chatting to the then Bristol City chairman, Leslie Kew. He said to me: 'Are you still interested in Cole?' My reply was: 'Yes, if our manager is still interested and if the price is right.'

The fee previously quoted for Cole had been prohibitive, bearing in mind that he had not then been fully tried out at the highest level. If my memory serves me correctly, they had been asking in excess of £2 million.

'Newcastle and Liverpool are both messing us around,' said Leslie. 'If you are serious about wanting him you can shake my hand at £1.2 million.'

It seemed an excellent deal to me, knowing of Ron's interest, so I shook his hand on the condition that it was subject to the manager's approval and confirmation.

Leslie Kew accepted the principle and, though he had a train to catch, was prepared to wait while I telephoned Ron there and then from the FA offices, hopefully to set up the deal. I recall that it was approximately one o'clock lunchtime, a time in the day when you would expect to be able to track your manager down somewhere or other.

However, for the next half-an-hour I made telephone calls, to the training ground, to Villa Park, his home, his mobile number, all to no avail. No one seemed to know where he was.

Eventually, Mr Kew pointed out that he was in danger of

missing his train back to Bristol and would have to go. As he left, I promised to call him at his home as and when I was able to speak to my manager. I never made that telephone call to Leslie Kew. To this day I don't know where Ron was. The nearest I got to finding out were suggestions from some people to whom I spoke that he was 'abroad'.

The outcome of that sorry situation was that Andy Cole signed for Newcastle United in March 1993 for a reported £1.75 million and was very successful at St James' Park before his £7 million move to Manchester United just under two years later.

I would sometimes see Atkinson's face on television, or hear his voice, from various places in this country and abroad, when I had no idea that this was where our manager happened to be.

If I wanted to talk club business with him, I had to ring him at the training ground or at his home. Even the courtesy of an occasional visit to my office for a chat would have been better than these periodic phone calls.

Talking of offices, one of the early breaches in my respect for his managerial style came over a match-day office we had specially prepared for him. It was in the building that was originally the Lions Club and later the club shop and promotions offices.

A players' lounge was created there with a manager's office next door to it, strategically placed, I would have thought, for obvious reasons of supervision.

Ron looked at the office and said he didn't want it. Instead he plumped for another room, well away from the players' lounge and right next door to the directors' private guest room. It was intended for apprentices and reserves on match days to save them from hanging around the corridor, but was taken over by the manager.

The walls were very thin and not soundproofed, and Ron and his match-day guests, usually including the opposition manager, tended to get a little noisy when they were winding down with a drink after games.

Sometimes, the raucous hilarity echoed around the directors' room to everyone's embarrassment. No one minds a laugh and a joke, especially when the day's job is done, but it wasn't the most discreet of signals for the manager to send out if his team had lost and possibly played badly.

I well recall one visiting chairman saying to me: 'You're not the Doug Ellis I know if you are prepared to put up with that sort of behaviour…'

And, talking about his team, they were well away from him with their own guests, drinking at the club's expense – often for a couple of hours after a match.

Some of those guests bordered on being rated as undesirables who did not conduct themselves too well, especially after several free drinks. They caused embarrassment to security men who were rightly trying to close the club for the night on more than one occasion.

It seemed to me that if the manager had accepted the office that had been sensibly planned for him, his very presence nearby would have prevented some of those excesses. The manager does, after all, have a free hand in terms of the players' code of conduct, and their discipline.

Another factor, incidentally, that truly does annoy me, is when things are reported in the press about the club, and players in particular, that I know nothing about. I always expect managers, and other executives at the club, to keep me fully informed each day about what is going on. There are few things more embarrassing than being stopped, sometimes by an ordinary supporter in the street, and being asked about matters which have appeared in the press, when, as the chairman, I know nothing about them. To be fair, all but one of my managers have understood this request and complied with it by keeping me informed to the best of their ability.

# CHAPTER FOURTEEN

# ATKINSON'S DOWNFALL

Ron Atkinson's second season coincided with the start of the Premier League, the Sky TV money and all the revolution in football finance that these advances entailed.

Ray Houghton had joined Steve Staunton as an Irish Republic international import from Liverpool, but Cyrille Regis had been a short-term stopgap as main striker and needed replacing. Another inquiry at Anfield was Ron's answer, this time for Dean Saunders. The Welsh international had scored twenty-three goals for Liverpool since moving from Derby County, including a record number of European goals yet, strangely, he was not unanimously regarded as a success there.

A club record figure of around £2.5 million was being discussed for the Welsh international, manager to manager, around August–September, but I'm afraid more strain was placed on our relationship when I became convinced that a better deal could be achieved for Aston Villa FC. As a result, I made some overtures myself before the negotiations were successfully concluded for £2.3 million.

As a result of my intervention we had, indeed, secured an

improved agreement, but it meant a delay of a week or two while Liverpool and the player pondered our bid. This caused speculation in the press about the chairman interfering with the manager's transfer policy. I heard subsequently that the usual group of local football writers, who assembled each Friday in Ron's office at Bodymoor Heath, got the impression that the deal was almost clinched on that particular day and they waited outside for further news. Apparently, it was at this time that I informed the manager that I wanted to talk to Liverpool myself. The press was able to glean from his subsequent demeanour, allied to the fact that the deal had not been clinched after all, that there was some friction between us.

Speculation about all this in the papers led to my having a chat with him along the lines that he should be putting out the message that we were all pulling together for the benefit of the club.

The reality was that we had not started that season especially well, and the last thing we needed were reports of internal unrest. Early home attendances were below 20,000, only one of our opening six matches had been won and this sequence included two draws and one defeat out of three at home. By now the team contained some seven players whom Ron had signed himself.

As a result of my chat with him on the question of relieving public fears about our working relationship, he was persuaded to go out onto the pitch with the microphone before the kick-off against Crystal Palace on 5 September to assure the crowd that the Dean Saunders signing would be completed shortly and that everyone at the club was pulling in the same direction. But were we...?

The game was won 3–0 and Saunders arrived in time for the next match, against Leeds United at Elland Road. By this time, Ron Atkinson's transfer account balanced out about even, with £20 million-worth of sales and a similar amount spent on players. No complaints about that at all, and the arrival of Dean Saunders gave everyone a boost.

# ATKINSON'S DOWNFALL

A 1–1 draw at Leeds preceded Saunders' home debut, against his former club Liverpool, when nearly 38,000 fans flocked in and Deano scored twice in a memorable 4–2 win. Dalian Atkinson also scored and the pair became a popular strike pair with the public, who now had high hopes that the team they called 'Big Fat Ron's Claret-and-Blue Army' was on its way to big things.

It proved an outstanding season with a challenge being made to become the very first Premiership champions. This wasn't to be, but we did finish as runners-up behind Manchester United without any further signings being made or with any noticeable friction between the manager and myself. All the signs looked good.

The 1993–94 season, with our magnificent Coca Cola Cup victory over Manchester United following on to runners'-up place in the Premiership the previous season, was basically an encouraging period for everyone concerned. Our long-term aim to be challenging for league honours and a place in Europe each season – a reasonable objective I have always maintained for a club of Aston Villa's stature and volume and loyalty of our support – seemed to be on track.

Playing progress was there to be seen. Ron had skilfully nurtured two superb young players in goalkeeper Mark Bosnich and defender Ugo Ehiogu, while Andy Townsend had been signed from Chelsea for £2.1 million. The fee, we conceded, was a touch high for a thirty-year-old, but the manager said he would be good value and he was to be proved absolutely right. We had also signed striker Guy Whittingham from Portsmouth for £1.1 million.

A UEFA Cup place had been secured and though we were dismissed in the second round by Deportivo La Coruna, the Spaniards proved themselves to be one of the strongest teams in Europe at that time.

It was in the Coca Cola sponsored Football League Cup that

Ron Atkinson's team shone. Even when left 1–3 down to Tranmere Rovers in the first leg of the semi-final at Prenton Park – a ground with such nostalgic connections for myself – we came back to reach Wembley after equalising almost on ninety minutes and going on to win the penalty shoot-out in thrilling fashion.

The atmosphere of the refurbished and modernised Villa Park that memorable afternoon was absolutely electric: the supporters were right behind the club and Ron Atkinson was confirming the managerial skills he had previously illustrated elsewhere.

If that was exciting and rewarding, the final was an even more momentous occasion as Alex Ferguson's Manchester United were totally outwitted and outplayed. Atkinson demonstrably loved the cup competitions and taking centre stage at Wembley, where he provided great leadership with his personality, experience and self-confidence.

To keep things relaxed, he had his personal friend, Stan Boardman, the scouser comic, on the team coach on the way to the stadium and in the dressing room, keeping the lads amused and any Wembley nerves at bay.

Stan was at our banquet afterwards while Big Ron was up on stage with his rendering of 'New York, New York', which he changed to 'Dwight Yorke, Dwight Yorke'. It was a terrific atmosphere with excellent input from our manager who, during his career, had now won the FA Cup twice for Manchester United, the League Cup for Sheffield Wednesday, by beating his former club, and had repeated the dose for Aston Villa.

No one admired his achievements more than I did and no one wanted to see him build on the foundations that he had put down more than I did. Sadly, however, this proved to be the peak of Ron Atkinson's success at Villa Park, not the start of a plateau of achievement, and the downslope was unexpectedly steep. By the end of the season, when we had drifted to tenth place in the Premiership with only three League wins in fourteen matches since the Coca Cola Cup semi-final at the end of February, there were very clear danger signals.

We had several players, albeit quality ones, who were around the thirty-mark and over. I don't profess to be a football manager, but anyone who has watched the game over a lengthy period of time gets a gut feeling about certain things. Mine was that we needed to strengthen our squad with some top-class, younger players, during the summer. In short, fresh legs were essential.

There was absolutely no doubt in my mind that a large proportion of our supporters felt the same, even though Big Ron had become something of a cult figure by then. Imagine my surprise then, when in chatting to him, I discovered that he was firmly convinced that his squad, as it was, would be Premiership top-six material for 1994–95 without any additions.

Frankly, I disagreed with him and wasn't convinced that his best place for a portion of that summer was in the USA covering the World Cup for television; we're always told by those managers who want to see the World Cup that it is an essential part of their football education, but I saw no evidence of Villa benefiting from Ron's USA trip.

I do recall, while he was there, that the Manchester United chairman, Martin Edwards, told me that Dion Dublin was available for transfer. That, I felt, could be valuable information.

The general feeling among Villa folk was that while Dean Saunders and Dalian Atkinson had obvious strengths in attack, we lacked what might be termed an orthodox centre-forward type.

By way of passing on this information to Atkinson, I telephoned him in the United States, but it seemed that he was having a meal at the time and was most reluctant to speak to me. If my memory serves me correctly, he indicated that 'he did not fancy' Dublin, so that was the end of that.

In the event, the only signings that close season, when Ron returned from the World Cup in the immediate run up to the season, were Ghanaian Nii Lamptey on loan from Anderlecht and Phil King from Sheffield Wednesday, before thirty-one-year-old John Fashanu was signed for £1.35 million from Wimbledon.

Another mature pair of legs. Also, of course, Fashanu had extensive business interests, apart from having to record instalments of the *Gladiators* television programme and was some sort of travelling ambassador for UNICEF. Because of these commitments, he did not have to train or play if he did not wish to do so.

In fact, he played only thirteen games, scoring three goals for us before his playing career came to an end. Early in the season, he was out with Achilles tendon trouble and then, at Old Trafford in February, he was stretchered off after a challenge with Ryan Giggs with what proved to be serious cruciate ligament damage.

It was soon clear that he would not be able to continue playing, so we naturally took the necessary steps to implement the appropriate insurance policy covering the cost of his transfer.

This necessitated written expert opinions from two specialists that his injury made it impossible for him to play on in League football. One of these specialists, based in the south-west, was one he selected himself.

Both of these medical reports stated that he was unfit to continue playing professional football because the knee damage could not be put right by surgery.

Here I have to concede that I found John Fashanu's IQ to be as high as any player with whom I have ever had dealings. His ability to negotiate articulately was unsurpassed in my experience.

When we put it to him that his career was over and that we were to claim the insurance cover, he replied that unless he received fifty percent of that cover, he would continue to visit specialists for further opinions because, in his view, he could get himself fit again. He would work hard on his knee until, eventually, he would be able to play again.

The next two specialists he visited, he told us, would be in France and Canada respectively. Meanwhile, he would remain on our books, we would pay him his wages and our medical and recuperative facilities would be available to him whenever he required them.

Had he done this, we would not have been able to make our legitimate claim to our insurance company as compensation for the loss of his services after having paid out the £1.35 million fee.

In the event, he agreed that it was potentially impossible for him to continue in professional football and, as we parted company, we handed him a cheque for £250,000 as an ex-gratia payment.

Another transfer that caused me a great deal of irritation was, rather oddly, the movement of a player between two clubs in a foreign country. This was when David Platt went from Bari to Juventus in June 1992, a year after he had left Villa Park following his record signing for Bari.

When Platt left Villa Park, part of the agreement was that we would receive half of any profits if and when he was sold on, but when that situation arrived, I'm certain that a spot of tactical planning went on which cost us some £1.25 million.

The figure quoted to us for Platt's resale was £5.5 million, the same figure that Bari had paid: all very convenient. However, I established that two players, Allessio and Di Uri, had moved from Juventus to Bari on top of the fee, taking the actual value of the move up to an estimated £8 million. Thus Bari's profit amounted to £2.5 million, of which we were entitled to receive half. To this end, I appealed to the club to honour our agreement.

Receiving no response, I then took on the services of a lawyer in Italy who appeared to be putting the necessary case together for us to appeal through UEFA and FIFA when, out of the blue, he telephoned me to say that he could no longer pursue our inquiries. He would not explain why, not on the telephone, and that was the last I heard from him.

My next move was a further appeal to a contact at the club. In reply to this, I received a remarkable fax message saying that if I continued with the process 'he feared for my future'. Naturally incensed at what seemed like a thinly veiled threat, I recall ringing Ron Atkinson at the training ground to discuss what we should do next. There was a brief silence and then a hoot of laughter. 'I would leave it alone if I were you, chairman,' chortled Ron, or something like that. 'Otherwise you could find yourself wearing a concrete overcoat and holding up an Italian motorway.'

I decided to take Ron's advice, though, as a last throw of the dice, sought a second opinion from the chief constable, who said he would make inquiries. One week later, he recommended that I should 'forget it'.

It became crystal clear to me during the club's close-season tour of South Africa in 1994 that there was no way that Ron Atkinson and I would ever forge a constructive working relationship in moving the club forward. The Coca Cola Cup win should have been the basis for a period of consistent success. Just think about the opportunity that existed: we had returned to European competition, financial stability was there in terms of resources – available for the right kind of signings – and a large enthusiastic support was bursting to help us achieve more honours. Had we all been working together, there is nothing that we could not have achieved.

Sadly, the reality was very different. The only communication between the manager and myself came as a result of my contacting him. It was never the other way around. On that tour – on which he was accompanied by his wife – it was very evident to me that he desired no manager-chairman relationship whatsoever if he could avoid it.

His rapport with players seemed to me to be equally selective in terms of there being certain senior players whom he favoured and treated one way and others with whom he was far more distant. Dalian Atkinson was, for instance, the one and only player who could get away with back-chatting and wisecracking with the manager, sometimes I felt in a way which other players could have resented bearing in mind how, unlike Dalian, they had to be very careful with what they said and did.

All this I could just about have handled had team affairs been successful or even satisfactory. Quite distinctly, as the disappointing season progressed, they were not.

Premiership results in the closing weeks of the previous season, dating right back to the Coca Cola Cup semi-final success over Tranmere Rovers, had been continuously poor.

True, the 1994–95 season had started encouragingly enough with three draws and two victories in the opening five Premiership fixtures leading up to the UEFA Cup tie against Inter Milan.

The home leg win over Inter, with the nerve-wracking penalty shoot-out, was one of the many highlights of Ron's time at Villa Park but, worryingly, league results then went into serious decline.

Without wishing to rake over too many unfortunate memories, I have to point out that the record books show us that the squad which the manager insisted was capable of finishing among the top six, had taken just one point from a possible twenty-four up to the fateful night of 9 November when we played Wimbledon at Selhurst Park.

At that time we were nineteenth in the Premiership with only ten points from thirteen games, one place behind our opponents. With some half an hour to go in that game we were leading 3–1 and apparently looking at a victory that might just have been the turning point of the season.

Andy Townsend had been sent off before half-time, somewhat harshly we all felt, but the ten men remaining ought to have been well capable of defending a potentially winning lead after scoring their third goal early in the second half.

However, in the last half-hour, we virtually came apart at the seams and were left looking at a 4–3 defeat and a record of one draw and eight defeats in nine games. Dreadful.

Had I been able to have regular, constructive meetings with the manager to discuss any problems he had openly, make signings and support whatever constructive changes he wished to bring about, then maybe we could have halted our alarming slide towards possible relegation. As it was, time was running out and I was more likely to see Ron Atkinson on television explaining where other teams were going wrong than to sit over a quiet drink with him and talk about Aston Villa's failings.

More than one supporter and shareholder had talked to me critically at that time about Ron's television work and his capacity to recognise the shortcomings in other teams when our own was losing match after match.

After that defeat by Wimbledon, I didn't sleep too well. The fact was that if the other directors felt as I did at an emergency board meeting I had called at Villa Park the next day, then the manager's hours, let alone days, were numbered. In the event their feelings were totally unanimous, as fellow directors Tony Alderson, the late Dr David Targett and my son Peter Ellis expressed precisely similar misgivings to my own.

I was asked afterwards how I felt about dismissing a manager with such a high public profile, one with a big following among grass-roots supporters, one who had led us to a Coca Cola Cup victory only the previous season, one who was so liked and admired by all sections of the media.

My answer to that was that while it is never pleasant telling a professional man that he has lost his job, I was more certain that I had taken the correct course of action on this occasion than with any of the other previous managerial sackings that had earned me my nickname.

Once the decisions had been discussed openly by the board, and had been proposed and carried, I asked my secretary to telephone Ron and request that he attend a meeting at Villa Park as soon as he could get to us.

When he arrived, I called him into the boardroom and, with no need to beat about the bush, informed him that it was the unanimous decision of the Aston Villa board that his contract be terminated in order that we could seek a new manager.

It was a very brief meeting. I honestly believe that he was taken completely by surprise, even though I personally felt that the case for his departure was beyond dispute. It seemed to the board that if he carried on as manager we would be relegated. I never changed that view and nothing about his subsequent period as a manager at Coventry City, Sheffield Wednesday and Nottingham Forrest undermined my judgement. Indeed, as events later unfolded, I had numerous strangers approach me to say that, while they fiercely opposed the sacking of Ron Atkinson when it happened, they later came to appreciate that it had actually proved in the best interest of Aston Villa.

Odd, too, that he presumably rediscovered his appetite for travelling from Worcestershire to Sheffield, though this only proved the case until the end of the 1997–98 season when his contract was not renewed.

Anyway, we sincerely placed on record our appreciation of the successes he had brought to the club and were disappointed that his reign was no longer working out. As in the case of his predecessors, we were ready to settle his contract, less an amount to cover tax requirements, there and then. He could have gone home with the appropriate cheque in his pocket.

For whatever reason, he declined this offer in favour of asking his accountant to deal with the matter and this, of course, meant that we simply carried on paying him his monthly cheque until the settlement was agreed. He is the only Aston Villa manager, in my time as chairman, who has opted to stretch the matter out in this way and that, of course, was his contractual right.

More pressing matters were now on the agenda.

Approximately one-third of the season had elapsed, relegation was threatening and Aston Villa were, once again, managerless with our supporters roughly split into two 'camps'. On one side there were those who supported the view that it was right for Ron Atkinson to be replaced and, on the other, there were many who were incensed at his departure.

The media, by and large, fell into the latter category, though radio and newspaper reporters are, inevitably, influenced to some degree by a manager's past record and by the amount of co-operation they receive from him and the headlines he inspires.

What sort of successor could adequately fill Big Ron's shoes?

# CHAPTER FIFTEEN

# THE JOB'S YOURS, BRIAN

Not for the first time during my quarter-of-a-century association with Aston Villa FC, I found myself plunged into an avalanche of controversy, this time over the dismissal of Ron Atkinson. If the critics were right and I was wrong, then we had shamefully discarded their charismatic leader, a larger-than-life character who would have guided us forward to ever-greater triumphs. On the other side of the coin, if the board happened to be right and the fiercest of the critics badly wrong, then our change at the helm had not been made one moment too soon. The latter scenario was my own unshakeable opinion.

As I have indicated before, as a general rule you tend to find that if things are going well at a club the manager is a genius. When affairs go the other way then the public wants the chairman's head to roll.

Looking back to that particular period, however, I still find it ironic that for all the cast-iron evidence to the contrary, there were still those who felt that the manager had the playing affairs of the club on the right lines.

This conveniently overlooked the number of players we had

who were operating on what, in Premiership footballing terms, were ageing legs, plus the smaller number who were not giving the necessary level of performance. Results are the bottom line of any manager's account and Ron's had been awful for some considerable time.

As for choosing someone to replace him, I was totally certain that I would do so without even trying. To be absolutely honest, I mentally had my new manager lined up even before Ron Atkinson was fired.

What the dissenting supporters, many of them clamouring to get their letters published in the Birmingham *Evening Mail,* were not to know, was that I had known for the previous three years that Brian Little wanted to become manager of Aston Villa as and when the next opportunity arose.

I knew beyond doubt that when he became aware that the job was vacant, his interest would be sparked, just as it had been in the summer of 1991, before Atkinson succeeded Jo Venglos. If folks wondered why I appeared, in the circumstances, to be keeping a very low profile, that was the reason. Brian Little would be our next manager. It was only a question of the date and the terms of his contract.

How could I be so sure? Simply because he had telephoned me for a little advice a few days before we appointed Ron Atkinson in the summer of 1991. Brian had been approached by Leicester City, but wondered if he stood a chance at Villa Park, the job he most wanted.

By this time Atkinson was our choice, but in any event I advised Brian to take the job at Filbert Street in order to add to the experience he had gained with Darlington. To this I added a crucial final promise that was to become the essential basis of my confidence that he would succeed Atkinson.

'If the vacancy occurs again and you remain interested, then you have my absolute assurance that you will be considered for it,' I told him in 1991. 'You will not even have to apply, I will remember.'

It was that particular sentence that held the key to the controversy that subsequently raged about whether or not we made a wrongful approach to him in November 1995. Bluntly, we did not. We didn't even need to. Brian Little already knew that he was under consideration if he wished to be.

In the event, we went through the normal procedure of advertising the vacancy in a national newspaper and this produced some fifty replies. About thirty of these could be instantly discarded because they were from applicants with no previous experience of managing a professional football club. The other twenty included some well-known names and, despite what might have appeared in the newspapers at that time, we did not interview anyone, much less offer any of them the job, even though we were dangerously managerless. In the short-term, we put the assistant manager, Jim Barron, in charge of team affairs and, typical of such situations, we went to White Hart Lane for our next fixture, and reversed the seven-goal Wimbledon scoreline for our first victory in ten Premiership matches.

By now I had made a formal request to the Leicester City chairman, Martin George, for permission to approach their manager. This request was refused, leaving the ball distinctly in Brian's court.

What now? To my relief it didn't take long for the promise I had given to Brian three years earlier to take effect. Through an intermediary, a reporter to be precise, I was sounded out as to whether his Villa appointment could be guaranteed, subject to contractual agreements if he decided to leave Leicester City. The assurance went back to him that it could, depending on discussions and the approval of the entire board.

As a result of that assurance, Brian Little chose to walk out on Leicester City and the following day he spoke to me for the first time.

I invited him to my home in Four Oaks for 'secret' discussions about wages and conditions, well away from the prying eyes and ears of the media – or so I thought.

The discussions took us about an hour, but what we didn't know was that photographers and reporters were hidden away near my home and Brian was pictured both getting out of his distinctive four-wheel-drive vehicle on my drive and also walking through my front door.

News of his impending appointment was thus virtually common knowledge via local radio and newspapers before our contract talks had even been completed. One thing I had learned long, long before was never to underestimate the probing powers of the press: they don't miss a lot, believe me. Indeed, as 'neutrals' they can often be quite useful as middle men.

However, all that truly mattered to me was that I now had my tenth, and hopefully last, manager on board, in whom to entrust the playing affairs of Aston Villa FC. Subsequent attempts by Leicester City to slap an injunction on his working for us and/or to bring the wrath of the FA or the FA Premiership down around our ears were abortive, simply because Brian had merely exercised his right to leave one employer and apply for a post with another. In due course, two other ex-Villa players, namely his assistant manager Allan Evans and his coach John Gregory, also left Filbert Street to rejoin Brian at Villa Park.

There have been many difficult searches for a new manager under my chairmanship but, for all the controversy that stretched on for weeks, this one was the easiest both to decide and to implement.

One significant factor in Brian being appointed to the job he so badly wanted was the input of the club's former commercial manager, Eric Woodward, whose ex-secretary, Heather, was Mrs Little, the manager's wife. Eric rang me on several occasions each time we were seeking a new man, to commend Brian to me.

Constantly, Eric stressed that beneath his courteous and friendly exterior there was a band of steel, a stubborn determination to achieve his objectives in life. Since the cruel injuries which had ended his magnificent playing career at the age of twenty-seven, he had, bit by bit, taken on board a whole range of impressive qualifications.

As a starting point, Eric claimed, the former star forward was a true Villa man whose allegiance to the club since his days as an apprentice had never wavered. After he finished as a player, he spent a spell on the commercial side, including time as a lottery agent along with Abdul Rashid, who went on to become our commercial manager.

Also, he had talked to Eric about press and public relations and had generally shown an interest in wider matters than playing affairs. Added to this was a spell as a Villa youth team coach, a period as coach and team manager for Wolverhampton Wanderers and then further experience coaching for Middlesbrough, when Bruce Rioch was manager at Ayresome Park. As his own man, he had sampled relegation from the Fourth Division of the Football League to the Vauxhall Conference in the role of manager of Darlington, followed by a return to the Fourth Division and promotion to the Third.

It was at this point in his career that I advised him to accept Leicester City's offer and learn the ropes at a higher grade, which he did by steering them to the Wembley play-offs and into the Premiership.

Eric rightly saw this as the ideal managerial CV and nothing I witnessed in Brian's early years at Villa Park contradicted that judgement. On day one, for instance, he had the players in a circle around him at the training ground when a particular individual arrived late, wearing an American baseball cap backwards and hovering on the fringe of things, perhaps his normal practice.

As the story filtered through to me, the new boss took him aside, informed him that if he were late again it would prove very expensive and told him to remove his inappropriate headgear.

Players saw clearly that they could not take liberties with Brian and this applied to *all* players, with no selected exceptions. Life changed very quickly, I'm led to believe, at the Bodymoor Heath training ground, though it was my rule to be rarely there to see for myself. The training ground is not my immediate responsibility.

Villa Park is my domain, where, I was delighted to discover, a shift in routine and manager-chairman relations was equally evident. After morning training each day, the new manager's set routine was to move to his office at Villa Park and from there, assisted by Allan Evans, to conduct his wider duties. How very different to his elusive and uncommunicative predecessor.

At last there was a sensible, regular rapport in a relaxed atmosphere with the feeling of supporting each other to pull in the same direction. Quite naturally, I waited with interest to discover how he assessed the playing staff, which had begun the season being tipped by Ron Atkinson – and as I recall, Alex Ferguson – as being of top-six calibre. It was a fairly brief wait.

Before very long, Brian informed me that he was deeply disappointed with the strength of his squad of players and that, the following season, widespread improvements would be urgently necessary.

To be perfectly fair, there were many exceptions to this judgement. Ron Atkinson's replacement was fortunate to take over such excellent players as Dwight Yorke, Mark Bosnich, Ugo Ehiogu, Michael Oakes, Andy Townsend, and yes, 'old man' Macca, the incomparable Paul McGrath.

In the shorter-term, however, fighting off the threat of relegation was the all-embracing priority. In the circumstances, he did not wish to undermine the confidence of the players he had inherited by giving his misgivings a public airing.

The records show that he successfully achieved his first objective, no mean feat in itself, albeit by a narrow margin, and when this became mathematically certain with a 1–1 draw at

Norwich in the final match, we mutually became a touch emotional for the first time.

It reminded me forcibly of the afternoon at Swindon when Graham Taylor's team took us into the old First Division and any of the normal reserves were shed in a tide of relief.

Phase Two beckoned for Brian Little. He was to build his own squad.

# CHAPTER SIXTEEN

# WORKING IN HARMONY

The summer of 1995 was a highly important period for the club, because Brian Little now had both the freedom and the necessary financial support to illustrate whether or not he could operate successfully at a major club.

Since the previous November, apart from comparatively minor adjustments in his predecessor's squad, he had been operating from match to match, desperately looking for survival points and forging a working relationship with both myself and the club as a whole.

By this time he had, as I have already pointed out, expressed deep dissatisfaction with the quality and average age of his first-team players. Some managers in this situation would have metaphorically snatched the chequebook and gone on a shopping spree. Not Brian Little. His modus operandi is far more considered and selective than that.

What especially impressed me was that, unlike some previous managers, he had no hang-ups about discussing his thoughts with others, including myself, even though he was mentally tough enough to ensure that the final decision on team affairs was always his own.

For example, I well recall him coming into my office one afternoon and asking: 'What do you think about us going for Gareth Southgate from Crystal Palace?' 'I've seen him a few times,' I responded. 'I recall seeing him score one cracking goal. He's a very good player. I'll back you if you want him.' It is quite possible that he did not truly need my opinion, because I've no doubt that by this time he had already made up his mind and done his homework on the player's character. But he was happy to observe the courtesy of asking my opinion and seeking my co-operation. What's more, he fully accepted my golden rule that while managers and coaches assess team affairs and nominate players to be sold or signed, it is the chairmen and/or the chief executives who conduct the financial negotiations.

As a matter of fact, long before I became known as 'Deadly', I had, in some quarters, taken on board a quite different nickname. 'They ought to call you "Mr Ten Per cent",' I was informed by one individual in the game, simply because it has always been my objective to pay at least ten percent less than any asking price.

I have managed to achieve this almost without exception, though I must confess that I am never too willing to operate the ten percent rule the other way. When buying players from Crystal Palace, there was always one man to contact and one man only: their then chairman Ron Noades, with whom I had many dealings on various committees.

Any reputation I might have about being a dictator at Villa Park was nothing compared to the way that chairmen like Ron Noades at Selhurst Park and Ken Bates at Stamford Bridge always kept their fingers on the pulse at their particular clubs.

Ron would no doubt have liked to have kept a player of Gareth's undoubted quality, but Palace had been relegated and the player wished to leave, so he had little alternative but to talk business. As a result, I was quickly able to inform our manager that he could go ahead and meet his man, a deal had been struck. That to me was another example of how the chairman-manager relationship should work, as Southgate became our record club signing for £2.25 million, though he was not to remain the most expensive player for long. Running side-by-side with that deal was another proposed incoming transfer, where again there had been a beneficial level of co-operation between us. Dating back a considerable time, from before Ron Atkinson had signed John Fashanu, it was blindingly obvious to all that we needed a new striker. This was not just my view, it was Brian's, too, and he was combing through the possibles to find someone of the right age and of international-class strength.

As a result of my position on the FA's International Committee, I had fairly regular access to Terry Venables, then the England manager. One day I asked him if, from his knowledge of European football, he could recommend a player who could score us twenty goals a season. 'Not easily,' was his reply. But he promised to keep us in mind.

Some time later, he contacted me to say that he and Bryan Robson, an England coach and by then the new manager of Middlesbrough, had been most impressed with the young Yugoslavian international centre-forward of Partizan Belgrade, Savo Milosevic, a leading scorer in European competition.

In addition to having watched him in the flesh, they had a video consisting of clips of him in action and they were both very impressed with what they saw. Terry agreed to send me the video by special delivery on the understanding that if we did not go for the player that we should let him know straight away because Bryan Robson would have then pursued an interest on Middlesbrough's behalf. 'I've asked Bryan [Robson] to let you have first refusal because you asked me some time ago,' said Venables. 'And he's agreed. But if you don't go for him, then he will.' When the video arrived the next day, I passed it on to Brian Little, who had been eager to see it. Some other managers would have recoiled at the thought of following up a player recommended in this way.

Brian's reaction was one of acute interest once he had seen Milosevic's undoubted talents, albeit only on video. The mention of Partizan Belgrade brought an image to my mind of a tall chap whom I had met while attending UEFA Cup draws in Geneva. I checked for a name in the *European Football Yearbook* (Sports Projects) and I felt sure that the Partizan secretary, Zarko Secevic, whose name I had found in the publication, was the person whom I had met. Putting a call into the club in Belgrade, I was pleased to discover that he also remembered me and he quickly confirmed that Milosevic was for sale.

There was just one 'minor' snag. That very day, the president of the Italian Serie A club, Parma, had sent his private aircraft to Belgrade to collect Milosevic for talks after a deal had more or less been struck between the two clubs. Unless we were to miss out, we had to move quickly.

'Please get in touch with the player,' I urged him. 'Ask him not to sign for Parma until he has spoken to us. We will match their terms... We're coming over on the first available flight.' Come the time to get off to the airport and Brian Little was still out on the pitch talking to the media about the Southgate deal as the player posed for the usual crop of signing pictures.

When a member of staff was sent out to the manager to inform him that the chairman was waiting for him to set off, little did the reporters, whom he left virtually in mid-interview to join me for the Belgrade flight, realise that our record fee would be overtaken that very day.

When we arrived at Belgrade airport, we were met by Partizan officials and were assured that Savo had taken our 'advice' and not signed for Parma, but that he would not be back in the former Yugoslavia for some four hours.

We were taken to the impressive Partizan Stadium for discussions so that we could work out a package that would be suitable to both of us, though this time I was pretty certain that I would not be able to observe my 'Mr Ten Percent' rule. More likely, I suspect, they got more out of us than Parma had been ready to pay. If so, you could hardly blame them.

Incidentally, I do recall being shown around their marvellous stadium and seeing a trophy room that makes Liverpool's look under-stocked. However, the news came into the committee room, where we were still talking, that Savo had now arrived, accompanied by his close friend Igor, a former Yugoslav tennis champion and a sports presenter who appeared regularly on their television screens. The pair were summoned into the meeting and it was very evident to me that the players were kept very much 'in their place', rather like things used to be in this country.

During the talks that followed, Igor spoke perfect English and took very good care of his pal Savo's affairs. We found Milosevic to be a big, impressive young man who had once been an outstanding basketball player.

After our manager had held discussions with the powerful Serb, helped by Igor, a deal in principle was soon struck, though we insisted that he had to accompany us on our return so that he could see what we had to offer him in terms of facilities and a stage on which to play, while also undergoing the necessary medical. This was also agreed.

By now it was around midnight. It had been a long day. Time for some shut-eye? Apparently not... Our hosts insisted on taking us out for a meal, since none of us had eaten for several hours, and we found ourselves at a restaurant on the outskirts of the city where, to our amazement, bearing in mind that it was now the wee small hours, the place was alive and buzzing.

It was rather strange to reflect that we were in what had become known as 'war-torn former Yugoslavia', where terrible civil unrest was going on between the rival ethnic factions of Serbs, Croatians and Muslims.

As we sat enjoying a delightful meal and a bottle or two of wine, innocent people were being caught up in the strife not all that far down the road and UN mercy missions were having a hard time attempting to restore some stability. It was only later that we learned that one of the reasons Savo wanted the funds he would accumulate from his £3.5 million move was to help move his family from an enclave where they were virtually surrounded by warring groups, to a 'safe-haven' flat in Belgrade, where peace reigned.

We eventually went to bed at about 4am, having arranged to meet Savo and Igor at the airport in good time before our flight.

Brian and I were there in plenty of time. But no Savo. Time ticked away. Still no Savo. Warning signs began to flash. 'Is he going to let us down,' we agonised as it got perilously near to departure time.

Panic stations were not too far away when through the departure lounge strolled Aston Villa's potential record signing, along with Igor, ready to begin what was to become something of a roller-coaster ride in a claret-and-blue shirt.

There was never a moment's doubt in my mind that Brian Little would grow in stature at Villa Park once his first, desperately difficult season had been completed with the club's Premiership place successfully defended.

This confidence increased as, painstakingly, player by player, he dispensed with many of those he had inherited and replaced them, usually with younger models in accordance with our agreed transfer policy.

I mean no disrespect to outstanding players such as our former captain Kevin Richardson, Ray Houghton, Dalian Atkinson, Dean Saunders, Garry Parker, Bryan Small, John Fashanu, Shaun Teale, Earl Barrett, Graham Fenton and Guy Whittingham, but they had been given their chance to consolidate on Villa's League Cup victory and, instead, the club had almost been relegated.

A new manager, as always, wanted his own squad, comprising players whom he had selected and signed himself

Heidi with two football heroes – David Ginola, *above* and England captain, David Beckham, *below*.

At the graduation when I was awarded an honorary degree from Central England University.

*Above*: Prince Charles opened the Trinity Road Stand at Villa Park in 2004

*Below*: The club worked in conjunction with the Aston Rotary Club to raise money following the Tsunami. We raised over £100,000 and purchased forty-two fishing boats for two villages. Each boat provides a living for nine families.

Dressed for action at the age of eighty to fly at 9,000 feet, monitoring the control of eight warships in an exercise with Exocets, in the Northern Atlantic.

Rubbing shoulders with former South Africa president, Nelson Mandela.

We celebrated eighty 'deadly' years at a birthday dinner held at Villa Park in 2004.

*Above*: I was presented with a silver plate by all the Premiership teams to congratulate me on my eightieth birthday.

*Below*: Arsenal Vice-Chairman, David Dein, *left* and David O'Leary, Aston Villa manager, *right* were also at the birthday dinner.

Villa Park has become my second home over the years.

and had introduced into the code of conduct he expects of professional athletes.

The names of the players he recruited are there in the record books and it is interesting to look back and recall that there were seven of his signings in the team which beat Manchester United 3–1 at Villa Park on the opening day.

From there we simply took off and, by May 1996, we had regained the Coca Cola Cup with a sparkling Wembley victory over Leeds United, were back in Europe, had reached the semi-final of the FA Cup and were fourth in the FA Premiership.

Brian Little had successfully challenged leading managers in Britain, as I was certain that he would, and I was more than delighted to secure his services on a new contract to keep him at the helm into the 21st century just as he, at that time of current success and encouraging signs for the future, was delighted to stay.

As he himself wrote, without my knowledge at the time:

> I have known the chairman ever since I came into football and I don't think the word 'fear' has ever come into my thinking about anyone, least of all Mr Ellis. I find it quite funny that people call the chairman 'Deadly' and even try to avoid him in some instances. Actually, I go out of my way to make sure I see him most days and, although I feel it is a very important role for me to play, I can assure all the doubters that it is not an act. The chairman is always interested in my thoughts and I have no worries about relaying those thoughts to him.

These were Brian's unsolicited words, not mine, in his book *Return of the Little Villan* (Sports Projects).

Strange how, despite such public statements from him, folks still jumped to the conclusion that he was 'pushed' when he subsequently left the club, quite against my wishes.

However, back to his happier days at the club. From a season of almost total, non-stop enjoyment at seeing such progress being achieved, one little scenario sticks in my mind and when I describe it I am aware that perhaps it will appear to be a mere ego trip. In reality it was more than that to me, a demonstration that after years of battling, sometimes against pockets of public opinion, I had won a place in the hearts and minds of at least some of the supporters and had recovered from the psychological buffeting I had undergone after dismissing Ron Atkinson.

I had arrived at Wembley for the League Cup final against Leeds United and was walking up the steps to the main entrance when I heard my name being chanted behind me and turned around to see an army of at least a thousand claret-and-blue bedecked fans.

These people are the lifeblood of the club, without whom we couldn't function. Of course, it goes without saying that we greatly treasure our sponsors, our executive box-holders and our long-serving season-ticket holders. But, by and large, they are not the people who paint their faces claret and blue, who tog up in zany get-ups, who sing the songs, follow the team to every away game, friendlies and all, who spend their last pound of pocket money on the club and who are always there, come what may.

It was a gathering of those sort of supporters who were making music for my ears as they chanted: 'There's only one Doug Ellis...' Imagine that! Eighteen months earlier they had been chanting 'Big Fat Ron's Claret-and-Blue Army' until they turned on me as the chairman for having the temerity to dispense with the services of their charismatic leader. It was the change of attitude embodied by that chant that provided a fillip for my heart. And what a day it proved to be.

At the Cup-winning banquet in central London later that night, I had Heidi and the family around me and was one very proud man indeed.

The events of the remainder of that season, with fourth place in the Premiership, which had been achieved following an FA Cup semi-final, confirmed our potential for further progress and also strengthened our resolve to continue the upgrading of Villa Park, which had already been going on for several years.

There is no need for the full details of the various development schemes to be outlined here, but our desire to make the stadium meet the demands of the 21st century was to lead to some of the most insulting, almost malicious, comments being made about Villa Park. To say that I was incensed by certain observations about the appearance of Villa Park, and its adverse impact on the Aston landscape, would be the understatement of the decade, bearing in mind the neglected relic of former years.

Some background is necessary to understand the outrage we felt when a controversy about the state of Villa Park exploded in the local press in early April 1997.

Since the post-Hillsborough Lord Justice Taylor Report we, like all other clubs, had modernised the stadium, step by step, to meet the legal requirements of its findings. All of the work carried out had, obviously, required planning approval and great care had been taken to blend the modifications into the local environment, including the nearby stately home, Aston Hall.

We had carefully kept Villa Park as near as possible to its traditional character with external brickwork, while adding modern roofing with matching facias on three sides.

We had now submitted a planning request to bring the main Trinity Road Stand into line with the other three sides and thus complete a matching four sides of the stadium. We had also made it clear that we wished for a subsequent further development of the North Stand, which houses the club offices, with the ultimate intention of bringing the ground's all-seater capacity to some 50,000.

I must point out here that Villa Park does not have the look of the modern, custom-built bowl like, say, Molineux or Derby County's new stadium, Pride Park. Since our ground was originally built in 1897, there is no way it could and, in any case, there are very many people who are proud of the stadium's more traditional appearance. I am certainly one of those people.

Imagine, then, how we felt when, in delaying permission for us to carry out the Trinity Road improvements in the summer of 1997, pending a detailed plan containing a scheme for the North Stand End, councillors made insulting comments about our stadium. The council's refusal – they called it a deferment! – to accept the plans submitted to build the extension to the Trinity Road Stand in the summer of 1997, cost the club more than £600,000 in wasted fabricated steel alone despite, as we understood it, the council's professional planning officers having recommended that our plans be approved.

The planning committee chairman was quoted in the local press as describing Villa Park as 'an ugly mess' and 'a hotchpotch of four different sheds'. Another official was quoted as saying that Villa Park spoiled the appearance of the vicinity when viewed from the nearby Aston Expressway between Spaghetti Junction and the Birmingham city centre.

Surely, most people who have driven that stretch of road and glanced past Aston Church steeple to Villa Park would not feel that the stadium spoiled the view? The disgraceful phrase 'Ugly Mess' was a banner headline in the *Evening Mail* on Thursday, 3 April, hardly the publicity we expected as a result of applying for permission to spend yet another £3.4 million on improving the West Midlands' best-known and most historic football stadium.

This, remember, is a stadium which the Football Association had regularly chosen for FA Cup semi-finals and which attracted huge praise from all sides when Euro '96 matches, in the European Championships, were so successfully staged here. Anyone following the progress of Villa Park's gradual redevelopment during the 1980s and 1990s and who recall the tumbledown, antiquated decay of 1969, when the first flotation took place, would possibly regard the abusive language to which I have referred as being grossly out of order.

Our only course of action was to meet the council's request to provide a more detailed scheme, outlining our intentions for the North Stand development alongside the Trinity Road plan, while leaving the public at large to decide for themselves on the quality and appearance of the ground and its impact on the local environment. The eventual cost of bringing the stadium capacity up to 50,000 seats was calculated at more than £16 million.

All of which reminds me of the mess that surrounded plans for the new National Stadium...

# CHAPTER SEVENTEEN

# WEMBLEY: WRONG LOCATION

When I was a member of the FA Council and the international and finance committees, I became increasingly disgusted with the commercial arrangements for major matches held at Wembley Stadium.

Due to a long-standing contractual agreement, Wembley Stadium plc took, in my view, a disproportionate amount of the commercial income from internationals, cup finals, replays, promotion play-offs and the like.

Not only this, but Wembley could not offer the quality of facilities that the modern-day spectator quite reasonably demands and this includes getting to and from the stadium without unacceptable delays.

Wembley's very location hampers the arrival and departure of large crowds as the lines of motor vehicles – as anyone who has experienced the problem – will testify. Those who live in the south-east can just about put up with the traffic jams and the pressure on public transport, because they, at least, are otherwise reasonably close to home.

Those who have to drive a hundred miles and maybe twice that far once they are eventually clear of the stadium – and that, remember, could be after a night match – find that getting to and from Wembley is an absolute nightmare.

It could easily take a couple of hours just to get out of the car park and thus it could often have turned midnight before they even started their drive home. The whole infrastructure around the stadium conflicted with the requirements of seventy-odd thousand people and it was difficult to see how they could make truly significant improvements. The last time Aston Villa played in the Coca Cola Cup final, against Leeds United in March 1996, our staff coaches took over two hours to get to the stadium – despite the short distance from their hotel in the West End of London – and they only just arrived at their seats in time to see the kick-off. This sort of thing had been going on for years. When we drew against Everton in the 1977 League Cup final on a Saturday afternoon, a banquet was staged at the Metropole Hotel near the National Exhibition Centre just outside Birmingham. By the time all the coaches had fought their way through miles and miles of traffic, the function had been delayed late into the evening and was as good as ruined.

Even the official FA party for major matches was affected as badly as the long-suffering public at large. We used to leave from White's Hotel, Bayswater Road, near the former FA headquarters in Lancaster Gate, and we had to give ourselves at least two hours to get to Wembley. Getting back was even worse, unless you waited at the stadium for a couple of hours to allow the traffic to ease.

It has been interesting to note that certain London writers, who tend to be defensive about anything concerning the capital, have written newspaper articles expressing doubts about whether Wembley is the ideal location for our national stadium of the future, which it manifestly is not.

OK, now to 'dream up' that Fantasy Football Stadium, not just for those who live in London and its surrounds, but for the benefit of the national and international football family in its entirety.

In my opinion, the location for the new stadium had to be central to suit the majority. The site needed to be adjacent to a motorway network feeding in all directions, near to an international airport and railway station and on a large rural site with plenty of car-parking space. In addition, massive capital funds had to be available as well as a blueprint that would suit all of the FA Premiership clubs and other potential users of what would be one of the finest, most ideally situated stadiums in Europe.

Fantasy satisfied? Well, this scenario was not a fantasy, but a potentially feasible proposition. I argued in FA Council that football was a working man's game with its roots in the north of England, Scotland, the Midlands and elsewhere.

With this in mind, a state-of-the-art stadium to accommodate 85,000 people from all points of the compass, in comfort, with plenty of leg room, had become absolutely essential. In my opinion, the centre of England was the logical site for it.

A green site where environmental considerations could be met alongside all the other requirements of convenient travel was the obvious location and we had such a proposal adjacent to the National Exhibition Centre that, because of its own huge success, has simply grown and grown. A new stadium nearby would surely prosper in similar fashion.

The £100 million plan that our Midland-based group put forward was for the stadium to be in a bowl with part of it submerged below ground level so as to be concealed from view.

It was immediately adjacent to the M42, a motorway which leads to the M40, M5 or the M6-M69 and the M1, roughly an hour's easy drive to the outskirts of London, Manchester, Liverpool and Sheffield, a stone's throw from Birmingham International airport and a London-line railway station and with ample car-park space to accommodate some 30,000 vehicles.

There was a moving walkway scheme direct to the railway station, where additional platform space would be provided along with speedy access to the airport. A running-water moat would surround the stadium, which would be built in 110 acres of land.

Part-funding would come from the sum of £40 million spread over five years to be provided by the members of the Premier League, who would thus have a vested interest. When I put this financial proposition to the Premier clubs at their monthly meeting on two occasions, there were no dissensions from any of my chairman colleagues.

I was also quite confident that the remaining £60 million would be forthcoming from lottery funds over a similar period, because of the number of sporting and leisure activities for which such a magnificent stadium could be used, including major music concerts.

There were massive business opportunities for the surrounding West Midlands commercial community, including Solihull, whose planning permission was required. We had deeply researched the possible annual usage and turnover and had come to the conclusion that the scheme was entirely viable.

As concerns about the new Wembley continued, it is interesting to note a letter that I sent to Southampton FC chairman, Rupert Lowe, at the time:

Mr R Lowe

Chairman
Southampton Football Club
The Friends Provident St Mary's Stadium
Britania Road
Southampton
SO14 5FP

# WEMBLEY: WRONG LOCATION

Dear Rupert

FA Finance and Wembley National Stadium

Thank you for your circular letter dated 28 February 2003 addressed to all Chairman of the Premier League.

Unfortunately your concerns have been voiced by me a hundred times during the past 2 years whilst promoting the National Stadium to be built in the Midlands at a total cost of some £200 Million less than the present figure quoted for Wembley. To remind you, the location immediately adjacent to the M42, some 8 miles from the City of Birmingham provided 120 acres at a peppercorn rent from the City Council, providing 90,000 seats with all the modern facilities equal to Wembley (Adam Crozier asked me would I have any objection to the Birmingham plans being utilised for the Wembley site).

The cost of the building was £145 million and section 106 was £122 million and that provided a moving half mile walkway from the International Railway Station connecting to an overhead railway for a further half mile into the International Airport.

In brief Rupert, the total cost which was maintained right to the death was £572 million. In addition it had 7,500 car park spaces plus spaces for 500 coaches immediately around the Stadium with two bridges across the M42 in to a further 15,000 car park spaces. The whole project was to be managed by the National Exhibition Centre whose administrative costs would be negligible in comparison to the completely new setup at Wembley. They were treating it as just another Hall in as much as they already accommodate five-and-a-half million visitors per year.

We spoke to the Managing Director of Multiplex, who have the contract to build Wembley, who said he would be delighted to build in Birmingham as his financial risk would be far less plus the fact that Birmingham City Council were underwriting on the income. We also employed an Australian firm who specialised in selling all the facilities of modern stadiums throughout the world. Their Chairman and Managing Director spent six weeks around the UK visiting existing Wembley box holders and sponsors and were confident of securing contracts at least to the extent of two thirds of the prices being obtained at Wembley and this was before we were in a position to guarantee our location.

Despite all I write I have had to accept that Wembley has won the day and it is too late to go baaack, but I can only repeat my expressed concerns at the whole Wembley project in comparison to what I, together with the City of Birmingham were offering.

You are probably fully aware of what I write but briefly I can only add my concerns at the FA's inability to distribute funds to the extent that they have been doing in the last 2 years due to the excessive commitment thay have for the Wembley project. We will see each other on 22 March when no doubt we can discuss the matter further.

Congratulations on your acceptance to represent the Premier League on the FA Board.

Yours sincerely

HD Ellis
Chairman


Yet, incredibly, when our project was considered along with one from Manchester and that of upgrading Wembley stadium, it was rejected by the Sports Council on the grounds that planning permission for the site had not been forthcoming.

Let me just examine this. I had met the Birmingham City council, along with Rick Parry, who was the chief executive of the FA Premier League. The deputy leader, Councillor Bryan Bird, had expressed the view that his Labour colleagues in Solihull would support the scheme, with all its multitude of benefits for the locality.

I had also taken the precaution of enlisting the presence of Graham Shaylor, Birmingham's retired chief planning officer and temporary chief executive of the city council, to act as a consultant. We all felt that we were well on the way to bringing the scheme to fruition. True, our planning application to Solihull had originally been rejected on the grounds of increased traffic, but the usual procedure for planning permission to build on greenbelt land necessitates that it is called in by the appropriate minister, who then appoints an inspector to investigate all the relevant factors thoroughly. In cases where a national interest is involved, as was the case here, a local rejection can be overturned. I was confident that this is how it would have worked out. Had we been given the necessary six months breathing space to get the application called in by the minister, we would have won.

However, to reach that stage, the Sports Council would have needed to include us among the possibles. This they failed to do. I wonder why…?

Certainly, to be thrown out at the first hurdle, as unbelievable lobbying for Wembley Stadium went on behind the scenes, was absolutely heartbreaking. It was just as unbelievable as Birmingham's excellent Millennium Celebration scheme, with its structure already in being, had been defeated by a rubbish dump in Greenwich.

So, will the 'new' Wembley justify the decision? Only time and traffic jams will tell, but even if a satisfactory stadium emerges, the point remains that the location will be unacceptable to a large section of the football community.

Not one to give up the fight too easily, I made it known to Graham Kelly in April 1998, when it became known that Arsenal had ditched plans to possibly play at Wembley – and the stadium's future at that point remained unclear – that the centre of England project still remained an option. If it were backed with the full weight of approval from all interested parties, planning permission could be obtained, of this I remained confident.

Possessing a stadium fit for the next century is one important issue. Preparing the England team to live up to its splendour is even more desirable and this aspect came firmly under my wing when I was chairman of the Football Association's technical control board, the body that supported Howard Wilkinson, the director of coaching, in his task of improving the nation's skills for future years.

In this particular capacity, my belief was that, as far as individual skills are concerned, we are light years behind major European football countries, especially Holland and France plus others including Germany. This was why our committee, representing the FA, put our weight solidly behind the proposals to transform the old United States airbase at Upper Heyford in Oxfordshire into a magnificent multi-purpose British Academy of Sport that would incorporate a national football academy.

Unhappily, the subject, like the national stadium, then became a political hot potato, when Chris Smith, Labour's Culture and Sport Secretary at the time, talked of excluding 'team sports' such as football, cricket and rugby from the academy plans, before having second thoughts and talking of centres of excellence all around the country.

Thus, regrettably, the topic was shrouded in controversy and political in-fighting, just at a time when the need to meet the continentals on a level playing field in terms of nurturing outstanding young footballers from a very early age became more pressing.

The Sheffield bid, which was an excellent one, was the one to be accepted: however, from football's standpoint, Upper Heyford was a heaven-sent location for a National Academy.

The US Air Force left behind outstanding and varied facilities and was in good condition; it also included a sixty-bed hospital as well as many useful amenities. In addition to this, a hundred acres of valuable space could be allocated to football pursuits on the old airfield. Also, the potential deal with the Oxfordshire local authority was favourable in the shape of a ninety-nine-year lease on a peppercorn rent subject to receiving a grant from the National Lottery of £30 million to provide capital and maintenance.

Along with Howard Wilkinson and our FA colleagues, we firmly believed that the location, with all the facilities that could be created there, was ideal for producing young footballers with the quality and calibre required to bring England up to the level of the best in Europe and the world.

What I thought was a good opportunity to convince the government of the benefits of Upper Heyford ahead of the Lilleshall and Sheffield projects came in Paris. When Tony Banks, the then Minister for Sport and myself, attended the final of Le Tournoi between England and Brazil. I gave him a lengthy ear-bashing on the subject and was very hopeful that it would have an effect until Chris Smith's comment cast doubts about that and Sheffield won the day.

The fact is that we have continued to fall behind the other major footballing nations in terms of scientific preparation of young players, as I realised forcibly when attending France's National Academy at Clair Fontain, near Paris. It is a magnificent establishment with every conceivable aid to teaching young players the basic skills and then building on them as they, the

Dutch, the Germans and others have continued to do, sometimes to our embarrassment.

To encapsulate my personal feelings of total frustration about the dual situation, let me sum up what might have been: one of the finest football stadiums in the world situated in the very centre of the nation and with a magnificent Academy of Sport, equipped to employ every modern technique, a comparatively short drive away. All of this, remember, within easy reach of London and with a viable financial package on hand to bring it all to fruition.

What other enlightened nation in the whole world would need second thoughts about integrating such a package? If players from those nations proceed to show greater technique than we do and to beat us in the international arenas perhaps, as a nation, it is our own fault?

As the new £747 million Wembley is about to open in 2006, I still question its enormous cost – which, incidentally, nearly bankrupted the FA – and even though 'location, location, location' is apparently everything, I still have major doubts as to whether Wembley is in the right place!

# CHAPTER EIGHTEEN

# THE UPS AND DOWNS
# OF FLOTATION

A lady of mature years walked into the Birmingham office of stockbrokers Albert E Sharp in the spring of 1997, produced a sheaf of Aston Villa share certificates and asked how much they were worth.

The charming lady had read that, with a flotation underway, Villa shares had sharply risen in value. As one of the club's thousands of long-standing shareholders, it sounded like very good news to her.

Her late father had left her with a substantial holding in the club, though until she had read recent newspaper reports it had not occurred to her that they were anything but paper value. As it transpired, however, the growth of the club over the years meant that she had a pleasant surprise in store.

The clerk who perused the share certificates suggested that she should come inside, sit down and enjoy a cup of tea while a more senior member of staff was summoned to discuss her shareholding with her.

What were they now worth with the stock exchange flotation looming, she had asked? The member of staff called up a more senior colleague to break the news.

'Are you sitting comfortably, madam?' he asked, or words to that effect. 'Your shares, being special shares, are worth an estimated £1.3 million. Madam, are you all right? Would you like another cup of tea?'

Our fortunate, if speechless, lady was in fact Mrs Barbara Nation and the news of her windfall was extremely nostalgic to my ears dating back, as it did, to the momentous affairs of 1968.

Mrs Nation's late father was Joe Heath, a self-made local businessman and one of the Villa directors who had forfeited his place on the board to make way for my new administration in that eventful upheaval in December 1968.

Joe, a friend of mine, was the person who had supported Bruce Normansell's vain proposal to have me elected to the board back in 1964.

In a way, this anecdote is a financial barometer of the twenty-nine years between the two flotations. The value of those bits of paper, purchased by supporters of all income groups as an illustration of their commitment to the club, had multiplied in value several thousand times.

Those who bought one share for a fiver, for instance, found that, at the market peak, their share certificate was now worth £1,100 and that a 'special share' was worth fifteen times that value.

Subsequently, it was a fact that, after the 1997 flotation, share values went down very significantly along with others in the same sector, and confirmed the fears that I had always held that the clubs who floated before us set their figures too high to the detriment of those who were to follow. Indeed, let me be quite explicit when I say that I was deeply sceptical about the whole idea for quite a while.

The start of it all was Manchester United's decision to 'go public', followed by a similar move by Tottenham Hotspur. As a result, we began to get approaches from banks and financial institutions, but in principle I still remained profoundly unsure.

# THE UPS AND DOWNS OF FLOTATION

City eyes had been attracted towards football by the turnover increases that clubs such as ourselves had achieved from around £13 million a year to an escalating £30 million a year, supplemented by unprecedented stadium improvements, the BSkyB television contract, other commercial interests and a general upsurge in the sport's following. The purging of the old hooligan problem by modern-day security measures was another positive influence.

The first individual to begin my gradual transition towards the idea was Adam Shutkeever, an exceedingly bright barrister and a young, diehard Aston Villa supporter, who was originally from Birmingham and who represented Deutsche Morgan Grenfell, the German owners of the big finance house. He wrote to me and visited me at Villa Park, outlining his estimate of the current stock-market value of Aston Villa FC. He and a colleague whom he brought along, set the figure at substantially over £100 million, probably double the value that I would personally have placed on the club at that time. Bear in mind that, since I had never had any intention whatsoever of selling any significant part of my Aston Villa holding, and certainly of never putting the club up for auction, talk of the club's paper value was no more than a passing concern.

I wrote back to each of the brokers who had approached us to say that I was not interested in a flotation at this time and, indeed, said as much to shareholders at the Annual General Meeting of August 1996. I was asked from the floor at that AGM if it were my intention to float and my perfectly truthful answer was that it was not. Basically I was concerned about the treadmill that one could get onto whereby the banks, investment houses, brokers or whoever, were telling you how to run the club.

Nevertheless, the City's interest in us persisted and since we were to invest more large capital sums into stadium improvements and as we also needed to give Brian Little further support in the transfer market, the possibility of substantial cash injections into our funds could not be ignored. Consequently, when we visited Old Trafford on New Year's Day 1997, I made it my business to glean whatever information I could about Manchester United's experiences as a public limited company and the various complicated procedures involved.

My misgivings at the danger of possibly outlandish values being placed on clubs and their share-price listings had led to my making an unscheduled visit to Sir John Hall who, at that time, had agreed to float Newcastle United. Press reports suggested that Newcastle were to float at what I felt was far too high a figure: £200 million was being suggested as their likely value.

The mechanics of going public are less complicated than some might imagine. Basically, a valuation is set and divided up into the relevant number of shares, at whatever individual price is selected, and then the stock markets sell them to institutions and individuals at an increasing, or decreasing, price as the markets fluctuate. The question remained as to whether clubs were overvaluing themselves and thus the price of their shares. Would we be in danger of 'killing the goose that was laying the golden eggs'? I was afraid that we would. In order to make my concerns known, I called on Sir John at a hotel where he was staying in London and got him out of bed for an informal but, I felt, a profoundly important chat.

It was well after midnight when he was eventually able to return to his bed but, by the time he had turned in for a second time that night, I felt that I had convinced him of the dangers of going for a sum far in excess of what financial advisers might set as the club's realistic market value.

My view was that overpricing in this way could crucially affect the performance of others in the football sector. In the long term, it could be extremely detrimental to us all and I never reversed this view.

I asked Sir John to reconsider his valuation and go for £160 million. This, I suggested, would result in a massive oversubscription while retaining his share price, rather than have them selling at a discount, i.e. less than their original value on flotation day.

A rapid fall in price could not be a favourable outcome, I stressed. However, a club like ours could not be seen to be floating at a massively lower figure than others of similar financial potential.

When I left Sir John, with whom I had an amicable relationship, I felt that I had convinced him of my theory.

Readers may feel that I was a touch presumptuous in approaching him in this way but, in fact, when he first became chairman of Newcastle United, he asked me if he could visit Villa Park to see how a football club should be run. He asked for two hours of my time but, after flying down to Birmingham, he was with us for double that period. Thus, in some measure, we contributed to his building of the St James' Park club. With this in mind, I had no qualms in seeking him out in an attempt to dissuade him from over-capitalising on the market valuation issue, since their price would inevitably affect not only ours but also others.

In the event Sir John took only limited account of my advice and lowered his figure from £200 million to £193 million. History now tells us that my fears were realised and that the Newcastle shares were soon selling at a substantially discounted price. For whatever reason, Sir John retired for a while until the headline-hitting problems at St James' Park led to him returning to the helm at a time when the club's place in the Premiership was under threat, as were the share prices.

So why did we eventually decide on a flotation ourselves? The men who finally convinced me were Martin Edwards, the chairman of Manchester United FC, and Sir Roland Smith, the chairman of Manchester United plc, during that Old Trafford visit for a 0–0 draw on New Year's Day 1997.

Sir Roland Smith had formerly been chairman of British Aerospace, Rover and several other well-known companies. By now I had been approached by some ten financial houses, and had seen three of them at their request, but had retained many of my original misgivings.

However, Martin Edwards assured me that he had been assailed by similar doubts to my own, but after being persuaded to go for it, he had discovered that the process had been less troublesome than he had imagined and that he now enjoyed and appreciated Manchester United's status on the stock exchange and his periodic visits to the financial institutions involved.

Sir Roland then took me to one side of Manchester United's spacious and luxurious boardroom and observed that, having known me for many years, I would also actually enjoy the change and that Aston Villa would unquestionably reap meaningful benefits. He had no doubts that we could handle the transition without any undue worries or difficulties. We should go ahead. That was the Manchester United advice, and I took it, not without a sense of history when I recalled the rather less spectacular flotation of 1969.

The one important proviso was the very same one that I had offered to Sir John Hall, namely to keep the price down as low as possible compared to other clubs in a similar situation and to allow for the possibility of shares increasing in value rather than being sold at a discount. Sir Roland also recommended the Birmingham brokers Albert E Sharp to handle the operation and I have to say that this proved very sound advice.

After the necessary lengthy discussions and outline planning, the arrangements we put into force set our market cap, as it is known, at between £120 million and £140 million. This would have created a competitive market and would almost certainly have resulted in shares increasing in value, but for one powerful, adverse force that we had not anticipated.

None of us, not Albert E Sharp, nor anyone at the club,

imagined that the original 8,000 shareholders dating back to the 1969 flotation would sell their shares as they did.

The trend that emerged, and I have to repeat that it took us by surprise, was that our existing shareholders, a high proportion of them season-ticket holders, cashed in on their investment to the extent of £1,100 each, while holding on to a reduced number. Unfortunately, one of the directors I had invited onto Aston Villa's board in the early 1970s, who had purchased £25,000-worth of shares, sold some of them for a very handsome profit. Similarly, the little old lady whose father had invested £30,000 in Villa shares, sold most of hers for £1 million – two transactions that seriously added to the discounting of our share value.

It was this that made it a seller's, rather than a buyer's market, forcing the value of our shares down in a manner that I had tried so carefully to avoid. As one shareholder put it to me: 'This has paid for my season ticket for the next three years.' Obviously, in the context of the flotation, plans for which we announced on 6 February, well in advance of the actual day, the mass profit-making was a big disappointment.

On the other hand, it did mean that those who had helped the club all those years ago had now been repaid for their faith beyond their wildest dreams. Since then, I have asked well-informed people in the stockbroking business whether they can name another £5 share, in any business pursuit, that cost a fiver and which could have been resold for up to £1,600. All I have received in reply is a shaking of heads.

Inevitably, I suppose, there are some who have criticised our flotation. These critics do not include Barbara Nation or many of the others like her.

Those who put their 1997 shares away and forget them for a few years may find that, just like them, they will receive a pleasant surprise one day in the future.

Without going into too much detail, it is a fact that 'going public' demands that a company gets its organisation on a very sound footing at all levels, especially financially, and with a structured management policy.

To this end we took on a new, executive financial director in Mark Ansell, a chartered accountant who was formerly head of corporate finance with Deloitte and Touche, Midlands. A dedicated, lifelong Aston Villa fan, he was an enormous help in advising on the many and varied requirements. We also strengthened the board by the co-opting of two non-executive directors in Tony Hales, the chief executive of Allied Domecq plc, and David Owen, a former senior vice-president and a senior partner in Edge and Ellison, Aston Villa's long-serving club solicitors.

But the wealth of experience and specialised expertise did not end there. One of our two senior vice-presidents was Mervyn King, who later became governor of the Bank of England. Mervyn King is a fanatical Aston Villa supporter, from his Birmingham University days on the Holte End, and who has, for some time, been a regular in our directors' guest room on match days. The other senior vice-president was Lord Howell of Aston Manor, formerly Denis Howell and ex-Labour Minister for Sport and international referee, another big Villa man.

Sadly and tragically, however, within weeks of the flotation, our board strength was reduced by the sudden and totally unexpected death of Dr David Targett, a director and long-serving club physician, a wonderful sportsman, champion of all things claret and blue and both a dear, dear friend and boardroom colleague.

His death on 18 May 1997, followed by the death of Lord Howell a year later, set me thinking very deeply about all such people, at various levels of the club, who have made such selfless contributions to its health and well-being.

# CHAPTER NINETEEN

# LOSING A LOYAL FRIEND

For some time, it was the custom for a friendly group of four of us to travel together to all, or certainly most, of our away games around the country. Our regular carload would consist of Steve Stride, Dr David Targett, Dr Barrie Smith and myself.

Brian Little's second full season was always in danger of being something of a 'follow-that' exercise, given the outstanding achievements of the 1995–96 season, and as our quartet travelled around we saw, again and again, just how difficult it would be to maintain and improve the standards that had been established.

Our defence of the Coca Cola Cup ended at Wimbledon in the fourth round and our attempt to win the FA Cup for the first time for thirty-seven years came to grief, also in the fourth round, but this time at Derby.

By then, our UEFA Cup return had not survived the first round, as the underrated Swedes of Helsingborgs IF put up the shutters in the second leg at home after a shock, late equaliser had given them a 1–1 draw at Villa Park. We were thus left with the Premiership as our one hope of more honours and, as our championship challenge faded, a return to Europe became our only remaining target.

Set against these slightly disappointing affairs were the increasingly encouraging attendances at Villa Park, a sure sign that our public had become as confident as we were behind the scenes that the club's old inconsistencies had finally been banished. Faith in the future had arrived at last.

The season saw our average attendance rise from 32,614 to 36,027 with seven full houses of 39,339 and ten games at which the gate exceeded 30,000. We knew we had to repay such confidence and this gave our campaign to grasp one of the UEFA Cup places on offer an increased importance.

As the pattern at the top of the Premiership and in the domestic cups took shape, so it emerged that fifth place in the league would be enough to achieve our objective. Our travelling foursome left after Aston Villa's final visit to the dear old Baseball Ground (replaced in 1997–98 by Pride Park) slightly unnerved by a second away defeat at the hands of Jim Smith's ever-improving Derby County. A home draw with Tottenham Hotspur kept the situation more than a shade tense and after another draw, at Leeds, we arrived at our final away game, against Middlesbrough at their new Riverside Stadium, knowing that a victory, or maybe a draw, would clinch that European place. What a day it proved to be, one I shall never forget, for all the wrong reasons, as long as I live.

I had always had it in mind that, since this was our final away game of the season, and one that would hopefully see our European target achieved, I would arrange a special end-of-season celebration meal for our travelling foursome on the return journey.

The venue was to be a favourite restaurant of mine, the Dovecliffe Hotel, just off the A38 near Burton-on-Trent, a short drive from home, though I deliberately left a decision until after the match. Maybe we would not feel like dining in style if we had not achieved the result we required?

## LOSING A LOYAL FRIEND

As it transpired, the Riverside fixture left us feeling as though our emotions had been put through a spin dryer.

We were 2–0 down at half-time, but then we staged a magnificent second-half recovery as Ugo Ehiogu and Savo Milosevic scored the goals to equalise for what looked, until the closing seconds, to be a 2–2 draw.

Then came the mental trauma of a highly debatable decision against us and Fabrizio Ravanelli netted a last-ditch penalty for a 3–2 scoreline in Middlesbrough's favour. Bryan Robson's team was fighting, vainly as it was to prove, for Premiership survival, so naturally enough their supporters were as delirious as we were deflated.

When we set off for our long drive home, I felt that our mood did not make for a cosy restaurant meal. However, you have to learn in football to pick yourself up mentally and, in any case, we justifiably had every confidence that Brian Little and his players would achieve the necessary points for European qualification when we met Southampton, another of the clubs fighting against relegation, in the final match of the season at Villa Park.

As we shrugged off our disappointment on the drive back, we used our mobile telephone to contact the restaurant and book a table for four. And why not? The whole purpose was to celebrate the fellowship we had enjoyed on our journeys throughout the season and not just the result of one match. In a now-convivial frame of mind, and all of us seemingly in perfect health, we enjoyed our meal and returned to my home where David and Barrie's car had been left for their drive home.

The events of the following few hours left an indelible mark on the club, and certainly on myself. When David arrived home, having said nothing to us about being in any way unwell, he told his wife he had a bad headache and was afraid he was having a brain haemorrhage.

Immediate arrangements were made for him to be admitted to hospital where his self-diagnosis proved accurate. He passed away on 18 May having spent his remaining days on a life-support machine. I just hope that news of our victory over Southampton got through to him and that he was aware that the European bid had been successful.

As I wrote in the subsequent Chairman's Report to be presented to shareholders at the first annual meeting of the now renamed Aston Villa plc:

> David enjoyed all kinds of sport and for many years was involved in boxing and speedway, but football, and particularly Aston Villa, was always his first love.
>
> Indeed, his loyalty and support for the club were such that, in the early years, when the finances were considerably less buoyant than they are today, he received little or no recompense. Professional football, by its nature, is a short-term career, but it is a measure of the affection and respect in which David Targett was held that many of the players he treated and advised down the years remained friends long after their football careers were over.
>
> Blessed with a wonderful sense of humour and a caring and concerned nature, David was a marvellous colleague and a dear friend to Aston Villa, its directors, players and staff. We all miss him.

Similar sentiments apply to the late Lord Howell, just plain Denis at Villa Park, another lovely man whose heart and soul was in Aston Villa FC. To talk about the positions he occupied and all of his achievements would be a book in itself. Just one anecdote, recalled by Steve Stride from the European Cup-winning year of 1982, illustrates his service to the club.

During the semi-final against Anderlecht in Brussels an English soldier, based out there, had run onto the pitch causing a stoppage. Subsequently, the Belgian club claimed that the stoppage had prevented a possible goal and called for the semi-final leg to be replayed. Denis Howell was chosen as the club spokesman at the UEFA hearing. During the proceedings, Denis asked the referee where he restarted the game after the stoppage. The referee's reply was that he restarted the game in the centre circle, to which Denis replied, in his best Rumpole fashion: 'Well, how could a goal have been threatened then...?' Obviously one couldn't have been.

Game, set and match to Denis Howell and Aston Villa... the latter being freed to beat Bayern Munich in the European Cup final in Rotterdam.

He was a true statesman, indeed, and another good friend who had passed on. Recording David and Denis' loyalty to the club in this way reminded me of how many part-time and full-time employees we are fortunate to have who have been with us for many, many years. Could this mean that, behind the scenes, I have been less 'deadly' with Aston Villa staff than I have been with managers who know full well that they are employed at salaries comparable to the captains of industry on a succeed-or-else basis? I am deeply proud of the number of employees who have devoted so much of their working lives to Aston Villa FC under my chairmanship.

First, though, I must recall the events surrounding the record £7 million signing of Stan Collymore from Liverpool. Not all transfers go through in as speedy a fashion as the Southgate-Milosevic deals and the whirlwind twenty-four hours in which they were sorted out. The £7 million Collymore signing was a classic example of how it is sometimes necessary for the prey to be stalked with all the patience of a cat after a mouse.

When we eventually got Stan to put pen to paper for yet another new club record fee in the close season of 1997, it ended literally years of his wanting to play for Aston Villa and Villa having had him on the wanted list without ever quite getting our collective act together.

If ever a signing illustrated the precarious nature of expensive excursions into the transfer market it proved to be this one, even though it was carried out in good faith and with the best of motives.

The public at large and, indeed, the media, have a cut-and-dried attitude towards signing players. They see it as a case of Club A wants Player B, never mind the asking price, the player's terms, the rival bidders and all the other complications, just go sign him. If only it were that simple. And if only the outcome were always as predictable as both the public and the pundits sometimes appear to assume it to be.

Over several years there were many reasons for his arrival at Villa Park being put off, but I will always suspect that the final delay, from before the March 1997 deadline for transfers to after the end of the season, was caused by our local evening newspaper. What's more, I also suspect, it resulted in the fee we paid to Liverpool increasing by a million pounds.

Successive managers at the club had known about Collymore, who has lived at nearby Cannock just outside Birmingham all his life, from his non-league days with Stafford Rangers and even before that. It is always a shade aggravating to find that, for all the schoolboy and youth coaching carried out by your club, a player of his calibre slips through the net.

However, we tried to sign him in the summer of 1993, when Ron Atkinson offered a package of £1 million and three players for him, but Barry Fry, who was manager of Southend United at that time, could not afford to pay the three players the kind of money they had been earning at Villa Park. Bearing in mind that in his youth Stan was a devoted Villa fan along with his mates on our famous old Holte End terrace, and that our training ground is a comparatively short drive from his home, it doesn't take much working out that he would have jumped at the move had a deal been worked out. In the event, Frank Clark agreed to meet Fry's £2 million cash demand and took Collymore to Nottingham Forest, where he was a huge success, scoring forty-one league goals in sixty-four appearances.

# LOSING A LOYAL FRIEND

I would have liked us to sign him before Forest got the chance, but our manager wished to stick to a players-plus-cash arrangement, possibly feeling that Collymore was too big a gamble beyond that point. Forest were thus the beneficiaries.

When he was subsequently sold on to Liverpool for £8.5 million in August 1995, with Brian Little now our manager, we again tried to sign him, but to be perfectly fair Liverpool were in a stronger position at that time and were successful in getting him.

While he was in Liverpool colours, he seemed to take great delight in joining with the likes of Robbie Fowler in inflicting upon us some most damaging defeats. Eventually there were hints that Liverpool were prepared to sell him and soundings were being made from Villa Park.

Brian Little and I had an offer in at Anfield amounting to £6 million, which seemed to be acceptable to them until, in October 1996, the Birmingham *Evening Mail* ran a public poll asking Villa supporters whether or not we should go for Collymore. There was an overwhelming 'yes' vote just as talks between the clubs seemed to be reaching a successful late stage. Then suddenly, coinciding with that pressure of public support for a Collymore signing appearing in the press, there was a change of heart at Anfield where, instead of seeming to us to be on the verge of accepting our approaches, their evaluation of the player increased.

Did they see the public pressure as a reason for us to be prepared to substantially increase our terms? That we will never know, though I personally believe it was. However, whatever the reason for it, the negotiations went from warm to stone-cold after the *Evening Mail's* ballot and the proposed transfer broke down until it eventually went through on 13 May 1997.

Collymore arrived at Villa Park amid media discussion about his 'attitude' to his profession, his occasional tendency to skip training and his liking for the Birmingham nightclub scene.

Looking back, Brian Little simply saw him as a dynamic goalscorer with the kind of talents he could blend into a team sorely needing them, and was confident of being able to coax the best out of him.

In reality there was very little anyone could tell us about Stan, his upbringing and his background, because our reserve-team manager, Malcolm Beard, had lived near to him and his mother since Stan was a schoolboy footballer and more or less saw him grow up. Malcolm had followed his career and noted his progress as a person throughout the entire period, so we had been kept pretty well informed.

My own first detailed association with our new striker came when, immediately after he had signed for us, Stan joined us on our ten-day, end-of-season trip to the United States to play a couple of games during a massive San Francisco Bay British promotion that was being staged in California and was opened by Prince Andrew who, incidentally, sat by me at the match and impressed me as being very good company.

I found Collymore to be modest, very polite and respectful and also extremely articulate. What's more, he turned out to be the only Villa player I have known in all the time since I first became chairman who has actually bought me a meal. No doubt he will take some stick from his mates for me telling this little story, but I'm sure he can take it.

While in Las Vegas, I went out with Dwight Yorke, Ugo Ehiogu, Mark Bosnich and Stan to the huge MGM Grand Hotel with its 5,000 rooms and every possible amenity including, naturally, a casino. The other lads were having a flutter on the machines or tables, as do most visitors, but I'd done it all before and Stan did not seem interested in the gambling, either, so when I suggested we go for a meal in a nearby Italian restaurant within the hotel precinct he was all for it, whereas the others seemed to be on a winning streak and preferred to carry on.

We had a pleasant meal, a glass of wine, and a friendly chat, and when the bill arrived he said: 'I will settle that, Mr Ellis.' Naturally I protested at first, but he insisted: 'Please, I would like to pay' and he did. That was, indeed, a whole new experience for me, because I've been the one to pick up the tab on more occasions than I would care to recall with other players, as you can well imagine and as I would expect.

The fact that Stan Collymore did not make the impact Brian Little sought and subsequently attracted the sort of headlines that his successor John Gregory correctly deplored, was a considerable disappointment to everyone and, as I observed earlier, illustrated graphically why team-building is as hazardous an occupation as it is expensive.

Collymore's arrival, followed by the signing of Simon Grayson from Leicester City, took Brian Little's spending to nigh on £30 million with around £10 million recouped by sales. Anyone who accused the club of 'not thinking big enough' would perhaps be taken aback by that equation at a time when huge outlay had also been necessary in refurbishing Villa Park.

All this wheeling and dealing had been carried out in a spirit of the manager and the chairman keeping each other informed and with the club's budget and wage structure firmly in mind. It had also resulted in the average age of the squad being substantially reduced and a well-balanced squad being carefully accumulated, bearing in mind the necessity to encourage our own quality young players, which the manager and coaching staff had done superbly well.

Under Little's management, we had seen the likes of Michael Oakes, Riccardo Scimeca, Gareth Farrelly, Lee Hendrie, David Hughes and others from our own youth scheme, given an opportunity to make progress in their careers. In the past, it seemed to me, we had not seen enough quality players of our own make their way.

Since the likes of Tony Daley and Steve Froggatt, there had been something of a drought where the arrival of top-quality home-produced players was concerned (given that players such as Mark Bosnich, Ugo Ehiogu and Dwight Yorke, were well into their teens when they joined us from other clubs).

The bottom line to all this, as the 1997–98 season approached, was that my 'feelgood' factor about the future of the club and the way that all the various activities were being run, had never been more optimistic. One of the many things I have learned in my time in football is that few things are totally predictable. It is foolish to make predictions or promises, because they can always rebound in your face.

# CHAPTER TWENTY

# FALLING FOR ROYALTY

Time, now, for a little name-dropping. Well, we all do it now and again don't we? Forty years of access to well-known people does not remove the capacity to be star-struck once in a while, and why should it?

I don't mind admitting that I cherish the fact that being chairman of Aston Villa has led me into the company of some of the world's most famous people, including members of the Royal Family.

I have been embarrassed while sitting next to Prince Charles, captivated by the late Diana, Princess of Wales, and awestruck by the South African president, Nelson Mandela.

Involvement in charity work, for which we have our own Aston Villa Charitable Trust, and club tours, are possibly the major vehicles for meeting the non-football celebrities.

My proximity to Prince Charles arose from the period in the early 1990s when I was a committee member of the Prince's Trust.

Basically, each year we 'adopt' a particular charity to support substantially, in addition to all the smaller good causes that we help in many ways throughout any twelve months.

Thus, it was in my capacity as the Midlands' representative of the Prince's Trust, which covered a whole range of help for under-privileged teenagers with various needs, that I was invited along with seven other similar representatives to have lunch with Prince Charles at Kensington Palace.

You may recall the time when his arm was in a sling as a result of a fall from his horse while playing polo. This 'arm-in-a-sling' appearance presented me with a simple point of contact to break the ice, not always easy on such occasions. I knew that he fished on a salmon beat not far from the one I frequented on the River Tay and I realised that his injury would be as big a handicap to him as an angler as it was as a polo player. 'Have you had to stop salmon fishing, sir?' I asked him. 'Not at all,' he replied. 'I'm learning to cast left-handed.'

To keep up the social chat, I mentioned that, at around 8.30 one morning, while crossing a narrow bridge near the salmon beat, I had felt obliged to back off my Rolls to make way for a Range Rover crossing from the other direction. When the Range Rover passed me the driver, who was completely on his own, waved his thanks as he drove on and it was only then that I recognised the man at the wheel to be HRH himself.

Being the perfect host and diplomat that he undoubtedly is, he claimed to remember the incident, though I must say I put this response more down to impeccable manners than expert memory. However, when it came to the time to sit down for our meal, he asked me to sit next to him and I'm not ashamed to confess that I was thrilled by the invitation.

He was a very chatty neighbour during the meal and, at one point, he made some amusing comment which caused me to laugh and lean back onto the rear legs of my ornate, antique chair which, literally, came apart at the joints, depositing me onto the floor surrounded by precious Kensington Palace debris.

Embarrassed? What do *you* think? Yet the impeccable manners were quickly in evidence again as the demolished remains were removed and replaced with the minimum of fuss. The incident was quickly passed over and dismissed as a mere nothing but, even though he had his left arm in a sling, together with his aides, he helped me back onto my feet.

Shortly afterwards, at another charitable event, this time a dinner for Turning Point charity, which is concerned with rehabilitating young offenders who have suffered from the effects of substance abuse, I was fortunate to be introduced to the Princess of Wales.

The function featured a concert by the violinist Nigel Kennedy, a dyed-in-the-wool Villa fanatic, at the Metropole Hotel. Master of Ceremonies was Dave Ismay, another staunch Villa supporter who was then a professional entertainer, but who was subsequently to undertake an important full-time staff role at Villa Park in charge of special projects.

In the light of her subsequent tragic death at the tender age of thirty-six, the fact that I was to enjoy the delightful experience of meeting the Princess is more poignant in my memory than ever.

To my amazement and amusement, when I was introduced to her she broke into that alluring laugh of hers which, at the time, could almost have been described as a girlish giggle, and said: 'Oh, aren't you the one they call "Deadly"?' I could only reply by saying: 'Well, yes, I believe I am.' But then, I added: 'Did you hear about the antique chair I broke at Kensington Palace...?' This time she really did laugh, and replied: 'Oh, it was *you* was it? Everyone was talking about it afterwards. It was a scream. I'm just glad it wasn't my chair. It was Maggie's.'

I'll never forget her saying: 'It was Maggie's.' It didn't strike me as being the ideal way for me to leave my mark on the Royal Household but, looking back on what proved to be her very high-profile and often sad life, my everlasting memory will be of an enchanting, captivating young lady who truly was a light in everyone's lives, Diana, the Princess of Wales, and that lovely smile.

Dave Ismay tells me that throughout the function she laughed, joked and chatted with those around her, visibly enjoying every moment of the occasion. The Princess was scheduled to go at a particular time, but she declined to leave until after she had seen Jasper Carrott's cabaret.

Good for her... the People's Princess, she undoubtedly was.

Dave was subsequently in her company at another function and she told him that the Turning Point dinner was one of the happiest she had ever attended. I have also danced with Princess Margaret at a function at the Town Hall. I actually went over to her, to invite her to dance, and she was very nice and accepted.

With all the wonderful years I have had in the game, travelling with Villa to different corners of the globe, I have met some of the most remarkable people.

Omar Sharif is a great friend... he loved my wife, you know! I have met prime ministers John Major and Margaret Thatcher and world-famous players from Sir Stanley Matthews and Tom Finney, to Franz Beckenbauer and Pele. During my time serving on the international committee, I have got to know players such as David Beckham, Paul Scholes and Gary Neville very well.

John Major asked me to give his son Jamie a week's trial, and I housed him with our kit manager adjacent to the ground.

Then, of course, there was the Queen and the Duke of Edinburgh. Five businessmen were chosen to attend when the Queen and the Duke opened a property locally; I was fortunate enough to have been one of those selected. I went out to meet and greet the Queen and the Duke and escorted the latter into the property. I said to him: 'You know that you and I have something in common. Both of us served in the Navy during the war.'

He asked me which 'water' I had served in and I told him the Indian Ocean and he asked me which ship. I told him I had returned with dengue fever. By this time, the Queen had joined us.

Not likely to miss the opportunity, I presented the Queen with a copy of my book – the first account of which had appeared nearly nine years ago. I said to her: 'Please accept this book of my life story, it is guaranteed to send you to sleep, my love.' I'm not quite sure whether I should have referred to Her Majesty as 'my love', but there it is! She simply smiled and said: 'I will read it, Mr Ellis.'

There is one avid Villa fan amid the ranks of the Royal Family: Prince William. He became a fan after being taken to a match by his mother. Now that is something: a future King of England a Villa fan.

Prince William was my first choice to open the new stand after his great-grandfather had opened the original stand at Villa Park. When I was dining with Prince Charles on one occasion, I took my chance to ask permission for Prince William to open the new stand, but Prince Charles said to me: 'If you don't mind, I would rather keep him out of the public eye.'

So I then said: 'How about you being my second choice and first reserve?'

He spoke to his man and said that he would be available and he did come to open the new stand.

Prince William did turn up to his father's fiftieth birthday celebrations wearing a Villa hat and combat gear... we are proud to say that he is one of our fans.

On my office wall here at Villa Park is a framed letter from Prince William that takes pride of place. On Highgrove-headed notepaper dated 6 December 2001, Prince William thanked me for the signed shirt and Villa strip we had sent him, especially when all he had been after was a pair of shorts! He passed on his best wishes and wished us a successful season. He also said that if he could find space in his diary, he would love to take up our offer to be a guest at Villa Park.

Meeting President Mandela, during the club's close-season tour of South Africa in May 1994, left as indelible an impression on me for a rather different reason.

At a reception that he attended, I was able to claim his attention to myself for maybe five minutes with his ministers and minders some few yards away. My purpose was to discuss with him the importance of sporting contact between nations that can transcend any political activity in cementing friendships. In my opinion, sport can make more progress in securing peace between nations than all the ambassadors and consulates that countries can provide.

No doubt, bearing in mind his lifetime spent fighting the obscenity of apartheid, he was more aware than anyone of how much the breakdown of South Africa's sporting involvement affected his country's relationship with the outside world. However, to confirm the point with more than mere words, I offered to set in motion arrangements for a multi-racial football academy to be built in Johannesburg, to promote the coaching of excellence in football among young people.

Aston Villa had already provided clinics to this end in Durban and Johannesburg. Ron Atkinson and his coaches recognised the excellent skills of many South African youngsters who now needed professional coaching if they aspired to represent their country.

I asked Mr Mandela if he would agree to having such an academy entitled the Mandela Football Academy and he replied: 'I would be honoured.'

During my meeting with him, I was deeply impressed with his modesty and humility, given that he stood a very erect 6ft 2in and kept his eyes firmly directed upon mine during the five minutes I spent alone in his company. I still find it difficult to believe that this man spent twenty-seven years in prison on Robin Island and came through the ordeal having retained his sanity and his sense of modesty, alongside an undimmed imperial aura of a born leader.

Regrettably, the academy scheme never came into being, despite my ascertaining that, with the association of Nelson Mandela's name, bank finance would be available alongside major company conglomerates providing sponsorship to the tune of some £5 million. When we returned to this country, I informed the English FA, as a councillor, of the window of opportunity that had been opened up and though we sent two representatives out there on a fact-finding, logistical mission for ten days, it was never followed through.

In my confident view, if I had been able to afford the time to go to South Africa myself for the necessary period of time, we could have made it happen. Maybe some of the kids from the townships would now be Premiership footballers and South African internationals.

# CHAPTER TWENTY-ONE

# BRIAN LITTLE: THE TRUTH

On the afternoon of Tuesday, 24 February 1998, at around 2.30pm, Brian Little walked into Steve Stride's office, dropped photocopies of three newspaper articles on his desk and said: 'I've had enough. I'm resigning. I would like you to inform the chairman for me because this time I do not want him to attempt to talk me round.'

The three cuttings were from morning newspapers that, presumably he had only just read, all of them critical of him, and one of them in the *Sun*, written under the name of Andy Gray, his pal and former playing colleague. I got the impression that Andy's piece had particularly upset him.

My first knowledge of the sudden turn of events was when, after Brian had left his office, Steve telephoned me on his internal line to pass on the news, adding that he was sending Brian along to confirm that, indeed, he had made an irreversible decision to resign with immediate effect. I was told that Brian was absolutely adamant this time and that there would be no talking him around. When Brian came to see me to confirm his decision, I expressed my sadness and said that I understood his reasoning.

Whatever else has been said or written about Brian's departure, those are the facts. No dispute, no mysterious occurrence behind the scenes, no abrasive comment from myself or anyone else at the club to prompt his leaving at a few minutes' notice as he did. Brian Little left Aston Villa FC because he chose voluntarily to do so and because a variety of pressures about the job had brought him to the conclusion that it would be in the best interests of the club and himself if he moved on.

As for my own reaction, I was taken by surprise at the timing of his resignation, coming as it did only four days before a most critical period for us when we were to play Liverpool at home in the Premiership on the Saturday and Atletico Madrid in a UEFA Cup quarter-final first leg in Spain three days after that. Having said that, I could not claim to have been surprised at his actual decision to go, only the timing of his departure.

To explain what I mean by this, and to put the record further straight, it is necessary to give details of two very private meetings I had with him only ten days earlier, after our removal from the FA Cup by Coventry City, which had further damaged a disappointing season during which we had gone out of the Coca Cola Cup at the first hurdle and slid disturbingly into relegation danger. It is my usual routine to go into the dressing room – win, lose or draw – to show my face ten to twenty minutes or so after a game in order to first allow a period of privacy between the manager, the coaches and the players.

After the Coventry game, the dressing-room door was open, but Brian Little was not inside. That was unusual. I found him in his room nearby with two or three of the coaching staff. When he saw me he asked them to leave, called me inside and locked the door behind us. 'I've had enough,' he told me, or words similar to those he subsequently used to Steve Stride. 'I'm resigning.' He added that, although he had not discussed it with his wife, Heather, he felt that it was in the best interests of Aston Villa that he should leave.

I do not wish to betray any confidences, but it is fair to say in broad detail that he had been deeply affected by the abuse suffered by his children who no longer wished to be taken to school because of it; by personal, foul-mouthed abuse he was receiving from members of the public seated near his place in the dugout, where extra security men had been placed because of it; and by critical letters and articles in newspapers.

Poor results would also, no doubt, have played their part, along with the problems that there had been with a number of players, some of whom had been playing neither to their potential nor to the size of their transfer fees. It would be easy to speculate that Brian's confidence was taking something of a battering and my own observations led me to suspect that this was the case and that it was taking its toll.

Having spent all of my working life in service industries, where people and staff are the stock in trade, I reckon I have become a semi-professional psychologist and, as such, I pay a great deal of attention to people's facial expressions. They can provide warning signs. Leading up to the time of his departure, both myself and others had noticed little things about Brian that suggested a declining confidence. This much was reflected in facial and physical reactions towards him from several senior players, particularly from the Christmas period onwards. The mood had changed in the dressing room and Brian was no doubt aware of it.

Despite the fact that the majority of the players literally 'loved' Brian Little as a man, I believe that some of them had lost confidence in his ability to motivate them. He admitted as much when he resigned.

However, the bottom line of our chat after the Coventry defeat was my urging him not to resign as a rash decision in the immediate disappointment of being knocked out of the FA Cup, but for him to reconsider, talk to Heather, and to come to my home the next morning for a heart-to-heart chat about things and to see how he felt then.

The role of a chairman and a board is to stand solidly behind their man, through good times and bad, until such a time as it becomes harmful to the prospects of the club to do so and we hadn't reached this stage with Brian. Indeed, we wanted him to enjoy more success.

My mind inevitably went back some twenty-eight years to the day Brian had first joined the club as an apprentice. I well remember Brian's parents coming down from Tyneside and his mother telling me that he would not sign for us because he did not fancy being so far away from home. He was a very shy fifteen-year-old then, from a family of Newcastle supporters, and felt that he would be happier staying in the North-East and signing for one of the local clubs up there who wanted him. I protested that this would be a bad mistake because Brian had obviously loved being with us for training and coaching. He had already been with our youth team abroad and there was no way he should sign for anyone else.

Then Brian's mother observed that he might be persuaded to sign for Villa if his brother, Alan, could come too. She said that Alan was different to Brian, who wanted to stay at home. I was assured by her that Alan would go anywhere and had the makings of a good professional so, just as in the case of the two Riochs, Bruce and Neil, we signed them both, despite the fact that when I checked with our chief scout at the time, he had no reports of Alan being of the necessary potential. In the event, he made a couple of appearances for us, but went on to have a good career elsewhere and became a successful manager of York City.

As for Brian, we all know what an outstanding player he became and, because of the feeling that Villa were required to take good care of him as a fifteen-year-old, I had a kind of father-son relationship with him from then on and it was on a similar sort of basis that I chatted to him at my house on Sunday, 7 December 1997. The outcome was that he had calmed down and went home in a far more cheerful frame of mind than had been the case the previous evening. He had decided to stay. So much for all those ill-informed 'did-he-leave-or-was-he-pushed' debates that went on when he resigned for a second time.

OK, so now it was around three o'clock on the Tuesday afternoon, we were playing Liverpool at home the following Saturday, we had lost our two previous Premiership games, at home to Manchester United and away to Wimbledon since the FA Cup exit, we were only six points above the relegation zone with one more game played than the bottom three and we were one week away from the first leg of our UEFA Cup tie in Madrid.

No, Brian's timing wasn't good. I felt he should have stayed, at least until the end of the season, but it was not to be and now we needed a replacement manager. And we needed one quickly. The first, and only, concrete suggestion, came from Steve Stride.

Earlier in the season, we had suggested to Brian Little, when first-team coaching was being reorganised, that it would make sense to contact John Gregory at Wycombe Wanderers, where he was now manager, and sound him out about returning to his former job, because he had never been adequately replaced. When we appointed Brian, Allan Evans and John, there was an attractive system of coaching in which ex-forward Brian took the forwards, ex-midfielder John took the midfielders, ex-defender Allan Evans took the defenders and ex-goalkeeper Paul Barron took the goalkeepers. It all worked wonderfully, until Gregory left.

Many people felt that his departure had been a factor in the team's decline in the Premiership, but Brian had rejected the idea of his return on the grounds that he would take over the coaching himself from Kevin MacDonald, who had been moved from the second-team coaching responsibilities after John Gregory's departure.

Brian later promoted Tony McAndrew from the youth team

post and, while there were impressive performances in the UEFA Cup, inconsistencies in the Premiership continued to undermine all else and it was difficult to refute the feeling in many quarters that Gregory had never been adequately replaced. Kevin MacDonald and Tony McAndrew are both excellent coaches, both of whom remained on our staff, but the proof of the pudding, at first-team level in particular, is in results, and ours hadn't been good. Even so, we remained fully committed behind Brian Little until he chose to leave.

Against this background, and with time against us, Steve Stride battled hard for Gregory's return. Meanwhile, we contacted the financial director, Mark Ansell, on his mobile almost the moment his feet touched the ground at Heathrow when he arrived back from a long weekend abroad. Anyone who carried on believing that Brian Little's departure and John Gregory's arrival had been set up beforehand, would have thought very differently had they seen the emergency exercise that went on behind the scenes.

An informal board meeting was quickly summoned as Mark Ansell sped up the M1 and, in these discussions, I made the point that, while I was also an admirer of John Gregory's coaching calibre, if we were to appoint him, we would be castigated in the media and by a section of supporters for not appointing a 'big name'. It was not a case of disagreeing with the feeling that his return would be beneficial, I was simply playing devil's advocate in expressing the opposite point of view for discussion.

By this time the news of Brian's departure had appeared on Ceefax and Teletext and on local radio and would shortly be hitting the major news bulletins. I was already getting telephone calls from second- and third-party intermediaries telling me that such-and-such a 'big-name' manager would like to come to Villa, but who couldn't apply in person because he was already in a job, or whatever. They were expecting me to go to them. The so-called 'deadly' reputation of mine doesn't seem to put these 'big names' off when there is an attractive vacancy on offer!

Just to give an example of the kind of speculation that goes on in these situations, the *Evening Mail* next day ran a phone-in service to enable their readers to phone for the 'candidate' of their choice. There were twelve 'possibles' on their list, namely Terry Venables, Bobby Robson, Andy Gray, Graham Taylor, Gerry Francis, Allan Evans, Bruce Rioch, Ruud Gullit, David Platt, Martin O'Neill, John Toshack and Radomir Antic.

Before their phone-in lines even began to hum, we were at the nearby New Hall Hotel with John Gregory discussing the terms of his contract and, by telephone, the compensation we would pay to Wycombe Wanderers for the remainder of his contract.

The previous evening, we had unanimously agreed that an approach to John would be made, provided that we received permission from the Wycombe Wanderers chairman, Ivor Beeks, and his board. We asked Steve Stride to 'get on his bike' down the M5 to meet up with John in a hotel in Bristol, where Wycombe Wanderers were preparing for a Second Division fixture with Bristol Rovers. I would have gone with him, but the first important action was to make the chairman-to-chairman contact. Steve had his mobile telephone switched on to comply with our mutual agreement that, if Mr Beeks declined our approach, then he would turn around and come back and we would turn our attention elsewhere.

In the event, Mr Beeks, a builder in High Wycombe, said that he was very sad to be losing such an outstanding young manager and engaging personality, but he would not stand in John's way of taking such an opportunity at a major club. This was the green light for Steve to continue down the motorway, meet up with John at the hotel in Bristol and arrange for him to meet us at 10am the next morning. Steve, Mark and myself met at New Hall an hour before his arrival, to talk all the details through.

Contract talks with John presented little difficulty, such was his enthusiasm to return to Aston Villa, a club he had loved with all the commitment of a supporter since his playing days, when he was signed from Northampton Town by Ron Saunders. Agreeing compensation with Wycombe by telephone took a little longer, but after a couple of hours of phone calls back and forth, all was amicably settled and John Gregory replaced Brian Little – approximately twenty-four hours after the latter's shock departure – on a three-year contract.

By four o'clock we were unveiling our new manager before a surprised media corps, leaving him just two full days to prepare to meet Liverpool.

Even then, the whirlwind nature of it all was not over. That same evening, our reserves were playing Preston North End, whose reserve-team coach was none other than Steve Harrison, another former Villa coach and the very man John wanted as his right-hand man. The reserve game also afforded the opportunity for some adverse public reaction to manifest itself in the form of a rowdy group congregating in the car park under my office window to hurl loud-mouthed obscenities in my direction for a considerable period of time. Efforts by our security chief, John Hood, to get them to disperse proved ineffective. I eventually went down to confront them and slowly the demo broke up. Interestingly, I'm told that these 'fans' did not follow my own lead in then taking a seat in the stadium to watch our reserves in action.

Predictably, the accusation of not appointing a 'big name' cropped up in the newspapers the next day and I was assailed by carefully selected anti-Ellis 'fans' on Central television's Thursday night *Late Tackle* programme. It was interesting to note how people were prepared to jump to entirely the wrong conclusions about the manner of Brian Little's departure and to deal in innuendo by suggesting that Brian had been 'pushed'.

Even when Brian himself gave interviews to local and national newspapers describing in detail how this was not the case, those who chose to disbelieve us both, preferring to dwell on the 'Deadly strikes again' theory, did so despite all of the factual statements to the contrary. I was reminded once again of my repeated experience that when things go right the manager is a hero, when they go wrong the chairman is a villain.

Football is very much a case of the mood of the moment and that mood can change even more quickly than in politics. Within little more than a month of John Gregory's arrival, we had taken twelve points out of a possible fifteen, with the same set of players who had previously lost three matches on the trot, remember – and those dissenting supporters, and the media folk who had shared their foreboding, were starting to wonder whether we now had a 'big name' in the making. Speaking personally, I could only hope so. John Gregory's two predecessors had both won us a trophy, made good progress in the Premiership for their first couple of seasons and had then slipped back. What I had always sought for Aston Villa was a lengthy period of prolonged success, something that had never been achieved in recent times.

One example of John's 'let's-go-for-it' attitude was when we raised the possibility of gaining late entry to the InterToto Cup, simply because its change of date to late July from June and its incentive of a UEFA Cup place for the winner, made it a far more attractive proposition than it had been before.

This had been brought home to us when we played Bordeaux in the first round of the UEFA Cup in 1997–98 and we realised that this was how their place in the competition had been secured. John was instantly prepared to give it a go for all the positive reasons. After the final match of the season, an excellent 1–0 victory over Arsenal, sandwiched between the Gunners becoming FA Premiership champions and winning the FA Cup, John Gregory's record in the league amounted to twenty-seven points from a possible thirty-three, a splendid start by any yardstick.

Misleadingly at that time, as it was to emerge, the final whistle of our season ended in an air of frustration as the news came through that Chris Sutton, who had scored a first-half hat-trick against us in our first home match of the season, had scored a last-gasp goal for Blackburn against Newcastle at Ewood Park to hold on to what could well have been the final UEFA Cup place.

Off we went to give the players a well-earned holiday, now clinging to the hope that Chelsea would beat Stuttgart in the final of the Cup-Winners' Cup and thus relinquish the UEFA Cup place – already earned by their winning the Coca Cola Cup – thereby pushing the qualifying places in the Premiership down to seventh… and Aston Villa!

The lovely Mediterranean sunshine island of Majorca holds some very special memories for me, as I have outlined earlier in these pages, but few rate as more pleasurable than the balmy night of Wednesday, 13 May 1998. As the Cup-Winners' Cup final was played out, John Gregory and his staff preferred to sit outside the hotel relaxing rather than put up with the tension of watching the final being screened from Stockholm. Not me. I was in there glued to the television set for every kick and yes, we did enjoy an extra little holiday celebration after Gianfranco Zola left his subs' seat to score that magnificent winning goal. To be honest, I found myself leaping what felt like 6ft from my seat to punch the air, before rushing outside to tell the others the news. Then the realisation dawned that there was still some time to go, so back I went to sweat through the finishing stages.

When the final whistle sounded, I nipped outside again to tell John Gregory and now it was his turn to leap several feet into the air before flinging his arms around me for a victory dance followed by the popping of a few champagne corks. What an achievement it was to earn that qualifying place.

To most of the rest of Europe, that goal simply meant that Chelsea were winners of the Cup-Winners' Cup. Full stop. For Aston Villa it meant much, much more. We were back in Europe by the 'front door', with no need to play in the InterToto competition while, as a club, we had been restored among the elite of European competitors by the excellent transformation we had achieved under John Gregory.

We had climbed eight Premiership places from fifteenth and the threat of relegation on 28 February, to seventh and a place in Europe, all in the space of eleven matches. I've no idea how many clubs have changed from relegation fodder into European contenders in little more than a couple of months, but that was the sensation we were able to savour as a new Majorcan memory was taken on board.

## CHAPTER TWENTY-TWO

# TAP, TAP, TAP...

It makes me laugh when I see how Arsenal made such a big fuss over the way Chelsea were supposed to have tapped up Ashley Cole in a meeting with Jose Mourinho and Peter Kenyon. The Premier League must have been wondering what all the hysteria was about because it has to be put into context.

First of all let me state the blindingly obvious: it happens all the time. By definition, that means that Arsenal must surely be up to the same tricks as everyone else.

There have only been two previous hearings on breaches of the rules relating to tapping, and both of the 'guilty' parties have been handed minor financial penalties. The most recent case involved Aston Villa, who were found guilty of tapping James Beattie and were reprimanded without any fine. The case involving Liverpool and Middlesbrough is more relevant, because it contained the accusation of a face-to-face meeting between Christian Zeige and Gerard Houllier, and again, with Liverpool found guilty, the punishment carried financial penalties, both to the club and the player, plus expenses and legal fees that combined all pitched in at under £100,000.

But Villa were not fined, and that did not go down very well with Rupert Lowe, the Southampton chairman who brought up the complaint in the first place. He reacted when he heard the verdict by shouting: 'No fine, no fine!'

Aston Villa were ordered to pay the sum of £16,500 for expenses when our case was heard, however, and that most definitely went against the grain. I was not happy about that. We also had to cough up £3,000 fees and expenses for the Premier League's QC. The final bill was £19,500.

The truth of the Beattie talks was that his dad rang Villa and let it be known that he was interested in joining us. Of course, his dad did the same with Everton.

The Everton chairman, Bill Kenwright, and I are great friends, but he is relatively new to football and I rang him and made a pact that we would both agree the same transfer fee and salary scale and leave it to the player to decide. We had to increase our offer by a further £250,000 to match that of Everton, but I told Bill that it was pointless bidding against each other as all we were doing was pushing the price up. Bill agreed and we settled on our fees. Bill assures me that he did not break the agreement and I accept that.

So it was a straight choice for the player.

James Beattie had decided to ditch his long-serving and highly respected agents Jon and Phil Smith at First Artist Management and took on a 'team' of his dad Mick, who works for a haulage firm, and a Manchester-based lawyer. Beattie senior can act as an 'agent' under FIFA's present rules and regulations. Lawyers, accountants and close relatives do not need to hold an official agent's licence. The lawyer they used specialises in players' image rights deals, and had given Villa the clear impression – when the player met David O'Leary at my house where we spent two hours discussing the move – that the centre-forward was heading to the Midlands.

A call from the lawyer brought the bad news, and I got an

awful lot of stick because we had failed to sign the player. The final decision actually had nothing to do with me, and indeed, the first decision, i.e. to go for the player, was again not my call. The choice of player is down to the manager, but I had done my homework and I have to say that I was never really convinced about the player. My research told me that he lacked a touch of skill, and I think I've been proved right since he joined Everton where he has not looked quite the goalscorer everyone was led to believe he was. Again, I stress that any decision about a player is not my judgement call and I will always back the manager. Perhaps David O'Leary would have moulded him within his own team to have got more out of him, who knows?

But there was something not quite right about the way the whole transaction was handled that made me wonder whether it was the right thing to go through with the deal. I didn't question the role of the player's father. Beattie senior could have properly expected a substantial sum for his 'advice' to his son to return to the north closer to his family, rather than move to Villa. Beattie's father didn't actually ask for a commission. Unfortunately, the tapping rules are breached with virtually every transfer and the Premier League only has to listen to the boringly obvious, Club A wants Player B, so agent Z taps up the player rigmarole when a chairman gets all hot under the collar about it. Every day, every transfer, every player is tapped up: we all know it and we all accept it as part of the game. Tap, tap, tap...

I did get annoyed on a couple of occasions when I was concerned that our players had been targeted by other clubs.

Gareth Southgate came back from Euro 2000 and asked for a transfer and refused to play in the InterToto Cup in 2001 to make sure that he was eligible to play in Europe for another club, presumably with a move to Chelsea in mind. Chelsea, of course, had made numerous offers and all of them had been turned down, but you cannot tell me that the player didn't know that

Chelsea were interested in him. Of course he did. Eventually, though, he ended up joining Middlesbrough.

I would consider Sir Alex Ferguson to rank among my friends, but that did not stop me telling him, to his face, that he had sounded out Dwight Yorke.

We eventually sold Yorke to Manchester United for £12.6 million and our manager John Gregory was so upset with him at the time that he famously said: 'If I had a gun, I'd shoot him.' He showed no interest in our opening match at Everton and joined United a few days later.

I was barracked at the AGM about our decision to sell Yorke, who was such a popular player: indeed, the annual meeting doubled in attendance to 1,000. But we did alright without Yorke, and went twelve consecutive games unbeaten – it was the best start in the club's history and had been helped by the acquisitions of Paul Merson and Dion Dublin.

I went to Old Trafford for a reserve game on my own and when I walked into the boardroom, there and sat at the top of the boardroom table, was Sir Alex. I sat down and Alex started without any ceremony by saying: 'I don't appreciate you saying in the press that I sounded out Dwight Yorke.'

I replied: 'But you did, Alex.'

Alex: 'No I didn't.'

I wasn't going to accept this response and said: 'Well, I didn't say it was you personally, but I am talking about Manchester United, and you're the manager, so it is down to you, and you sounded him out alright.'

Alex: 'No, I didn't.'

Finally I said: 'If you say that again, I'll have you before a tribunal, so let's just leave it like that, but I know that you did sound him out.'

Alex became a touch more conciliatory: 'Why did you say that?'

I replied: 'Well, the player together with his agent came into my

240

office three months before you signed him and Dwight begged me to let him go so that he could go and sign for you and Manchester United! He even told me the contract that you had offered him, so please, don't kid me.'

Alex got up, walked over and put his arm around me.

That was the end of the matter.

I had concluded a deal sometime earlier with the chairman at that time, Martin Edwards, and I had accepted a £12 million fee and Manchester United would have to pay the five percent levy to the Premier League, which brought the total to £12.6 million. It is hard enough to finalise transfer dealings domestically, but as we have all found out to our costs, it is so much harder when it comes to doing a deal abroad.

It looked at one stage as though we would acquire Patrick Kluivert when he was at his very best, before he signed for Barcelona. I was on exceptionally good terms with the AC Milan vice-president. We went out to Milan, but by the time we got there we discovered that he had been sold off to Barcelona. I was none too pleased.

More recently we wanted to sign another player from Milan. This time I reminded the vice-president about his promises over Kluivert. I said that I would come over to sign the player the following day, but he had to assure me that he would still be there and that the player would still sign. I was given an unreserved apology about Kluivert and when I went over to Milan the player we wanted was waiting for us and we signed him. That's how we signed Martin Laurson from Milan for £3 million in 2004 when the Italian club had paid Parma £9 million for him. Unfortunately, he was injured most of the time when he joined us!

Benito Carbone joined us on a free transfer from Sheffield Wednesday in 1999 and we did all we could for him, including setting him up in a £1 million house. However, nothing seemed to suit him, including the carpets! He demanded that we change the carpets. He complained that the fluff from the carpets in the house had exacerbated his child's asthma. I personally organised for one of our contractors to change the carpets, but he was still not satisfied. He was very untidy. When our contractors turned up there must have been fifty newspapers on the lawn. He really was a naughty boy, but boy could he play. His behaviour caused us nothing but problems and his life outside of the game left a lot to be desired too, but he sure did have an enormous talent. However, he was a disaster and, in the end, we were glad to get rid of him.

David Ginola arrived in 2001 and there have been a lot of stories about how I signed him. Once again, it is the manager who selects the players and John Gregory was keen to recruit Ginola from Spurs where he was adored by the fans. Alan Sugar squeezed every last penny out of me on that deal, and we finally agreed on a fee of £3 million.

By sheer coincidence, Ginola happened to be on holiday in Mauritius at the time I had a suite at the St Geran Hotel. When I discovered that we were in the same place, I invited him to come over to my hotel, but the next minute he was personally on the phone inviting us to his hotel. So, instead of Ginola coming to my hotel, my wife Heidi and I took up his invitation to go to his luxurious hotel.

A massive limousine arrived to pick us up. We went to his suite that was just sensational: a duplex, with two butlers! When we arrived, he had laid on a band outside of the hotel and, as we were taken up to his suite, a three-piece violin troupe played us in. One of his butlers even asked if he could clean my spectacles!

I know how disgusted the Spurs fans were that they had let Ginola go; I also know how delighted Gregory was to have captured him. Ginola and Alpay were paraded before our game with Celta Vigo in the InterToto Cup on 2 August 2000.

Ginola was a huge success in his first season and his brand of exciting football must have put something like 10,000 on the gate. Gregory and Ginola were huge pals and the French winger had wonderful gifts and scored some delightful goals for us.

But he fell out with Gregory when the manager suggested he was fat. 'Le Blob' headlines followed that remark and when Ginola scored his first Villa goal, a late equaliser in the 2–2 home draw against Manchester City, he took off his shirt to show off his fabulous figure and later insisted that his act of defiance was not aimed at the manager, but at the tabloid press. But we all knew he was aiming his gesture at Gregory.

In the summer of 2001, Ginola went as far as to threaten to sue Gregory over his comments about his thickening waistline, and there were even suggestions that he would hire Cherie Blair as an employment expert to take up his legal fight. It was inevitable that Ginola would have to go, and we sorted out a deal with Everton. In fact Graham Taylor was appointed on Tuesday, 5 February, and Ginola went off to Goodison on 8 February, but the deal had been concluded before Gregory resigned.

It would be reasonably fair to say that we have signed and then sold some amazing characters. Take David Unsworth, for example. He signed for us in 1998 from West Ham for £2.9 million and, just a week later, he told us that he wanted to rejoin his first club Everton because his missus had told him that she wanted to move back to the North! We sold him on to Everton for £3 million – he never played a competitive game for us.

Then there was Stan Collymore. We signed him for £8.5 million from Liverpool after he came up to me in Ronnie's Bar in Broad Street one night and said: 'Come and fetch me, I have always been a Villa man.' Now that's cheeky! As a player he was a big, strong fella, with bags of talent and a better class of player than most, who played many games for England. But his life outside of football... Perhaps it would be best to say that I shouldn't have taken him.

I remember one game driving away from the ground and

spotting his then girlfriend Ulrika Jonsson with a friend outside the stadium, no doubt having seen Stan play. I offered them a lift and they accepted. It was Steve Stride's car actually, but we took them back to their hotel.

We eventually sold him off to Leicester on a fee based on appearances, but he didn't actually manage to play sufficient games for them for the contract to have come into effect. We had to sell him after months of personal problems, including being admitted to the Priory Clinic in Roehampton for clinical depression. In June 1998, fans jammed the Villa switchboard calling for Collymore to be sacked following an incident involving Ulrika Jonsson in a Paris bar.

But we also signed some lovely people, such as Dion Dublin, who joined us from Coventry for £5.75 million and scored seven goals in his first three games. He was unlucky when he broke his neck, but he came back to become our penalty hero in the FA Cup semi-final.

Then there was Gareth Southgate, a highly intelligent person as well as player. He scored a very good goal against us for Crystal Palace before we bought him and then sold him to Middlesbrough for £6 million. He is also a very rich young man: I recall that he bought a house not far from mine for around £780,000 and sold it for £1.25 million when he left us.

We wanted to sign James Beattie in the January transfer window, but lost out to Everton, and I had allocated that sum, £6 million for new players. We signed just the one, Eric Djemba-Djemba from Manchester United for £1.35 million, plus £250,000 when he plays twenty games and a further £250,000 when he plays another twenty games.

Before I left for a break in Australia, I rang Manchester United's chief executive, David Gill, to ask if he had any players for loan until next season and he said yes Djemba-Djemba, but he would have to ask the manager first. Within forty-eight hours of my departure for Dubai en route to Australia, I got a call saying that Manchester United would not loan us the player, they would only listen to a sale. Our manager David O'Leary contacted Roy Keane who told him that he thought the player would do a sound job for us and that he should take him. The player had been bought for £3.5 million, as an eventual replacement for Keane, but clearly Sir Alex Ferguson wasn't that impressed; otherwise he wouldn't have wanted to flog him, would he?

# CHAPTER TWENTY-THREE

# BATTLES WITH BLATTER

Politics in football used to take up an awful lot of my time. I worked on FA committees, and also on one of FIFA's most high-powered committees, that dealt with media and television. As the media and television committee handed out television contracts for the World Cup, you couldn't really have been involved in a more powerful or more influential committee in world football.

When I was appointed to FIFA's media and television committee, I received an interesting call from a top executive of one of the world's biggest television companies, just to congratulate me! Now, I wonder why he was so keen to talk to me, nearly two years after I had first met him, and having never heard from him since?

When I was first introduced to this particular television mogul, whom I cannot possibly name, it was over a very convivial dinner with our respective wives. During the course of the dinner, I handed him my business card that contained my home telephone number. Of course, I never heard from him again, until within days of my appointment to the FIFA committee.

Although I never said a thing to him, it was most improper of him to have called me at home now that I was on the FIFA committee, and I think he must have thought I had just come up the Clyde on a squiggy.

However, my time on the FIFA committee was short, because Sepp Blatter sacked me for speaking my mind.

Blatter was heading up a presentation on the subject of the vast amounts of television revenues being generated by the World Cup and how it all broke down country by country. The presentation, with all the facts and figures, was on a giant screen. At the end of the presentation, Blatter threw it open for discussion and I advised him, given my experience in dealings in South America, that I wasn't entirely happy with the amounts being paid.

I reminded Blatter that, some time ago, there existed a cartel in England when ITV and BBC controlled the value of televised football coverage. At that time, the BBC and ITV alternated their coverage of European games and, when we were playing Spartak Moscow in the European Cup, I couldn't believe it when the BBC declined to screen our game when it was their turn. Apparently they were committed to showing something else and couldn't move their schedules.

I rang the head of BBC sport, the old Welsh fly-half, Cliff Morgan, and gave him a piece of my mind. I told him that I just couldn't understand how they could turn down such an important European Cup tie. He explained that they had bought the rights to a five-a-side competition being held at the NEC that was sponsored by a Japanese company, and that it had to be screened on that night. He felt that he couldn't take the audience away from that event by putting on another football game.

Cliff Morgan offered to send our club a cheque for £1,000 as a sign of goodwill, even though he was unable to put a camera into Villa Park to screen our game. I told him to forget it; he could keep his £1,000. I found a small television crew in Holland and brought them over to Villa Park. It was just a three-man crew: they filmed the game and I sold the rights to nineteen countries.

Instead of the £1,000 as a goodwill gesture, the club made £59,000 and just about every country I contacted took the game, with particular interest coming from Russia, who sorted out a satellite link. We beat Spartak Moscow and in the next round we drew Barcelona. This time I wasn't bothered whose turn it was to take the rights – ITV or BBC – and I didn't offer it to either of them. This match yielded £62,000, with RAI 5 in Italy paying more than anyone else, when they coughed up a £5,000 fee.

I told Blatter that television companies are the same all over the world; they have a cartel to ensure that they get the lowest rate, and when you go out into the field, you quickly discover how much more there is on offer.

I warned Blatter that FIFA were being ripped off in the same way, when it came to the sale of World Cup rights in South America. For example, it was thought that Argentina had researched an understanding not to sell on their rights to any other Spanish-speaking country. It therefore came as some surprise when they did sell. Now, the only reason I knew what was going on was because I was in the travel business and my contacts in the various countries were telling me how they had seen the games. The matches had been beamed to places like Ecuador and Peru, but I also knew that neither of these countries were paying FIFA or Aston Villa for the television rights.

I sent telexes – there were no such thing as faxes in those days – to all my agents around the world. I wanted to know if they had seen Villa's game against Barcelona being screened in their countries. I could then crosscheck to see which one of those countries had actually paid for the rights and who had been going behind our backs.

My advice to Blatter was to do the same with the World Cup rights. Each year the committee is nominated again, but I wasn't nominated next time round.

So, it has been a few years since I last appeared on the FIFA committee, but I still retained my position on the FA's finance committee. Again I was considered somewhat of a rebel because I questioned the high levels of fees that the FA had been paying to the firm of lawyers it retained. The fees were particularly high when the First Division reformed into the FA Premier League, and the FA employed Freshfields for such a highly complex transition. The Football League employed Herbert Smith to represent them and the fees between two of the best most expensive law firms in the country, were on their way to nearly £1 million.

I went absolutely mad when I discovered the level of legal bills that the FA were paying. David Hill Wood, who was then chairman of the finance committee, and I wanted the legal fees 'taxed', that is to see a complete breakdown of the fees and how they justified them. But I was told that you couldn't ask for such detail from so highly respected a firm of lawyers. That's not the done thing. I said: 'Oh yes it is.'

As a result, both Freshfields and Herbert Smith were taxed and, although no one liked it, it saved the FA between fifteen and twenty percent in legal fees. I wasn't very popular, but I thought that it was worth it to the FA.

I was also the founder chairman of a new technical control board at the FA and the Football League, and I served on that for six years until Robert Coar, the Blackburn Rovers director, took over from me.

The technical control board provided facilities to professional clubs to encourage youngsters to take up the profession. For the first three or four years, I worked alongside Howard Wilkinson. We now have thirty-eight clubs signed and on average it costs each club £2 million a year. However, the clubs had to meet some very stringent conditions to provide facilities for the nine-to-sixteen age group. We had sixty-five in our Academy at Aston Villa and we set an example to all the other clubs.

## BATTLES WITH BLATTER

I had another run-in with Sepp Blatter over an unusual transfer deal.

Deals conducted between two clubs in the UK are relatively straightforward. Outside of the country it is usually a nightmare.

We sold Gary Charles to Benfica in 1999 for £1.5 million and only recently got our money! The deal was structured in such a way that we would receive half down with the other half to come over a twelve-month period and the second half of the fee would be interest free for that year. But there would be eight percent interest if the second half of the payments was delayed for any reason. Knowing most Spanish and Portuguese clubs the way I do, it came as no surprise that they didn't come up with the second instalment and that is why I had insisted on the payment of eight percent interest if there was a delay. But it took more than *four years* to get the full amount, and then it has been bit by bit every three months with around six months to go. They haven't paid for him, but that didn't stop them selling him on to West Ham!

Now, the only way to combat such blatant refusals to pay up would be for FIFA to take a tough stance and refuse to allow clubs from signing any more players until they have fulfilled their other contractual obligations.

Maurice Watkins, the Manchester United director until he was ousted from the board by Malcolm Glazer, works for a Manchester firm of lawyers and we hired him to take our case to FIFA. He went to Zurich with Stephen Stride, my Operations Director at that time, to act for us in this case and to make representation to Blatter. We wanted to recoup the £750,000 owed to us plus eight percent interest, the total coming to around £800,000.

We finally got our money, but it was a long wait.

251

# CHAPTER TWENTY-FOUR

# TRANSFER DEALS

John Gregory did well enough when he first became my manager. He was very passionate and he had a great rapport with the crowd; they loved him.

The fans remembered him as a player here and he was very bright then. He was also extremely bright as a coach, and our results under him were reasonably sound for the first eighteen months to two years.

But then he went off to Argentina and told me that he had thoroughly enjoyed himself. He went out there to buy Juan Pablo Angel and I did the deal with the lawyer and the player's agent, a man who controlled much of South American football. It is not uncommon there for the agent to own part of the players, sometimes as much as fifty percent and that happened to be the case on this occasion.

When I started the discussions, I was told that the price was £9.5 million in cash. They insisted that it had to be cash, and all of it up front; there would not be the usual instalments. They wanted me to pay the money in differing proportions into four different banks in three different countries: America, Argentina, and Holland. I refused to do it.

The transfer was delayed for some considerable time, as we continued to haggle and argue about the method of payment.

Eventually I put my foot down and insisted that I would make one payment, in conjunction with the Football Association. I spoke with Graham Noakes at the FA and paid the full amount of £9.5 million to the FA and, quite correctly and according to the rules, the FA here transferred all the funds directly to the FA in Argentina. Now, coincidentally, the chairman of the Argentinean FA also happened to be the chairman of River Plate, the club from which we were buying Angel!

He was also a member of FIFA and, at that time, I was a member of FIFA's media and television committee – as luck would have it, he was the chairman of that very same committee! He spoke a little English, enough to make himself understood, and although my Spanish isn't perfect, it is good enough to get me by.

When we next met up for one of our committee meetings, he explained that the transfer fee had been shared between the player's club and the Columbian FA.

Juan Pablo Angel became a firm favourite with the fans and scored twenty-three goals in the 2003-04 season.

The FA hired two top-level private investigators to look into all the paperwork in the Angel transfer and two other deals and nothing untoward was discovered.

Besides Colombian striker Juan Pablo Angel, the FA also looked into the transfers of Turkish World Cup star Alpay Ozalan, a £5.5 million buy from Fenerbache in July 2000, and Croatian international Bosko Balaban, who signed from Dinamo Zagreb in August 2001 for £5.8 million.

Graham Smith, Balaban's agent, had a meeting with the FA at his home in Ojal, on the Californian coast, to find out what the former Chelsea director and Colchester goalkeeper, who played in the 3–2 FA Cup win over Leeds in 1971, knew.

The FA spent five days in Ojal discussing the details with Smith. Smith was contacted by Nikki Vuksan, an employee of Mamic

Sport Agency, a company run by Dinamo Zagreb's vice-president Zdravko Mamic. Smith says: 'The call came out of the blue. I had done a few transfers involving Croatian players. They were looking for a FIFA-registered agent, and I am registered. I wasn't involved in negotiating the transfer fee and I haven't the foggiest clue what happened to the money once Aston Villa wrote the cheque.'

Smith has presented the official invoice for his £125,000 to the FA. He adds: 'That is the entire amount I received. Nothing more, nothing less. The money is logged in my company accounts, which are registered with the tax authorities in the US.'

Smith says: 'My role in this was minimal. I put the two sides together. That was it.'

Balaban played just eight league games as a substitute and is now with Bruges in the Belgian League where he is their leading scorer.

Graham Bean, the FA's compliance officer talking about the general problem of undisclosed payments expressed himself to be 'disillusioned' that his FA bosses were dragging their feet in tackling the transfer bungs and soccer scams and their lacklustre attempts to pour the resources into tackling it.

Mohammed Al Fayed hired a team of forensic accountants, lawyers and fraud experts in France to look into the question of bungs. The Fulham and Harrods owner had reached into his own pocket to discover the truth, because he is suspicious that the FA are so underfunded in this department that they cannot take on the case load. Al Fayed is frustrated with FIFA, UEFA and the FA in dealing with their suspicions. Gregory, clearly upset at the position he found himself in, commented publicly as follows:

It has been going on for two years and I have not worked since I left Derby, but all these so-called investigations have shown absolutely nothing and I now feel free to resume work. I should be back at work. I know that I am a bloody good manager and a bloody good coach, but I know people have put the boot in whenever I have applied for a job. I feel

I have been persecuted alright, ever since I left Villa. I walked out and the club didn't receive compensation.

It all started days after leaving Villa in January 2002. But no one at the FA has spoken to me, no one at the Serious Fraud Squad has spoken to me, no police have spoken to me. The Inland Revenue has been looking into all my affairs going back over the last four or five years. They've had all my bank statements, everything, and even went back to 1998 when I sold a property in Windsor before anything came up about a number of transfers at Villa.

The FA, the Fraud Squad and the police didn't initiate any enquiries; they were provided with all the paperwork by Villa. It seems to me that Villa were saying: 'Have a look at all this and no doubt you will find some irregularities.' Well, if they've looked, they have found nothing because I have not heard a word.

But I have applied for a few jobs and had a few interviews, but I am sure they have picked up the phone and spoken to certain people who have said 'don't touch him'. The whole business is shameful, and it's hard not to feel resentful. My attitude has been to sit back and say 'get on with it, I've got nothing to hide'.

John had a very close association with Paul Stretford, a well-known football agent who has been involved with Wayne Rooney through his company Pro Active Sports Agency.

*Private Eye* suggested that thirty-three out of thirty-six transfers going in or out of Villa during Gregory's time as manager were conducted by Pro Active, which also represents Gregory in his moves as manager. That figure was vehemently contested by both Gregory and Stretford.

*Private Eye* also reported that although Gregory complained bitterly about lack of funds at Villa, he bought players for £71.5 million and sold players for a combined total of £46 million.

# CHAPTER TWENTY-FIVE

# CAPPING PLAYERS' WAGES AND AGENTS' EXORBITANT FEES

Agents have become a major problem in the game and I have tried to make my Premier League chairman colleagues see sense in bringing in tough regulations. We need to have a formula for paying agents and we all need to abide by it. The Premier League and the FA are currently working on a new code for agents, but you simply cannot get everyone to agree to it.

It's odd really because it's difficult, if not impossible, to get all the twenty club chairmen to agree with capping agents when they are in committee meetings, yet when we discuss it outside of the formal gatherings they are all for it!

A fundamental principle should be that the agent shouldn't be paid twice for the same transaction that invariably at the moment he is, because the club pay a commission and then the agents also charge the player.

More often than not, the agent is paid by the clubs in instalments over the period of the player's contract, but then he shouldn't also be charging the player.

The agent will threaten the club by saying that he will take the player elsewhere if you don't agree to his 'fees'.

We have been meticulous at Villa in trying to get agents to submit reasonable commissions, and in some cases we have refused point blank to meet an agent's demands. You have to applaud Manchester United for coming clean with the precise amounts they have paid agents, but they were coerced into doing so because of a legal row between their manager Sir Alex Ferguson and their leading shareholders at the time, John Magnier and JP McManus. The shareholders demanded explanations of the club's payments to agents and, in the event, the legal dispute was settled. In the process, however, the club published all of its payments to agents.

Other clubs have not followed suit. In my view, it should be all or nothing. All clubs should be compelled to declare such payments; otherwise they should all remain confidential. Considering that Manchester United declared that they paid in excess of £5 million to agents in one year, I feel that, in comparison, we have been moderate here at Villa, although of course Manchester United do pay £30 million for one player!

In the past few years we have paid £2 million in fees to agents, but we are doing all we can to cut back on such payments and we will continue to negotiate as hard as we can. What is required, though, is a common practice among the entire twenty clubs and, until that happens, the agents will try to charge whatever they like.

Willie McKay wanted to 'sell' Amdy Faye to Aston Villa. McKay operates from his mobile in Monte Carlo. McKay had negotiated a ten percent cut of any money Portsmouth made over and above £2.5 million for Faye. He almost pulled off a deal last summer, with Fulham agreeing to sign Faye for £3.5 million, but the midfield player failed a medical and the deal was called off, costing McKay an additional £100,000 to whatever other commissions he had already negotiated.

McKay is on record as saying: 'Doug Ellis has offered me

£50,000 for my commission for Faye, but I told him: "Don't pay me anything, but if in a year's time he is sold for anything more than £4 million then I get ten per cent." ' He was tempting the market to enable him to earn his commission. Faye subsequently signed for Newcastle.

All commissions have to be registered with the FA and the Premier League and the rules block payments from both clubs or one club and the player. Suspicion persists that agents are circumventing the rules, however. The players are being ripped off and they haven't got a clue.

We have been asked for huge amounts of commissions from agents and I simply won't pay it. It has become a business within a business, and you simply can't stop it. Agents are making millions and are doing much of it by phone from places like Monte Carlo…

Players' wages are already high enough, and additional payments to agents means that outgoings from the clubs are on the increase year on year. Something has to give.

Some chairmen want to cap agents' fees: the idea of capping agents' fees is an issue that the Premier League has looked into at various stages, but has never got to grips with. I fully agree that agents are asking for ludicrously high amounts and it's about time that there was full transparency in the game, and that agents' fees were subject to vigorous scrutiny.

I raised the issue of agents' fees at a Premier League shareholders' meeting of all the clubs around two years ago. I advocated a capping of agents' commissions for facilitating transfers and for negotiating their clients' new contracts. I wanted a minimum payment of £20,000 and a maximum sum of £50,000, although, no doubt, moving on and with inflation, those figures would be much higher now. Manchester United and Liverpool were among the top clubs who opposed my plan to cap agents' commissions.

The topic of capping players' salaries is also one that I have raised at chairmen's meetings at least two or three times – the first time was as long as ten years ago. A subtle and workable formula has to be found, but in truth no one is in the mood to sort it out. Of course, you cannot simply cap individual salaries because that would be against the law.

However, we could, if there was the desire to do it, cap the amount that each club could spend in any one given season, using the total gross figure. Then the club would have the option of to whom they paid £100,000 a week or £10,000 a week. It could even be a fairly high ceiling figure so that clubs would have plenty to play with. Liverpool and Manchester United have always been opposed to any form of salary capping. I can understand Manchester United's valid argument that they are a plc, who are responsible to their shareholders and who, therefore, must be free to do whatever they wish; I am sure they could be more flexible if they wished, however.

I have been savagely criticised by my own fans for being too cautious with the club's money, but the realisation that big spending doesn't guarantee success – and can lead to financial ruin – has suddenly hit home when examining the incredible rise and fall of Leeds United in just two years.

Moves in the Premier League to attempt to revitalise an ailing transfer market have me worried. I have argued against altering the twelve-month rule in a recent meeting whereby the Purchasing Club pay 50 per cent down and the other 50 per cent over the next twelve months. I told them that the reason for the introduction of the rule in the first place was to protect them from overspending; from spending money that they don't have and can't afford. A lot of them went silent, but the motion went through anyway and it will be rubberstamped at the AGM.

Clubs will now have the option of negotiating the fee to be paid over the length of the player's contract. That, however, can only be achieved if the selling club agrees. The proviso that the selling club must accept the payments over a longer period of time may not encourage an increase in transfer activity, which was the main objective of these changes.

Clubs have got to consider the financial impact of relegation and they need to budget accordingly. One sensible way is to register players' contracts with specific salary changes relating to moves between divisions. Therefore, if a club is promoted to the Premiership, the players' salaries will have to be worked out in advance. Clubs can then work out players' wages should they be relegated.

# CHAPTER TWENTY-SIX

# MY THIRTEENTH MANAGER –
# LET'S HOPE HE'S MY LAST

If you include Graham Taylor's double stint as manager, then David O'Leary is my thirteenth manager.

Of course, as we have already established, my moniker of 'Deadly' comes from my fishing exploits and not from my reputation for sacking managers and nothing would give me more pleasure than never having to sack another manager.

It is all very simple. Managers are judged on results. If the results are bad, then the manager goes. Now, that is not just my reasoning, it is common practice within football, not just in this country but just about everywhere.

Graham Taylor was managing the club in his first stint when the FA came calling and wanted him for the England team. How could you refuse a man who wants to manage his country? You can't. He came to me and said: 'Will you let me go?' I said I would and that I understood, but I also insisted that the FA paid compensation, perhaps not the full amount because it was the FA, but they would have to put some money into the kitty for me to find a replacement.

I did the deal with Bert Millichip who was the FA chairman at that time. Dear old Bert died right in front of me on 18 December 2002 when we were having a meal together. He went face down into his plate of food and I tried to revive him, but he was already gone

I got on very well with Bert. He even offered me the presidency of the FA. He said to me one day that he would like to see me, and said that I had served on so many FA committees that I qualified to become FA president. I had been on the international committee for nearly fifteen years, the finance committee and the Charity Shield committee. However, I had too much on my plate at Villa, so I declined.

Anyway, Graham Taylor did not last long as the England coach and I eventually took him back here. He had a wonderful track record at club level and I considered him to be the right appointment at the time, despite his experiences with the England team. But it was an error on my part to bring Graham back to Villa, and I will be the first to admit it. It might have worked out, but as we know it didn't. Once again I found myself looking for a new man to coach the team.

How can I sum up David O'Leary? Well, he's a good, sound Irishman. I first met him, oh it must be five years ago now, in an airport lounge. I was heading off somewhere and he was going to the States at the time when he was a coach at Leeds United with George Graham as the manager. It was at Heathrow Airport and both of our flights were delayed, so we had the opportunity to talk for some time. He talked mostly about his love for Arsenal, and I talked about mine for Aston Villa.

Graham Taylor resigned, perhaps knowing that he didn't have much time before the inevitable, and rather more unpleasant, end would have come. I respect him for that.

However, the results were bad at the time and he knew very well that I was not happy. He beat me to the punch by resigning! I would say that he beat the sack by a week or so, no more.

As is always the case when your looking for a new manager,

the media have a field day and Villa were linked with a profusion of names. But David O'Leary was out of work at the time, and that was a big help — I didn't have to pay any compensation to any club that he would normally have been tied to by a contract. We had fifty-seven applications for the job, forty-five of which you could have removed immediately as they had no chance. There were a few surprising names among the applicants, a dozen of which were very experienced managers. There were also a number of high-profile players who wanted to become managers.

I didn't have a shortlist and I didn't need one. I wanted David O'Leary.

It wasn't long before David's name was being linked with a move back to Leeds United, and then to succeed Sir Bobby Robson at St James' Park. I was not approached by Freddy Shepherd for the services of O'Leary and the Newcastle chairman would have been wasting his time if he did. I would have taken the issue to the High Court if necessary and that would have tied up any decision in litigation for at least six months.

O'Leary pledged his unflinching loyalty to the club and to his chairman when his name was first mentioned as a potential candidate the instant Sir Bobby was surprisingly sacked. David had two more years left on his Villa contract, which did not possess a compensation clause. We have since sat down and renegotiated the contract, extended it and now it does contain all the necessary clauses.

David now has a contract that lasts until 2007 and his assistant has the same length of contract; an appointment that the manager wanted.

As a member of the International Board, I was consulted on the appointment of the England coach, but of course it was not ultimately my decision. However, when I was asked my opinion about Sven-Goran Eriksson, I was not too enthusiastic at the time.

Kevin Keegan had just resigned after England's World Cup

qualifier defeat against Germany at Wembley, and his departure had left a vacuum. I was not asked officially inside any International Committee meeting, but I was sounded out about my views by Noel White, the chairman of the international committee, who was seeking opinions among other members of the committee. He wasn't that sure about the idea of appointing a foreign coach, and I also had my reservations. I said: 'Surely there is someone good enough from among our own coaches.'

I thought of Terry Venables. I thought that he would be the best man for the job. He had done it before and I thought he was worthy of another crack at it. I have subsequently been proved wrong. He was past his sell-by-date, but no one really knew it for sure just at that time. But his spell with Leeds United proved to me that he would have been the wrong choice to return to the England job.

However, I must admit I fancied the appointment of Terry purely on his coaching ability. We all know that he comes with a lot of baggage, but I have never been afraid to appoint a manager if he has the right credentials as a coach.

# CHAPTER TWENTY-SEVEN

# THE FUTURE

There have been two occasions when I thought that there was a possibility that I would wind things up at Aston Villa. There is only one reason that I would go, and go willingly, and that is if I could find a buyer who could take the club on a stage from where it is today.

A serious possibility of that emerged with the very real and serious offer from Trinity Mirror Newspapers. Rupert Murdoch tried to buy Manchester United with his media empire behind him and, quite properly, I felt obliged to explore the distinct possibility of a company as powerful as Trinity Mirror buying Aston Villa.

When you think of Trinity Mirror, anyone would immediately think of the *Daily Mirror* and their other national titles but, of course, Trinity Mirror is in fact the biggest and most powerful owner of local newspapers in the country, and had just taken over the *Birmingham Post and Mail*.

Trinity Mirror offered me £30 million for a twenty-nine percent stake in Villa in 1998, which would have left me with thirteen percent of the company. The deal was an attractive one, as it would have meant that I would have remained as chairman for the rest of my life, or for however long I wished.

I met with their chairman at that time, Sir Robert Clarke, who told me some wonderful stories over lunch at Browns in London about their MD, David Montgomery, who had been introduced to the company by Kelvin MacKenzie.

I wrestled with that offer for several months, and it was a very good one. However, I eventually turned it down because I wasn't 100 percent sure that it would, indeed, take the club forward in the way that I wanted. There are always risks aligning yourself with a group of newspapers, because their rivals are always going to present a powerful opposition.

Of course, it wrangles with me that our supporters don't realise how close I came to selling up because there was such a good offer on the table, but I turned it down because it was not one that I was totally convinced would be good for Villa. Those supporters accuse me of all sorts of things, but so little do they know. No one loves this club more than I do!

I also have in my possession – and I kept it in my bottom drawer – an indicative offer made much more recently by the senior partner in Seymour Pierce, Keith Harris, who used to be chairman of the Football League and who has been working hard to put forward a plan to combat the takeover bid of Malcolm Glazer at Manchester United.

Two years ago, Keith came to see me and made me an indicative offer of £63 million for Aston Villa on behalf of his clients. There would also be big money coming into the club and no doubt quite a bit of that would have been allocated for the kind of spending sprees that the supporters have been wanting. I have the offer in writing; the letter is dated 22 July 2003. The bid was in cash. It was most definitely tempting.

But again I was hesitant. I was worried who might be behind the bid. There had been a lot of debate about Colonel Gaddafi's son wanting to invest in a Premiership club and, although I have no idea to this day whether or not he was involved, I was deeply concerned when Keith told me that Bryan Richardson, formerly with Coventry City, would be involved in the consortium. However, in the end they would not or could not confirm that they had the necessary funds available and the decision was made for me. At the time Bryan left Coventry they were £60 million in debt. Not the kind of track record I was looking for.

The most recent offer arrived via Ray Ranson, the former Birmingham City and Manchester City full-back, who had been involved in helping clubs to finance the purchase of players. He approached me a year ago in March. I met him together with Richard Thompson, the one-time QPR chairman, at Thompson's London offices. Steve Stride was present at the meeting. I was made an offer, but it was verbal. It was clearly Thompson's money involved. They wanted me to stay on as chairman and Ray Ranson would be chief executive, but they started talking about sacking this one and sacking that one and I thought 'forget it'.

There was a lot of speculation about other offers, one in particular from a source in Colombia, but it never materialised. However, the two offers I have talked about were very real indeed and most people would have jumped at them.

I would love to have a bottomless pit of money like our friend Roman Abramovich, but I haven't. Funnily enough, I was having a break in the south of France not too long ago and my yacht harboured next to this almighty massive yacht. I wondered who could possibly own such a yacht, only to discover from the captain that it was the new Chelsea owner.

When he discovered that I was the Aston Villa chairman, he invited me on board and said that Mr Abramovich would be delighted to see me. I declined, of course, but a little later, when we played Chelsea, I spoke with Abramovich's aides and they told me that he would have been delighted to have had me on board, and I have been invited back at a later date. I have met him, naturally, when we have played them and I get on very well with him. I like his lovely wife, Irena, immensely.

You can't take it away from him. He is a genuine football fanatic, despite what anyone else might say about him. Unfortunately, someone like Roman Abramovich has made it harder for the likes of myself to make it an even playing field, and that even includes the likes of Manchester United and perhaps even Real Madrid.

I understand Abramovich makes £1 million a day in interest alone, at least so I am told. Well, good luck to him.

Generally speaking the rest of us have to balance the books, and the experiences of clubs such as Leeds United should tell football fans everywhere that there are risks involved in spending more than you can actually afford.

Fans mistrust directors and owners, but that is hard to understand from where I am coming from. There are so many genuine people in football, such as Delia Smith at Norwich.

Delia wrote me a wonderful letter three or four years ago when she first got involved in Norwich and I invited her down here to Villa Park and we had lunch together at the Corner Flag restaurant. She was highly impressed with our catering and said that it was out of this world. We now serve up to 3,200 meals before every game and have done so for the past three years. This place is unrecognisable from when I first became involved in Villa. We have spent a fortune on the ground and we have spent a fortune in the transfer market, but there is just no pleasing some of the fans.

I was fascinated to see Delia getting down on the pitch and making her speech to the fans. 'Let's be having you,' she told them. Sometimes I fear that I hear too much from some of our fans.

One of the criticisms that the 'Ellis out' brigade frequently raise is that I have never personally put any money into the Club but, as usual, their comments are based on a lack of information. I could list countless ways in which I have made millions for the Club and here are just three or four examples. Going right back to 1969, I purchased what is known as the Serpentine Site for my own building company but was persuaded by our then Commercial Manager, Eric Woodward, to give it to the Club for car parking. Many years later I bought our Siemens site for just over £1 million in total. These two sites alone are now worth £20m.

Then there was the NTL deal. I was professionally advised to accept £18m from NTL for 9.9% of Aston Villa shares. I went to London to meet the Chairman and CEO of NTL and pushed it up to £26m to include their name on our shirts. It was a tremendous deal for Aston Villa and the money we received enabled us to fund the £20million development of our Trinity Road Stand, which is widely regarded as one of the best stands in the Premier League.

They also forget that for many years, although I spent most of my time working for the Club, often to the detriment of my own businesses, I did not take a salary until 1982, and even then at half the rate which most other Club Chairmen are paid.

I make no apology for blowing my own trumpet; I've given half my life to the Villa and kept them solvent with no debt and not many football Chairmen can say that. My maxim has always been 'to earn my corn' whenever I complete a deal for the Club and I think it is fair to say that I 'earn my corn' more than most.

Villa Fans Combined made a public announcement that they would be handing out 20,000 red cards prior to the Middlesbrough game for supporters to hold up to demonstrate that they 'have had enough of the mediocrity, underachievement and lack of backing given to the managers of the club over the past twenty-two years'. There were only around 5,000 as it turned out, but even so, it is so demoralising because those fans simply fail to understand or appreciate what I am trying to achieve here. To say I lack ambition is absurd. No one wants to see Aston Villa be more successful than I do. No one. And I would do anything I could to see that happen.

The VFC believe that I have gone back on my word to make funds available for strengthening the squad. They claimed that: 'Spending on players, after sales, amounts to between £4–6 million per season.'

I can show you the figures for the transfers coming in and going out, and I can show you the salaries that we have been paying in recent seasons, and I believe the figures do not show a club that is reluctant to spend over the last four seasons.

Under the last three managers, covering the period from the start of the 1998–99 season and the projection of those salaries for players for the 2004–05 season, this club has paid out close to £150 million in seven years – that is an average of £21.5million a year.

Over the same period we have spent £77.5 million under Gregory, £12.3 million when Taylor was back in charge, and now £30 million under O'Leary: a total of £119.8 million. We have sold players over that period to the value of £57.1 million. The total transfer deficit is £48.1 million.

VFC also claim that we have failed to back the manager in signing players, despite promises to that effect in the summer and that they had seen an injury-hit small squad fail to be bolstered and fall away from the progress made last season.

Of course, they are entitled to their view. But at that Boro game, we emerged from our recent slump to claim our fourth win in sixteen games, yet David O'Leary was on the receiving end of the criticism as well. He reacted furiously to two supporters behind the home dugout, turning around to shout at them during the match and poking fun at them afterwards.

O'Leary said: 'They are perpetual moaners. I am told they moaned after Villa won the European Cup because they didn't win it in style. One bloke was calling for my head after my second game and again when we didn't make the Champions League last year. No one has ever heard him cheer the team, so I wanted to ask him if he was happy this week. All he said was that it didn't make up for last week. I have players on the pitch who are brittle. If their first pass goes wrong then they know they are going to get it. I can cope with it and handle it, but it is no good to the players.'

I have always said that the fans who pay their money are entitled to moan if they want, but they have no idea what I am trying to do for this club and what I plan to do in the future with a number of plans going ahead right now. Ok, I am proud to say that Aston Villa have won the first football hospitality award for corporate food. Eat your heart out Delia!

Before the kick-off at match days at Aston Villa, you will find six queues bearing down on the 'refreshments' counter under the Holte End. There is a selection of burgers, balti pies, pasties or pizzas on offer, the kind of fast food most football clubs will have on offer to their fans. But it is becoming far more sophisticated these days, especially at Villa Park. Clubs now cater for corporate clients, executive box holders and VIPs.

The Corner Flag restaurant serves the quality of food that puts some of the best-known London restaurants, in the shade.

We offer an excellent three-course lunch with fine wines. It is the norm. As such, as I mentioned, Villa scooped the first football hospitality award for the food it serves to its VIP guests on match days. Among those who commented favourably on the meals served in the directors' dining room were Chelsea's billionaire, Roman Abramovich, and Norwich City's Delia Smith.

'Delia first came here with her husband about four years ago, when she was looking at ways of developing the catering at Norwich,' recalls Peter Reed, the executive chef at Villa Park. 'They weren't even in the Premiership at the time, but she knew that we were among the market leaders.' And was she impressed? 'Well, she gave me a signed copy of her book, *How to Cook*.'

Not that he needed it. Reed has been overseeing a team of forty chefs catering for eighteen function suites and 125 hospitality boxes. There are just over 40,000 fans inside Villa Park for several matches and just under 3,000 of them enjoy corporate hospitality.

I am proud of the way that this club has grown off the field, but I do share the fans' frustrations and I also want to achieve success on the field. Believe me, I am trying to do all I can to achieve it and have a couple of land deals going on that will release more funds for that purpose. One piece of land I bought for my building company, Ellmanton, in 1969 for £10,000 which I subsequently gave to Aston Villa for car parking at the behest of Eric Woodward our Commercial Manager and it is now worth millions.

The aim is to be playing in Europe during those two years left on David O'Leary's contract, and it would also be a bonus if we have some silverware on the table. If we don't get into Europe, the bottom line is to maintain a respectable position in the top half of the Premier League, making reasonable advancements in the FA Cup and Carling Cup competitions, playing entertaining football to the satisfaction of our supporters – of which we have 600,000 names on our database and an average home gate crowd of just under 38,000.

No, I don't believe in retirement. I know from bitter experience that when you retire you can become mentally unfit. I learned that during my many years' experience as a travel agent. Many of my clients wanted to retire abroad and bought properties with the aid of my foreign-currency exchange contacts. Over a period of time, I must have helped more than 100 people relocate to all sorts of places all over the world. I always advised them not to do it; it is one thing to enjoy a place for a few weeks on holiday, it's another actually living there in retirement. On average I must have helped to bring back six bodies a year. I am convinced they were simply bored to tears and stagnated in retirement.

# THE FUTURE

I was last asked about when I plan to retire by a young journalist on television: 'Are you thinking of retiring?' he asked me.

'My son,' I replied. 'I'll hold my own mentally with anyone twenty-five years younger than me and I would even physically challenge them to a game of tennis.'

The interview was on Sky and just about everyone fell about laughing, because the interviewer was forty-two!

After a six-hour operation and six days in the intensive-care unit during the summer, my operation at the Edgbaston Priory proved a success although I have returned on three occasions to the operating theatre. At the time I was only thinking of being able to say 'good morning' to someone at that stage. I wasn't thinking about anything else. Was I frightened? Naturally. Did that make me think about the future? Of course. It was serious. But as time went on, I was in touch once, twice, three times a day with Villa's operations manager, Steve Stride and the company secretary, Marion Stringer to find out what was going on. I never left Villa really, apart from those six days in ITU.

I have lost two stone in weight but I do feel fitter and I have been back salmon fishing, shooting, and back in my office sorting out the complexities of the most recent offers to buy Villa.

You can imagine how I felt when we beat Birmingham and then our manager David O'Leary performed his jig across the pitch (nearly as bad as David Pleat's) in support of me just days after I had been given a hard time at our AGM by one or two supporters/shareholders.

The main point is that I still have a lot to achieve in life. Look, nothing would give me greater pleasure than to see Aston Villa win the Premier League before I go. Now wouldn't that be a wonderful legacy. There's an old saying that you should only quit at the top, but I am selfish and wouldn't consider retiring even then.

First of all, I would want to make sure that the right man was there to take my place and that he will continue, whoever he is, to maintain the stability of the company just as relentlessly as I have worked to do – without any debt.

# APPENDIX

# WHERE ARE THEY NOW?

*(A random look at the whereabouts of some of the main personalities mentioned in these pages.)*

CHARLIE AITKEN... Villa Park regular, residing in
   West Midlands.
WILLIE ANDERSON... living in the United States, working
   on television promotion.
RON ATKINSON... TV analyst, residing in Barnt Green.
AUDREY, my first wife... still a good friend, residing in
   Four Oaks.
TONY BARTON... deceased.
RON BENDALLL... deceased.
ALAN BENNETT... semi-retired in Leicestershire while
   retaining Leicester City connection.
BRIAN CLOUGH... deceased.
HARRY CRESSMAN... Retired and residing in the Bahamas.
VIC CROWE... Villa regular, retired and residing in
   Sutton Coldfield.
STAN CULLIS... deceased.
JIM CUMBES... commercial manager at Lancashire
   County Cricket Club.
TOMMY DOCHERTY... popular after-dinner speaker.
DOREEN... my sister... residing in Chedworth, Gloucestershire.

SIR WILLIAM DUGDALE... landowner in Coleshill-Atherstone area.

BRIAN EVANS... still a Villa fanatic. Property conveyance specialist, residing in Ireland.

SIR TOM FINNEY... President of Preston North End.

BRIAN GODFREY... still a Villa man at heart, living and working abroad.

JIMMY GREAVES... media freelance residing in Essex.

PHIL 'TIGER' HART... deceased.

JIM HARTLEY... deceased.

HARRY KARTZ... retired and residing in West Midlands and Florida.

BRIAN LITTLE... manager of Tranmere Rovers.

ROY McLAREN... residing in Australia.

BILLY McNEIL... residing in Scotland.

PAT MATTHEWS... a businessman residing in Marbella.

JOE MERCER... deceased.

BRUCE NORMANSELL... deceased.

HARRY PARKES... residing in Birmingham.

BRUCE RIOCH... residing in West Midlands.

NEIL RIOCH... instigator of Aston Villa Former Players' Association, residing in West Midlands and running his own business.

RON SAUNDERS... retired and still residing in Knowle.

GRAEME SOUNESS... manager at Newcastle United.

TONY STEPHENS... based in Meriden, representing top players including Alan Shearer, Dwight Yorke and Michael Owen.

DICK TAYLOR... deceased.

GRAHAM TAYLOR... journalist and media pundit living in Four Oaks.

PETER TAYLOR... deceased.

BRIAN TILER... killed in road accident, Italy 1990.

GRAHAM TURNER... Chairman and manager of Hereford United.

Dr JOZEF VENGLOS... actively involved in football in Slovakia.

JACK WISEMAN... vice-chairman of Birmingham City FC after a spell as chairman.

RON WYLIE... retired and living in Sutton Coldfield.